70 Years a-Growing

by

Jean Westlake

Folkmoot – The Annual General Meeting of The Order of Woodcraft Chivalry

70 Years a-Growing

by

Jean Westlake

with Photographs from the Westlake Archives

and Illustrations by the Author

Hawthorn Press

Published by Hawthorn Press, Hawthorn House, 1 Lansdown Lane, Stroud, Gloucestershire, GL5 1BJ, UK
Tel: (01453) 757040 Fax: (01453) 751138

Cover Photograph from Sandy Balls Photo Library.
Cover Design by Patrick Roe, Southgate Solutions, Stroud, Gloucestershire.
Typesetting by Hawthorn Press, Stroud, Gloucestershire.
Printed in the UK by Redwood Books, Trowbridge, Wiltshire.

British Library Cataloguing in Publication Data applied for

ISBN 1 869 890 37 X

Dedication

To: my two Sons, Eden and Ashley and the memory of my Mother and Father. This little book is dedicated to all discerning people who revere the past, cherish the present and look forward to the future.

My two sons – Eden and Ashley

Acknowledgements

My grateful thanks to the Fordingbridge Neighbourhood Magazine for permission to use many of the articles first appearing in their monthly publication 'The Gate'.

Also to the Bio-Dynamic Agricultural Association for allowing me to include material previously written for their bi-yearly Journal 'Star and Furrow'.

To "Hampshire" for permission to quote from an article by John Cheeseman 1966 entitled 'Grith Fyrd – Sandy Balls as a haven for victims of Depression'.

Grateful thanks to the Order of Woodcraft Chivalry for extracts from their bi-monthly magazine 'Pine Cone' and especially to Doris Salt, an early member, for her account of Father as a young leader in the 1920's.

To Angela Coombes for the lovely photograph of the washplace at Grith Fyrd.

To Juliette de Bairacli-Levy for the use of several photographs from her archive collection.

For permission to use the line drawings of Braziers by my friend Bonnie Russell, foundation member of Braziers Park School of Integrative Social Research.

To ITF (International Timber Foundation) for permission to use the photograph of Richard St. Barbe Baker on page 82.

To the Salisbury Journal for permission to use the photographs taken by them, included on pages 165 and 203.

My grateful thanks to Penny Pope and Lynn Dyer who typed the text, to Brian Bush who made this possible and the many people who helped and encouraged me.

Contents

'Sandy Balls, 100 acres of woodland, overlooking the Avon Valley, in Hampshire'

Introduction

This book is about different types of growth: Chronological – the growth of plants and animals and systems of growing; of understanding and ideas and of a family inescapably linked with the growth and development of a family estate and holiday centre.

Sandy Balls, 100 acres of woodland on the edge of the New Forest overlooking the Avon Valley, in Hampshire, was bought by my Grandfather, Ernest Westlake, seven years before I was born, so I have been associated with it all my life.

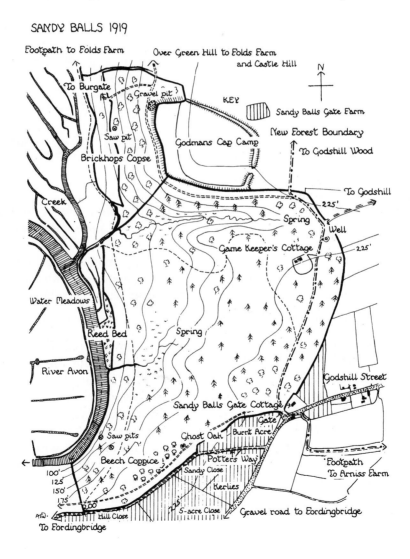

On Monday 28th April 1919, by direction of Sir Hamilton Hulse, 1040 acres of the outlying portions of the Breamore Estate were put up for sale by auction. In 1915 the 7th Baronet, Sir Edward Hulse, had been killed at the battle of Neuve Chapelle. Only 26 years old when he died, he left no heir and was succeeded by his Uncle, Sir Hamilton. On such a large estate death duties would have been considerable, especially as the recent Finance Acts of 1894 and 1909 made large changes in the duties payable on death. Most of the so-called Godshill Estate, including the Manors of East Mills and Folds were listed in the comprehensive Sale Catalogue. There were 67 lots in all, Sandy Balls being Lot no. 14.

The 'Charming Cottage' mentioned in the Sales Catalogue.

At auction, Sandy Balls, including a 'charming cottage', was sold for £3,150 to a Mr Ormond of Ringwood, a timber merchant. The standing timber was valued at £3,500, making a total of £6,650 in all – a large sum in those days.

Grandfather had every intention of buying it himself, thinking it an ideal place where his educational ideas, the Order of Woodcraft Chivalry, founded by him in 1916, and his great inspiration The Forest School could find practical expression; so together with his agent he attended the sale for this purpose. However, when the agreed figure was reached and knowing his client's financial position, the agent refused to bid higher and Sandy Balls was sold to another. Without consultation Grandfather instructed his agent to see Mr Ormond after the sale and offer him a few hundred more for Sandy Balls.

Imagine the consternation of the family, my father, his sister, Margaret and faithful family retainer 'Old Tatsie', sitting at supper in their home on Godshill Ridge, when the agent arrived and handed Grandfather a piece of paper bearing Ormond's signature! My father, recently qualified as a Doctor, and soon to start his medical career as a General Practitioner in Bermondsey, South East London, was dismayed, for he knew that if sufficient money was found to pay the mortgage, there was none to pay the mortgage interest. But Grandfather, with the far-seeing eye of one 'who knows', stated quite calmly that everything would be alright. Sometime later Mr Ormond arrived on his bicycle in an agitated state - saying he had no idea what had come over him, he had no intention of reselling Sandy Balls and wished to be released from his commitment. Grandfather stated quietly that Sandy Balls was now his and that was that!

Chapter 1

The Quaker Family

Let us take a brief look at the life of a remarkable man who saved this lovely woodland from the feller's axe. His memorial stands today in the heart of Sandy Balls surrounded by the pine trees he loved so well. The inscription reads as follows –

ΘΕΡΕ ΙΣ · ΜΑΤΕΡΙ ΠΑΙΔΑ

HERE · ON · WOODLING · POINT
OVER · LOOKING · HIS · NATIVE
TOWN · LIES · THE · BODY · OF

ERNEST

WESTLAKE

F·G·S: 1856 — 1922 FRAI
FOUNDER · OF · THE · ORDER · OF ·
WOODCRAFT · CHIVALRY · ITS ·
FIRST · BRITISH · CHIEFTAIN ·
AND · HONOURED · AS · FATHER ·
OF · THE · ORDER · HIS · FORESIGHT ·
AND · PUBLIC · SPIRIT ·
PRESERVED · SANDY · BALLS ·
FOR · LOVERS · OF · NATURAL ·
BEAUTY · AND · FOR · THE ·
TRAINING · OF · YOUTH · IN ·
HIS · GREAT · INSPIRATION ·
THE · FOREST · SCHOOL ·

Memorial to Ernest Westlake in Sandy Balls.

* Appendix 1

We can see all around us the natural beauty of Sandy Balls, but you may well ask – 'What is this Order of Woodcraft Chivalry; why was Grandfather its first British Chieftain and honoured as Father of the Order? It all sounds so very bizarre and strange, and what happened to his great inspiration The Forest School?

So to begin at the beginning: - Ernest Westlake was born on 16th November 1855 (not 1856 as was supposed). The family lived in a spacious but damp cottage by the bridge in Fordingbridge, Hampshire, known as Southampton House. In 1869 they moved to Oaklands – this was a substantial country mansion set in its own grounds and designed by his father, Thomas Westlake*. 'It was built of white bricks from Fisherton, slates with an extra deep lap, 11-inch floor joists, plate glass windows and everything solid and of the best. I think a fair estimate of the price would be £2,500; the land cost £1,118'. Thomas was the third of the three sons of a respected Southampton Quaker family who could trace their ancestors back in direct succession to John Westlake, one of those converted by George Fox (1624-91) at the beginning of Quakerism.

Thomas Westlake (1826-1892)   *Hannah Sophia Westlake (1833-1857)*

He was now a successful sail-cloth manufacturer at East Mills, one of the major industries of Fordingbridge, employing about 200 hands, in partnership with his Uncle, Samuel Thompson – having left Southampton in 1843 at the age of 17 years. In addition to business his two main interests were preaching the Gospel and Astronomy.

Ernest's Mother, Hannah Sophia Neave, belonged to another large Quaker family, living at Bicton a village on the Avon, 2^1/$_2$ miles from Fordingbridge. Her father was a miller. Hannah died of tuberculosis when Ernest was only 18 months old

Oaklands - The Family Home in Fordingbridge

with another baby on the way. She requested that her sister Agnes should care for her child and six years later Thomas married Agnes Neave. They went abroad to marry, for in those days it was illegal to marry your deceased wife's sister. This may well have conditioned their life together, for although they were devoted to each other, they had no children of their own and 'Oaklands' was a sombre home, where 'it was almost a sin to smile'.

Social contacts at this time were largely confined to small Quaker communities and other acceptable non-conformist groups, but within this limited sphere there were considerable cultural activities, and science too was beginning to make itself felt. Quaker religious outlook was not circumscribed by the set religious forms of the established Church; their practice of waiting in silence on the Lord during Sunday Meeting for worship gave them a spiritual freedom untrammelled by the dogma of conventional thought and practice.

They believed that religion is inseparable from everyday life and indeed life in all its forms should be seen as sacramental. They felt that there is a divine spark within every man and woman and that no intermediary, in the form of priest or minister, is necessary between an individual and his God.

Ernest Westlake aged 8 years (1863)

They tended however to be too extreme and puritanical in regard to morality; they condemned dance and drama, even some forms of music and were very conscious of good and evil. Family life was of paramount importance to them and even if a little restrictive to its members, it was also ordered, caring and secure, and embraced the whole unit – family and servants alike.

Quakers or members of the Religious Society of Friends became known over the years for their integrity, persistence and trustworthiness: their word was their bond. This characteristic enabled them to found the English banking system and to prosper in commerce and business. Lloyds, Barclays, Cadburys, Rowntrees and many other well-known firms, remain household names today.

Ernest grew up to be a lonely, sensitive, only child, brought up by a stepmother and two maiden aunts, who, although well-meaning, never understood him. All was not gloom however – a delightful picture is given by Grandfather, later writing of himself, as a young boy in the garden of Southampton House. It appears that he had invented a machine using waterpower to crush charcoal for firework making. 'So the bright water ground my black charcoal, while I sat on the bank among clumps of flowering osmunda, feeling all the mechanics' pride in having got the water to work for me. The music of the fall in my ears, enhanced by the whirring and clatter of the machinery, celebrating as a never-ending chorus the triumph of mind over matter.'

We can imagine this sensitive boy exploring and delighting in the unspoilt countryside of the Avon Valley. The age of power and progress had not yet disturbed the rural scene with its slow natural rhythm of the seasons, or destroyed the many rural crafts and the social structure of the district. These experiences and impressions of early boyhood must have had a profound effect on his later development.

ADAMS & STILLIARD   SOUTHAMPTON

Ernest Westlake aged 16 years (1872).

At the age of 12 years he was sent to Olivers Mount School in Scarborough. This episode he later recalls as one of the happiest of his life. He admired and respected the Headmaster, Thomas Walton, whose encouragement, combined with the freedom of this school, provided just the right environment for his special qualities to develop. His deepening love of nature and science fostered here, remained with him all his life. Leaving school he studied under a private tutor before going to University College, London. Here he devoted himself to Science under the great masters of the day, especially Biology under Huxley.

On returning home he joined the family sail-cloth business but his father soon realised that he was 'a fish out of water' and said very wisely that, as money was no problem, he could follow his own inclinations in the field of science. In 1859 Darwin's "Origin of Species" had been published and the controversy between

Religion and Science was at its height. The scientific field was wide open for just such a mind as Ernest possessed; for he was gifted with a powerful and brilliant mind combined with a tolerance and breadth of vision which were a revelation to all those who came to know him. Besides the scientist and naturalist he was a geologist, anthropologist, interested also in spiritualism, hypnotism and psychical research; he was a founder member of the Society for Psychical Research and knew the great figures of that time, among them Sir Oliver Lodge and F.W.H Myers. He was also an accomplished scholar. The Greek on his memorial comes from Sappho's "Ode to the Evening Star" and translated reads "Thou bringest the child back to its mother". During the last years of his life he learnt Greek so that he could make his own original translation of these Odes.

There was never any real understanding or intimacy between father and son, for Thomas with his strict puritanical upbringing was unable to cope with the new concepts of the age. His brother, Richard, in a Memoir written after his death from pneumonia in 1892, says "His well-balanced mind never allowed him to go astray on the lines of scientific research as opposed to Revelation. The contradictions that appear to some to exist between Science and Religion never troubled him. He believed that in the Scriptures God has revealed himself to man and made known His will.

The Rutter Family. Ernest Westlake 3rd from right, Lucy Westlake seated 4th from right.

*Appendix 2

On 1st May 1891, at the age of 36, Ernest married Lucy Anne Rutter, youngest daughter of a large Quaker family living in Mere, Wiltshire – her father , a country solicitor practising at Mere and Wincanton.

Years later Ernest, writing to his Uncle Richard after Lucy's death in 1901, tries to explain and justify the loss of his substantial fortune.

'I married in 1891 and my son and heir at this time, 1895, was just two years old. Although I was comfortably off and had no need to earn a living, having time and money to spend on my main interest – field Geology – I decided to do better for my family. In 1895 money was cheap and could be borrowed from the bank at 3 1/2%, so I put it into American Railway Bonds returning 5%. I also had an interest in St John de Rey Co, the shares were standing at 34/-. I transferred some of the bank's holding and the shares declined to 14/-, so I bought more to cover my loss. I also had priority shares in the New Elkhorn Co., having properties in Montana and Colorado; delay caused by a strike and the share value also dropped. I had an interest in three West Australian Companies, one of which, the Hampton Plains Exploration Co., showed a market decline.

The bank now wished me to sell all these depreciated shares, but to sell shares after a fall of nearly £6000 would be suicidal, as nothing could be recovered on my securities which did not fluctuate in value.

Before investing I made a careful and complete study and was satisfied of their intrinsic merits and honest management (not the Exploration Co – the enquiries were not satisfactory). That I might be forced to sell out at the bottom never occurred to me until a few months ago. Since then I have been doing all I can to pull my position round and through the kindness of Pardoe Yates acquired 1000 additional new preference shares in his company.

Then came the sudden death of Pardoe Yates and the failure of Yates and Co. (The Wilton Carpet Factory). The discovery that he had been falsifying the books for years and the dividends of the company had been paid out of capital (he was twice Mayor of Wilton and active in public matters). The final loss for the firm amounted to at least £140,000, his personal misappropriation was £2,000, comparatively small.

It was a local industry, established for a century and had a security of £90,000. The manager (Pardoe Yates) was my brother-in-law behaving as a friend; the solicitor my wife's brother and her trustee. Preference shares were held by all her family and by my step-mother on the advice of that most careful of men R.H.Penny. The accounts were audited twice yearly by professional auditors and the shares at a premium and held by insurance companies as permanent investments.

...and yet the whole was completely rotten.

By that time all my wife's money and nearly all mine was in £50,000 of preferred shares which were supported by the £90,000 of ordinary Capital. But none of the shareholders except some debenture holders recovered anything. Where other members of the family lost hundreds we lost thousands.

Struggling to keep our lovely home in the Vale of Health, Hampstead, my wife, Lucy, took in paying guests. Then after the death of her Father on 26th December 1899 we moved to the family home at Mere to sort things out. By the following January we were installed in a rented house in Salisbury, halfway between the two family homes – Mere and Fordingbridge. Here, worn out by work and worry she contracted pleurisy; the doctor gave her morphine to ease the pain and she died within the day. She was only 36 years old.

I am now left fortuneless, homeless, wifeless with two motherless children to support and now the family wish to take my children from me – but I will not let them go".

The name of this unfortunate man, native of Fordingbridge, purchaser of Sandy Balls Wood in 1919, Ernest Westlake, my Grandfather!

Ernest Westlake aged 66 years
(1855 - 1922)

The Avon Valley – View from Sandy Balls.

Chapter 2

Ernest Westlake

and the Order of Woodcraft Chivalry

Although Grandfather's life was completely shattered by the tragic death of his beloved wife, he was not daunted by the task of bringing up his two young children, my Father aged 7 years and my aunt Margaret aged 4 years. He resisted all attempts to take them away from his influence. Giving up the house in Salisbury they returned to the family home in Fordingbridge and the children spent their time between Oaklands with their Father and step-grandmother and Uncle Clarence and Aunt Mary with their six children – three boys and three girls – at Wincanton, Somerset. A close link developed between the children; and later my

The Rutter Family – Uncle Clarence and Aunt Mary with their six children (Cuthbert aged 8 years old, (second on right), later Head Master of Forest School. – Aubrey Westlake, aged 19 standing behind

father says of this time – "We were more like brothers and sisters than cousins". In 1905, thinking it cheaper to live abroad and a valuable experience for the children, Grandfather decided to take his young daughter, now 9 years old, on a

Sketch map showing Route

Cycle-Camping Tour 1905

cycle-camping tour of France and Spain; their Estonian Governess, Fraulein Saas, accompanied them (a Governess being a prerequisite of a well-to-do Victorian family). He planned the tour with meticulous care. The strongest bicycles were purchased with the lightest accessories; everything prepared with particular forethought to ease of travelling and comfort in camping. A complete record of this adventure, in the form of letters to a friend, remains.

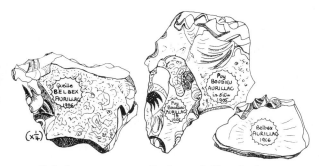

Eoliths - scrapers, flake and Hand chopper.

So in the early Summer they made their way slowly down through France, creating quite a stir as they passed by. Held up in Aurillac in the Cantal by the non-arrival of his fortnightly allowance from Clarence, (£4 a fortnight), grandfather discovered a deposit of geological interest, undisturbed in any way. He was sure it dated from the Eocene period (Dawn of the Recent) and that the flints or eoliths found showed the work of primitive man. If this proved to be correct the find would pre-date the arrival of homo-sapiens by at least two million years! Intensely excited, he decided to stay to make a comprehensive study of the site and a collection of the stones.

Returning home two years later with what the French Government described as 'part of the soil of France', (so large was the collection), he thought to spend the rest of his life cataloguing the stones, but one day, looking at the Tasmanian collection in the British Museum, he was struck with the similarity between the crude implements of the Tasmanian Aborigine to those at Aurillac. He spent two interesting years, 1908-10, in Tasmania and on his return was elected a Fellow of the Royal Anthropological Institute. He was already a Fellow of the Geological Society (1879).

By 1914, 42 acres of Purlieu-land was bought on Godshill Ridge for £800 and secured by a mortgage on his wife's eighth share of her Father's estate managed as a trust. A wooden bungalow was built and they had their first home together as a family in 14 years.

During this time, 1914-21, as a result of this settled home life, the geologist and anthropologist was gradually transformed into the humanist and educationist. He was intensely occupied in making what he felt to be a vital contribution to the preservation of civilisation and all the cultural and religious values he felt in danger of being swept away in the chaos of war and its aftermath. As a result the Order of Woodcraft Chivalry was founded in 1916 (and still continues today) and his great inspiration, The Forest School, became an integral part of his thinking and planning for the future. This also thrives as an independent adventure camping organisation, Forest School Camps Ltd. catering yearly for many hundreds of children in standing and mobile camps.

The whole conception of the Order of Woodcraft Chivalry was an inspiration and for a Quaker to have conceived it was remarkable – for Quakerism was associated with a narrow puritanical outlook. The name itself is unusual, but this combination of <u>Order</u> – <u>Woodcraft</u> and <u>Chivalry</u>, was a deliberate selection by Grandfather to express, as far as it was possible, its essential character.

<u>Order</u> was chosen to signify an organisation with a definite religious outlook – indeed Christian outlook; a religious movement in its profoundest sense.

<u>Woodcraft</u> embraced the recapitulatory theory of education – that is, for a child to retrace in its own development the whole evolution of the race. By working through the primitive state as personified by the young child or early man; by learning from first hand contact with nature; by participating in the life of the wilderness, the forest, the hills and the sea; by discovering the craft revolution begun in the neolithic age and experiencing civilisation as it progressed and produced greatness in the arts and learning in the sciences. He felt that this heritage was the true riches of mankind and together with his community spirit had made man what he is today. Through a complete evolutionary system of education, children became in their own right the "heirs of the ages". This was to be the inspiration for the Forest School.

"We believe that a child who has been rooted and grounded in Woodcraft will be able to use the higher crafts without injury and books without pedantry. In this way traditional learning and social culture will have full opportunity to complete the wisdom and refinement necessary to his highest functioning".

<u>Chivalry</u> meant the quality of caring in the deepest sense, in my Grandfather's words: "It takes all sorts of culture to make a man, but it needs chivalry to make a gentleman".

"The Order for him, while standing for simplicity, also stood for complexity, that complexity which is expressed in the exuberance, richness and splendour of life. Life which consists of the bare essentials is poor indeed, it can only become rich by adding the fullness of colour, beauty and passion of existence, whether in human form, music, ritual, drama, revelry or in other colourful ways".

So the Order of Woodcraft Chivalry (OWC), in its fullest expression, comes nearest (in this modern age) to a way of life which includes all aspects of the personality of man and his search to find a whole, balanced life in harmonious social fellowship and in harmony with his environment.

We cannot realise today how revolutionary these ideas were – Robert Baden-Powell (hero of Mafeking) had started his Boy Scout movement in 1908 largely as a result of his experience in the Boer war, but the OWC was to embrace a much wider concept, for girls as well as boys, men and women; non-political, non-denominational, it is based on the principle that the fundamental need of every individual is self-realisation.

In Grandfather's words: "We do not profess to offer a ready-made solution of the riddle of the world. The Woodcraft way we advocate is the way of the Saints. It is in the experience of life that every individual finds or loses his God. We aim, like the trainers of the knights of old, not to deny the darkness of the world, nor to explain it, but to train men to meet it. We cannot guarantee them victory, but we can help to make them strong".

The first children's camp was held in Sandy Balls from 28th July to 25th August 1920 with 12 boys from the Smoke Tribe, a Woodcraft group based in South-East London. The camp was organised by Father who took his annual holiday to run it.

The group of 12-13 year olds now experienced for the first time a primitive environment. They drew water from a well, cooked meals over wood fires, listened to the myriad sounds of nature and grew to accept the darkness of a woodland night away from the warm companionship of the campfire: They had a full and varied programme to work to and daily grew more proficient in woodcraft skills and the understanding of living together as a group. The camp was an unqualified success. A record remains: This was the beginning of camping in Sandy Balls.

In October 1922, Grandfather was killed in a side-car accident. Father riding the motorcycle had the trauma of seeing his Father killed before his eyes. His vehicle was squeezed against the roadside by other traffic, the side car turned gently over and Grandfather hit his head against the kerb. He never regained consciousness! No will was found and Father was declared 'heir at law'. His estate was divided between my Aunt Margaret who became outright owner of the Ridge property and Father, who took on the heavily mortgaged Sandy Balls and other properties which had to be sold off to maintain it. Father, now in General Practice in Bermondsey, married mother, Marjorie Gladys Harrod, on 28th April 1923; Mother's parents also came from two large Quaker families – the Harrods and the Crawshaws. Grandfather, Ernest Harrod, was a hide importer and travelled widely for his firm Heggaty Brothers, learning languages the while. My grandmother, Ida Ellen née

Marjorie and Aubrey Westlake on their Wedding Day April 28th 1923.

Four Generations. The Author aged 15 days, Keith 15 months with Mother, Grandmother, and Greatgrandmother April 1926.

Crawshaw, was a typical wife of her generation, kind and gentle by nature, she was subservient to her more dominant husband and seldom ventured outside the family home. Mother, elder of two children with a brother, Kenneth four years younger than herself, was brought up in New Cross, South East London and educated at Quaker Schools, Sibford and Saffron Walden. She was just 22 years old at the time of her marriage, Father was eight years older.

Father had been living in lodgings in Bermondsey, but on his marriage they set up home together in the recently vacated Doctor's house in Southwark Park Road.

Chapter 3

Woodcraft Education and the Family

A picture of Father as a dedicated young leader is portrayed by Doris Salt (a member of one of the early children's groups) in her contribution to the Memorial issue of Pine Cone entitled - 'Golden Eagle as I Remember Him'. (1985)

"It was over 60 years ago in the aftermath of the First World War when civil life was entirely disrupted and in order to support the war effort, extreme poverty resulted.

At that time two General Practitioners in Bermondsey were deeply concerned with the hopelessness of family life and in particular the plight of young people. Dr Alfred Salter, a serious Quaker of political convictions and Dr Aubrey Westlake, also a Quaker were especially concerned with the deprived outlook of the boys in their district. Dr Westlake was inspired to put into practice his Father's ideas based on the American League of Woodcraft being organised by the thinker and writer Ernest Thompson Seton based on the lore and culture of the American and Canadian Indians.

This idea took root in the mind and heart of Aubrey Westlake and with his Quaker connections at Sidcot School, he founded the Order of Woodcraft Chivalry and began the life work of giving these boys a new outlook on life. From his home and practice in Bermondsey the Beomond lodge was formed with great enthusiasm from the local lads. We children of neighbouring Peckham also became as enthusiastic and Revonah (reversal of Hanover St.) lodge joined in many of the activities of Beomond group. Cash and opportunities were in extremely short supply but undismayed, and with the leadership of Golden Eagle, plus the example of the American Indians we found a new challenge and inspiration in overcoming numerous problems and found a joy in doing so.

Golden Eagle and Appleblossom with Woodcraft Attendants.

With Dr Westlake as our Chief, the Order of Woodcraft Chivalry grew and in Woodcraft Indian style, suitable names were awarded to outstanding members. What name then could be more suitable for our leader, with his red gold hair and brisk red gold moustache than that of GOLDEN EAGLE?

A quiet intellectual, but an alert, forward looking young chief: Friendly, yet remote he had the

Mother and Father in Woodcraft Uniforms.

respect and admiration of us all. Especially so when he married Appleblossom (Marnie Harrod) at the Peckham Friends Meeting House. (Incidently my first attendance at a Quaker wedding).

An autocrat I suppose, but a welcome disciplinarian needed by the lads, starved by the war. So the Order grew and the Woodcraft Way of self sufficiency developed. Our badge shows clearly the education of physical ability with its axes, and its red cross representing service to others. Thus the "Order of Woodcraft Chivalry"

Sandy Balls Wood, bequeathed to Golden Eagle, became the chief O. W. C. camping site where the Annual Folkmoot was held each year when, with tremendous joy, we were able to renew friendships with the increasing number of Lodges.

These early attempts which gave hope to the young, gradually embraced all ages, in family groups or kindreds - from Babes, Trackers, Pathfinders, Waywardens and Wayfarers, so that the chivalrous aspect naturally dominated discussion Doubtless there are still those who recollect those fruitful meetings.

A Camp fire at Sandy Balls

For me as a 'Witana', well over 60, the precious memory will always be the morning Meeting for Worship round the Campfire at Sandy Balls, among the pine trees at Godshill. I wonder, do you still make tents out of proofed old sheeting, or make twisters of dough on sticks round the fire?"

Doris Salt

It is interesting to try and recall those early Folkmoots in Sandy Balls from 1926 - 1933 of which I was part. Admittedly in 1926 I was only a babe-in-arms and obviously remember nothing of that time - but it was at this camp that I was presented to the large gathering around the Ceremonial Fire and welcomed as a birthright member of the Order.

In fact, the Folkmoot of 1926 was the largest one ever held in Sandy Balls, attended by 284 members. The photograph shows the main camping ground, The 'Festive Circle' and of the Grand Feast in the 'Folkmoot Circle' below, with bracken-lined baskets full of apples, oranges and tiny chocolate bars and other goodies ready for distribution.

Folkmoot, Sandy Balls.

Folkmoot, Sandy Balls.

However, I do remember the atmosphere of the 1933 Folkmoot where Father announced his resignation. Mother and Martin were not present and Keith and I were staying with my Grandparents nearby in Godshill. The feeling of tension, even slight hostility, when previously all had been welcome and friendliness, were very tangible to me as a child. No wonder Mother chose to stay away.

…And so the Golden Eagle Kindred withdrew from the Order and the Order withdrew from Sandy Balls for many years. Strangely enough, I never liked to ask what really happened at this time.

My main memories of those early Folkmoots were of scents, sounds and colours. As we children ran excitedly to the Folkmoot Festival from the 'Eyrie', our little holiday home, we were aware of the scent of the surrounding pine trees intermingled with woodsmoke from innumerable cooking fires, the voices of children, the chop-chop of skilled axemen and the fragrance of newly chopped word.

'Great Bear', Grand Keeper of the Fire, of whom we were much in awe, taught us to respect the Everburning Ceremonial Fire and that it was just **not** done to run through the closely packed tents, tripping over the guy ropes.

'Great Bear' and the Woodcraft greeting – 'Blue Sky'.

We added our little voices, and arms in salute to the great crescendo of sound of the Order Watchword, 'Blue Sky' at the beginning and ending of each camp rally and joined in the Goodnight Song where age groups of children retired quietly to bed at the appointed time. We felt part of the pageantry and splendour of the Ceremonial Opening and Closing of Folkmoot, overawed by the magnificence of the Chiefs in their Ceremonial robes and in the knowledge that Father and Mother were Chieftain and his Lady and we should behave accordingly.

Later, when we were old enough, we pitched our own little tents, lined our camp beds with bracken which lulled us to sleep with its dusky fragrance and were wakened in the morning light by the haunting 'Arise Song' which echoed through the sleeping camp…and in my memory the sun shone every day and the skies were always blue!

The Zuni Arise Song
Rise, Arise, arise,
Wake thee, arise, life is calling thee,
Wake thee, arise; ever watchful be
Mother life god she is calling thee,
Mother life god she is greeting thee.
Rise, Arise, arise,

In the 1950's, Mother was asked to give a paper to the Conference of Educational Associations held yearly at University College, London, on the subject of 'Woodcraft Education and the Family'. Admitting she had no real qualifications for addressing such a learned gathering, Mother introduced herself as being first and foremost an ordinary housewife and mother with secondary interests of farming, gardening and all livestock.

She continues…

"It was my great good fortune to be intimately connected with the Order in its enthusiastic youth, and the birth and upbringing of my three eldest children coincided with its heyday. It was only natural that working in and for the Order, I should attempt to carry out its ideas on education with my growing family.

Having had a most orthodox, suburban upbringing myself, I was determined that my own children should have no such thing. That, as far as possible, I would follow the tenets of the O.W.C. - they should learn by personal experience - they should follow the Woodcraft Way, with all that that implied, although living in a congested part of South London it was not possible to follow this too literally."

She then goes on to give a charming account of her attempt to do just this. The first lesson to learn was Self Reliance, even to the extent of allowing Keith (a 5-year old) to go to the Zoo by himself when he had saved enough money to do so.

She continues…

"About 3 weeks later, a dull November morning, he came to me and said: "I'm going to the Zoo to-day. " A little nonplussed, I asked him how much money he had. He replied, "6d. for the Zoo, 6d. for the fare, and 6d. for the Aquarium. "I had to think quickly. If I made some excuse and kept him at home, he would never trust me again. About ^{1}/2 hour later, he started off - a postcard in the breast pocket of his coat, with his name, address, and telephone number clearly printed, and "No. 1. bus to the Zoo and back" - a carrier bag full of sliced potatoes for the elephants and greens for the deer, etc. in one hand, and one containing his own lunch and tea in the other. The one concession I made was to give

him money to buy a hot drink, and in case he needed to get someone to telephone me. With a notebook and pencil in his other pocket, he left the house about 10 a.m. As it got darker and foggier and nearly 5 0 'clock, I began to doubt the wisdom of my action, and to imagine the comments of relations and friends should anything unforeseen occur. However, about 5.15 he arrived back, quietly happy, not a bit tired, his little notebook full of the names of all the fish seen in the Aquarium, in large unsteady capitals. A lovely, lovely day. Yet strangely enough, he never asked to go alone again, although at intervals I continued to take all three.

Obviously, while living in town, the recapitulatory, or valley section, aspect of the Woodcraft Way could only be very partially followed. I therefore took the children, as often as possible, down to our Estate of 110 acres of woodland, sloping steeply to the R. Avon, on the borders of the New Forest. This, Ernest Westlake, the founder of the Order, had originally acquired, intending to use it as a centre for all Woodcraft activities, with the Forest School as its focus.

Unfortunately, he died before this was anything more than a castle in the air. It was a number of years before the Forest School came into being under the guidance of Cuthbert Rutter, its first Headmaster.

For one whole summer term I was there as a housemother, doing the cooking, washing and looking after the younger children, as I had firsthand experience of the life. Its keynote was simplicity and a deep belief in the importance of learning by doing. There was very little

Outside the Sunny Sleeping Rooms

The Study Room at the Forest School

equipment, so the fullest possible use was made of the natural resources of the place. The children climbed trees, made houses in them, using bracken and boughs. They played in a large natural sandpit at the back of the house, and dug clay from the seam in the back, from which they made elementary pots and persuaded me to bake them in the oven. They never tired of the streams and river or of exploring the wood and the edge of the New Forest. Lessons and meals were out of doors whenever possible.

Camping, nowadays, is taken for granted, but a quarter of a century ago it was considered eccentric, to say the least, particularly with young children, and I endured much well-meant criticism and advice from my more orthodox relatives.

Camping became an integral part of the children's lives. I made each a small tent, with stencilled animals and flowers all round - each had a camping eiderdown and a coloured blanket to match, and these, with a stout groundsheet, they stowed in a light-weight, showerproof rucksack, also homemade. They became adept at putting up their tents, helping each other when necessary, lighting campfires, making cocoa and simple meals, fishing with little more than a bent pin, and often catching perch, roach and dace. The perch made delicious eating.

Although they were all too young for Woodling Trials, we carried out a modified version of them. One I found particularly useful was the Trial of Cleanliness. Other Trials tackled were those of the Seeing Eye, Noiseless Tread, Keen Smell and Sharp Hearing. For the Trial of Neat Hand, the children made sand castles with very ambitious gardens, rockeries and summer houses, also a Tree house at the top of a pine – hoisting everything up by means of a stout rope.

The Golden Eagle Kindred dressed for Folkmoot.

We explored the whole wood, little by little, tracing the streams as far as we were able, watching the birds and squirrels in the part kept as a Nature Reserve, and every day we bathed in the river - the two eldest swimming quite presentably - then running about in the sunshine to get warm and dry.

When they were 7, 9 and $10^1/2$ we thought it would be good to let them have a few days' camping entirely on their own. We all went down to the wood, and after supplying them with the real necessities for camping, locked up our little bungalow and left them to themselves. We returned six days later, about noon. The camp site looked orderly and well cared for. No one was about, although it was evident that someone had just had a grand washing day - clothes were strewn all over the bracken drying.

The eldest came along with a bundle of wood for the camp fire, while the 9 year old girl hurried back from the store with some biscuits she had suddenly thought we should like with our cup of tea. She told us that she had sent the youngest to the store to buy $^1/2$d. of soap flakes, and to go down to the river and give himself a good soaping all over. He soon returned pink and shining.

Much thought had gone towards the lunch, I know, but I can now only remember that the salad contained an excess of Spanish onion, which we were forced to confess we could not manage, and that the pudding was a most delicious junket with apple cut up in it.

We learnt afterwards that the eldest boy had been rather tyrannical over mulligatawny soup - demanding it at each mid-day meal, when the others did not care for it - and insisting on an evening ritual of campfire, cocoa and singsong, when the younger ones were too tired to enjoy it. Apart from this, the experiment was an unqualified success."

Much more of human interest was presented to the well-attended meeting in the Lecture Hall of University College and Mother ended with the following thoughts -

"The qualities produced by this Woodcraft Way of life are, in my view, those best calculated to fit the coming generation to make good in the world which is now emerging.

Life to-day is becoming increasingly uncertain and insecure and particularly difficult for the young. The prevalent idea is, that so long as the parent provides his child with a good orthodox education, followed by a training for a profession or trade, he has done all that is required of him. I maintain that more important than all this is to provide him with a balanced, confident, yet adventurous outlook on life, and the rest will be added unto him.

Victorian education - to which we still largely adhere - was education for a stable future. What is urgently needed now is education for an <u>un</u>certain, <u>un</u>stable, sometimes almost hypothetical future, and this cannot be acquired or superimposed in a day. The aim of educationalists should be to fit children for anything they may have to meet, not coerce them into a stereotyped pattern.

The majority of people still think of education as that received in schools after the age of 8, overlooking the fact that the very foundations of the character and personality of the growing individual are laid down during the first 5 years in the home.

Hence the supreme importance of Woodcraft education in the family, for only in this way can we achieve what I consider to be the only true education for the future."

Woodcrafters dancing in the festive circle – Sandy Balls.

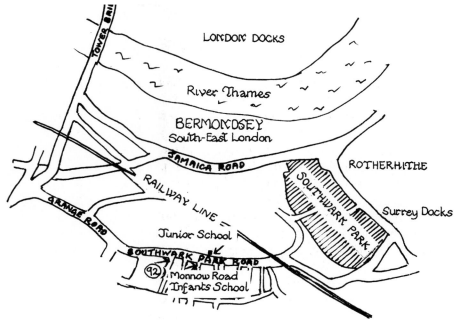

Sketch Map of Bermondsey.

Chapter 4

A Rich Kaleidoscope - Bermondsey

Our home in Bermondsey, South East London was a large bleak corner house facing Southwark Park Road on one side, Reverdy Road on the other. A back-yard was the only garden with a wall topped with broken glass, separating us from our neighbour; presumably put there to deter tomcats that caterwauled the nights away. It was a doctor's house with polished brass plate and morning whitened step; a house that was never left, for Father, the resident doctor of a large panel practice, could be called out at any hour of the day or night, and often was to birth or death or a child seriously ill with one of the many epidemics which devastated the poor during the 1920s and 30s. Indeed we children were not immune to the ravages of whooping cough, measles and chicken pox but, thankfully, never caught the dreaded scarlet fever or diphtheria. Off Father would go carrying his little black bag, walking or cycling through deserted lamp-lit streets on his errands of mercy.

Father was in partnership with Dr Alfred Salter, a brilliant doctor who later became a Justice of the Peace and well known Labour Member of Parliament; the only student to receive a triple first, a glittering career was forecast for him within the medical profession.

Trees planted in Bermondsey

Instead, dedicated to the well-being of the people, he became convinced he could achieve more through politics, and in the early days did good work opening health centres and beautifying the arid streets and factory areas with trees and gardens. Later the Labour County Council, under the leadership of Herbert Morrison, supported by Dr Salter, was to have more ambitious plans which necessitated pulling down the close-packed terraced housing and erecting modern purpose-built flats.

As senior partner of the practice, Dr Salter forbade us children to play in the yard. Mother, only young herself, felt this restriction keenly and took every opportunity before we were school age, to take us down to father's wooded estate, Sandy Balls, on the edge of the New Forest and the home of her parents, Ida and Ernest Harrod who lived nearby. Later in 1928, father built a little wooden bungalow for us all, in idyllic surroundings, with a gipsy caravan (a family heirloom) placed alongside as bedroom for my elder brother, Keith and myself. We were guarded, if guarded we needed to be, by grandfather's magnificent Red Setter, 'Bobby', whose charges we all were when we were there.

Bermondsey, a close built-up area in a poor working class district, had a certain charm of its own. Our daily walk was to Southwark Park, holding tightly to the pram, past the colourful market stalls that lined both sides of the road. The stall holders bought direct from Covent Garden, Smithfield and Billinghurst Markets, not so far away; straight from the country, this produce could not have been fresher. In Winter we stopped first at the chestnut brazier and mother allowed us to warm our hands at the rosy glow and buy a bag of freshly roasted nuts. The equally inviting hot sarsaparilla drink was forbidden for the glasses might not be clean! In Summer the pitch was occupied by an Italian ice-cream seller and the creamy white mixture containing thin slices of lemon was kept cold by deliveries of block ice. He did a brisk trade and we yearned to buy, but mother made her own delicious ice-cream in our refrigerator at home and it was equally forbidden.

All the stalls were fascinating to us as children; the rabbits and poultry hanging heads down, still in their brilliant plumage and soft furry coats, 6d a rabbit; mountains of spotted Canary bananas, four a penny; plump bright-eyed herring, 1d each; the cat's meat stall, where slices cut while you waited, showed the marbled iridescent graining of horse-flesh, the cat food of the day. Street hawkers were there too, especially at Christmas time, and strange dark men selling liquorice sticks, the blind match seller, the woman with streaming eyes and red raw hands grating fresh horse radish, favourite condiment for the Sunday joint of roast beef. And the many friendly shops. One that always held our attention, yet repelled us, sold live eels, large squirming ones in large containers, considered a great delicacy in Bermondsey, but mother never fancied them and neither did I; the ever-popular toy shop where Mrs Leach, a patient of father, took us through to her back garden to see three enormous black toads squatting by the lily pond. Were they not Princes in disguise? The high-class baker who advertised Angel and Devil's Cake (one so white the other so dark) and the low-class one who sold squares of bread pudding. This thrifty baker used up all his stale bread, enriched it generously with spices and fruit and, when the midday hooter sounded, sold the luscious snack to the factory workers.

Father had few private patients, for 2/6d a visit was a large sum and few could afford it, but the Jewish owner of the sweet shop was one and Habins, the draper, another. Everything sold at Habins was a bargain, from a yard of calico at $11^3/4$d a yard to a card of pearl buttons, $1^3/4$d. We knew exactly what a farthing would buy, for didn't we get four different kinds of sweets for our Saturday penny pocket money at the corner shop across the road? Lipton's the grocer was a great favourite of mine. Large tins of Peak Frean biscuits, straight from the local factory, took pride of place along the front of the counter. Sugar of every kind was weighed into strong, blue paper bags and large slabs of butter cut and patted to size on cold marble. Lovely fresh butter was kept in cool cellars below - an integral part of most houses in Bermondsey. And Woolworth's ... the shop that really did sell 'nothing over 6d'; a real treat for us was a tin of melon or pineapple jam at 6d a tin.

'Their bit of Heaven' – Back Gardens in Bermondsey.

A Modern Purpose Built Flat in Bermondsey.

On to Southwark Park we went, keeping our chestnuts warm, for it was bad manners to eat in the street. There, free at last, we ran ahead and climbed the steps leading to the bandstand and stopped - for we knew full well what the notice said – 'No Admittance under 14 years' – a great age to us and many years ahead. Under Mother's excellent tuition we closely observed the changing seasons from bud burst to leaf fall, the glorious bedding schemes of Summer; the mysterious beauty of plane trees during November fog and Winter frost. Returning home in the gathering gloom, the gas flares above the stalls hissed and thrilled and threw grotesque shadows on the passing people and pavement beneath.

Bermondsey was a close working class community, the extended family evident in every street. They had a dignity born of long years of hardship, suffering and childbearing and Father had a deep affection and regard for these hardworking people. Employed in the many factories and nearby docks he was concerned that this community was soon to be swept away, for the Labour Government and County Council were pledged to improve the lot of the people by building modern flats and tenements with safe playgrounds but <u>no</u> gardens, the delight and solace of the men-folk who called them 'their bit of heaven'. They kept pigeons, rabbits, poultry, cultivated gardens and along the long hot walls that divided garden from garden vines tumbled, producing an abundance of small sweet grapes in Autumn. So father launched his one-man campaign against the Labour Council. He organised a lecture series called 'Out of the Frying Pan into the Fire' and warned the authorities in every way possible that the destruction of this community would lead to an increase in mental and physical illness, alcoholism, vandalism and hooliganism - but he was a lone voice crying in the wilderness. The brewers took note and moved in in force, with a pub on every street corner and all that he predicted was sadly proved to be right. But all that came later.

All five of us children were born in Bermondsey, well within the sound of Bow Bells, and although we attended local schools and developed devastating cockney accents, however hard we tried we were never really accepted by the other children out of school hours. A form of inverted snobbery existed, for the parents did not think it right or proper for <u>their</u> children to associate with us – doctor's children. Strangely enough when we moved to Godshill in 1938, a tiny village on the edge of the New Forest, the reaction of the village mothers was exactly the same. I began to think that except within our own family we did not really belong anywhere.

During the summer time, regularly in bed by 7 o'clock, we observed, through net curtains, the happy children playing below. For the side streets were a vast playground – little traffic ever came along, perhaps a bicycle or two, the rag and bone man with his horse and cart calling his wares, the muffin man ringing his bell – but seldom a car.

The street games varied with the age of the child and season of the year – as the days lengthened yet another new craze swept the closely built-up area; tops, scooters, yo-yos, roller skates, ball games, singing games, skipping, hoops, hopscotch, hide and seek and rounders. November 5th brought out the guys and the begging bowls - 'A penny for the guy, mister?' Any blank wall resounded to the thud, thud of balls. 'Mothers and Fathers' was a great favourite, dressed up as perfect replicas of their parents, complete with babe in arms, they mimicked in greatest detail the drama of life. The dominance of the father and subservience of the mother were very evident even to a child observer.

Class 2 Six year olds at Monnow Road School, The Author centre by train 1931.

Once we had the great excitement of joining a group and going outside our own district to tie door knockers together and run away before being caught. It was all good-humoured fun. The Bobby on the beat sometimes gave chase and the boys received a cuff or two. I remember only one case of vandalism and it had a tragic result. Milk bottles were put out for collection round the trees that lined the streets and the boys took to pelting them with stones. A child got a splinter in his eye: it blinded him! This terrible news was given out in all the Borough schools and had a salutary effect on the children. The message got home for it never happened again.

School life was happy, even I think, for the runny-nosed, undersized urchins from the real slums, and classes of 40-50 were not unknown. There was an order and discipline and no young child ever questioned the authority of the teacher whom they often worshipped. I certainly did my first teacher, the gentle Miss Dougherty! My elder brother, Keith, 15 months my senior, had so far been taught at home by a friend of father's, but Keith was a precocious child and difficult to keep happily occupied, cooped up in the house, and Mother haunted the Montessori and Froebel shops for things for him to do. So, when I came to my 5th birthday, the decision was taken to send us both to the Monnow Road Infants School, not many streets away. On our first day, we arrived after lunch and entered a darkened room and made our way through tiny sleeping bodies. It was all very strange and not what we had expected at all! However it soon became clear, for the five year olds awoke, picked up their little folding beds and helped stack them away. It was siesta time.

The children who were not considered very bright sat at the top of the classroom; the desks rose up in several tiers as in a theatre. Here they sat, not learning very much but never disrupting the class. The front row was reserved for the able students. There was a great competition for 1st and 2nd place in front of the teacher. Every morning we had the daily ritual of singing our multiplication tables until the correct answer became automatic (an invaluable asset later in life much envied by my sons). Then followed mental arithmetic, but I much preferred painting and experimenting with patterns and colours.

An embarrassing incident occurred when I was seven years old. After a difficult winter, I was being built up with cod liver oil and malt but Father had read that garlic juice rubbed on the soles of the feet would prevent colds. On the day I was liberally treated, the afternoon sun shone hotly through the long windows and the room became warmer and warmer. With a long pole, the teacher opened the windows but the reek of garlic became overpowering. Looking everywhere to discover the source, she finally decided one of the local pickle factories was to blame and the windows were shut. Luckily the bell rang for the end of school. I never wore garlic again!

The Alma Road Junior School was equally happy for me, here there was a girls' and a boys' side, not co-educational as in the Infants School. Needlework, current events, long division and multiplication and even decimals were added to the curriculum. But Keith was not enjoying himself. He was selected to be a scholarship boy, so to ease the pressure on him he was sent for a few terms to A.S. Neill's now famous school at Summerhill.

Several terms later the headmistress requested to see my parents. She said it did no service to a doctor's daughter to be educated with girls of a different social class, so I too in January 1935, a couple of months before my ninth birthday, joined Keith who was by now at Forest School, an experimental school, the practical expression of the Order of Woodcraft Chivalry, based on grandfather Ernest Westlake's ideas in Sandy Balls, Godshill – Father's 100 acre woodland estate. It had opened there in 1928 with a handful of pupils and was now expanding. Father was chairman of the Forest School Company and he felt under a certain obligation to send his own children as they became old enough. Mother was not so keen but consoled herself with the knowledge that her Father and Mother lived close by and would keep an eye on us.

Forest School in Sandy Balls 1928-1938.

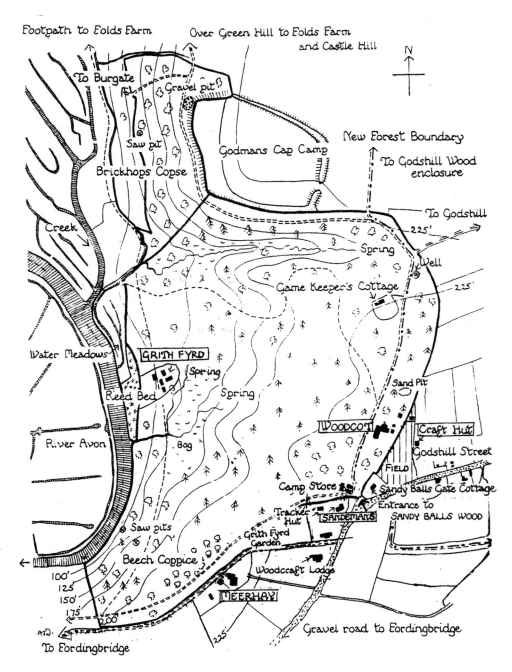

Chapter 5

Memories of Forest School

Forest School at this time (January 1935) consisted of two boarding houses 'Woodcot' and 'Meerhay', a school room 'Sandemans' and a Craft Hut – all timber built. Woodcot, to be my home for the next year, was a spacious, airy bungalow, a World War 1 reconditioned army hut with brick partitions including a large kitchen and bathroom. With the growth of the school an L-shaped extension had recently been added. The building had been put up originally in 1922 for the Mother of a friend of Ernest Westlake and on her death sold to the Forest School Company; it nestled among the Scots Pines in Sandy Balls with a 1½ acre field alongside for the school's pet ponies 'Cherry', an Icelandic, and 'Posy', a Shetland. There was also Smuts, now 4 years old, Cherry's offspring at the great age of 27 years.

Meerhay lay outside the boundary of Sandy Balls and had at one time been a guest house. There was a large garden and various out-buildings in the grounds.

Sandemans lay conveniently equidistant from both at the entrance to Sandy Balls with a large orchard and area for growing crops. It had three rooms – the large centre one for

Woodcot – one of the Boarding Houses, Sandy Balls.

Sandemans – the School House.

use of the Woodlings – the 8-12 year olds (the largest age group), the smaller ones on either side were entered not through the doors but by the windows, thus avoiding any disturbance by other age groups of lessons; for the doors between were kept securely locked. With about 40 pupils and staff at this time a large wooden hut (27 x 15ft) in the grounds of Sandemans was utilised for the Tracker boys (12-15 year olds). It was out of bounds for anyone else and even the headmaster had to ask permission to enter. Jealously guarded by the privileged occupants, the seven boys were expected to keep it neat and tidy. The Craft Hut lay just across the field from Woodcot. The only other habitation in Sandy Balls was a woodman's cottage, occupied by a widow, Mrs Sparks, and her two sons. She did washing and ironing for the school.

Sanitation was in the form of earth closets housed outside and 'friendly pots' under each bed, emptied by the children in the morning. There were three open fireplaces in Woodcot, an old Swedish Range and primuses in the kitchen, candles and oil lamps for lighting and bare boards on the floors polished every Saturday morning. It was very primitive indeed and cold in Winter but the staff were young, keen and enthusiastic and it was not Winter all the time. The one luxury was running water as mentioned in the Forest School prospectus of 1931: "The School has its own private water supply automatically pumped from a pure water spring in Sandy Balls Wood". A few other dwellings in Godshill had standpipes outside their homes supplied from Sandy Balls but no one else had the luxury of running water and a hot water system as in Woodcot and Meerhay. In the village the use of well and rainwater collection still continued as it had for centuries past.

Most of my memories of Forest School are happy ones, only once do I remember being slapped by the housemother in Woodcot. I insisted that I had seen the Great God Pan with his cloven hoofs in the woods and would not go to bed for I was so frightened that he would come and take me away. Myths and legends and ancient lore were high on the agenda for the Woodling age group of which I was one!

The other disquieting episode was my arrival at Fordingbridge station in January 1936 a few days late, owing to illness and nobody there to meet me. It was a dark night, I was a child of nine and school was $2^1/2$ miles away! Thinking to be met at any moment, I decided to leave the now deserted station and to start walking. On and on I went – through Fordingbridge and then on to the more familiar Godshill road. The most frightening part for me was passing the Gipsy Encampment on the crest of the hill as I approached the village. Never was I more relieved to see a light shining than the lamp that shone through the darkness from the kitchen at Meerhay and visible to me from the main road. I fairly flew the last little way and safe at last, collapsed in tears and was comforted. My parents were rightly concerned that though the school had been notified, I had not been met.

…And what of my most unhappy memory?

Sunday was staff day and we children were given a lunch packet after breakfast and expected to occupy ourselves until tea-time when we were allowed back in. I remember one Winter Sunday when I had a streaming cold and it was raining. Life was indeed pretty miserable then.

Father's cousin was headmaster, Cuthbert Kirk Rutter (1901-1946). Educated at the Quaker School, Leighton Park, Reading; Queen's College Cambridge, Housemaster at Borstal, Vice Principal of Toynbee Hall and now enthusiastic Headmaster of Forest School. Only 34 at the time, he was beloved by staff and children alike.

Coming from a Borough Council School in Bermondsey I found it very strange indeed that teachers should be called by their Christian names or even nicknames, and that Cuthbert, the headmaster, commonly called Kirk, should sleep on a mattress on the floor rather than in a bed! Camping yes – but not indoors! Each house had a housemother and father, other staff and a mixed age range of children.

Sandemans –
The School House.

Lessons in the Tracker
School Room.
(12 – 15 year olds)

Summer lessons in the
garden with the Elves
(5 – 8 year olds).

Coming from a class of 40 or more I found it rather lonely for there was only one other girl my age. Joycie Edwards was a few months younger than me; she was a delicate child and had a brother also there called Ormond, a fey little 7-year old, later in adult life to become a Priest of the Christian Community.

Bathing in the Creek.

Hide and Seek in Sandy Balls Wood.   A Riding lesson – Author and friend in background.

Looking back, over 60 years, various highlights of my two years at Forest School spring to mind, brought into clearer focus by the 20 letters written home and still in my possession. The Forest School prospectus describes the 'School Estate 100 acres of woodland, as a veritable children's paradise', and this was indeed true. We climbed trees, played in the sand pit, built dens and tree houses, stalked through the child-high bracken, laid trails, dug for clay and made pots, wove and plaited rushes, swam and dived in the Avon, sunbathed, rode the school ponies, cultivated our gardens, gathered wood and lit fires and in fact enjoyed everything that a primitive environment offered.

On the New Forest we walked far and wide over the vast stretches of heather and gorse and through closely planted enclosures. We played games, dammed streams, climbed the enormous old Douglas Firs at Sloden enclosure and dug for Roman pottery, picked wild flowers and in the summer went on hikes over the forest to the sea, camping as we went.

School work was not neglected either, lessons started at 9 o'clock on week day mornings – but my memory of Sandemans is not of lessons but of my trial of silence (trials for each age group were part of the curriculum at Forest School). I can see myself now, sitting at my desk by the open door looking into the garden and remaining silent all morning despite constant provocation. I was keen to keep my parents informed about my progress ' I am going onto book two now'. 'Can you tell mother that Beefy thinks I'm going to be on book three in Arithmetic soon'. Strangely enough, Arithmetic was the one subject that I found I was behind with when I returned to a Borough Council Secondary School in 1937.* From my Autumn report of 1935 it appears that we covered a wide range of subjects and although lessons were not compulsory, I for one seem to have been a regular attender for I was entrusted with the key to the Woodling Room and when it was cold to light the fire. 'Please send my gloves down, it is getting very cold in the Woodling Room, I light the fire every morning'.

The Wide Game was a favourite at Forest School and the one I remember most vividly was played during the school camp at the end of the summer term to which other children and parents were invited. A Forest enclosure was chosen about 25 minutes walk away. The idea I believe was to raid the enemy base and steal the flag – or was there more than one? Played in the half light in a little known environment I found the game frightening, my bare legs scratched by brambles and the worry of what I might be treading on. I took no active part in the raiding parties and breathed a sigh of relief when the gong sounded, signalling that one side had won and the game was over. Hot cocoa was enjoyed by all and ground sheets and sleeping bags laid out in the woodland clearing – then all was quiet. In the morning when I lifted my ground sheet, I discovered two squashed adders beneath! Indeed

* *Appendix 4*

adders were plentiful in those days. During our walks they lay sunning themselves on the pathways. The boys carried forked sticks with which to pin them to the ground, and nobody stopped or reproved them in any way for such barbaric practice. Today the adder is protected and there is a substantial fine for death or damage.

The boys were in many ways little savages and to a well-brought up child their manners left much to be desired. For some unknown reason they had developed a taste for formic acid and delighted in eating the swollen abdomen of the wood-ant, so abundant in Sandy Balls. There was a craze for making homemade wine but when some made from banana skins caused sickness, and the other made was strongly intoxicating it was forbidden.

Later a cache of bottles was discovered in the Tracker Hut and suitably disposed of. Once I believe a boy ate hemlock, thinking it to be parsnip and had to have his stomach pumped out, but at the time this was hushed up. On the whole, except for an outbreak of impetigo and infestation by threadworms, which I was riddled with for years, the children led a charmed life. When giving the Woodcot roof its annual tarring no one fell off, although Mother complained that Keith's clothes were covered in tar when he returned home for the Summer holidays. Visits from health and safety inspectors were unheard of – the children were examined monthly by the school doctor (Father) and cuts, grazes and minor ailments were treated by the staff. There had been a school San, but with no ill children and the school expanding rapidly, it was thought better to utilise it for staff accommodation.

Wilfred – The Riding Master.

The Author on George.

It was in the Autumn of 1935 that a Riding Master came – his name was Wilfred. He brought his two horses with him, a great big Chestnut, 'George', and 'Pizarro', an Arab Stallion. The care and knowledge of the horse and riding lessons, from an expert, now became part of the curriculum. I took to horsemanship like a duck to water and became Wilfred's favourite companion; this meant I accompanied him out riding in the Forest twice a week. I remember being fascinated by the way he opened the Forest Gates and closed them behind us without dismounting. One day an unfortunate incident occurred. Pizarro bolted with me down the main road and stopped dead at the 'Fighting Cocks', the village Pub. I was thrown off, shaken but unhurt and, as is the way in horsemanship, I re-mounted and continued back to school – I never rode Pizarro again! Wilfred was obviously relieved that I hadn't been hurt and impressed that I hadn't ruined his horse's mouth, but from that time on solid, unflappable George was my mount. At the end of the Spring term Wilfred left, taking his horses with him; we never knew why.

In the Summer term hikes were taken, one for the Woodlings and one for the Trackers. Woodlings were allowed to carry 8lbs on their backs and the rucksacks were weighed and surplus equipment either put in the trek cart, pushed or pulled by all in turn or by the accompanying staff. We were expected to write a diary every night and a letter home records that 'on the hike we walked 67 miles' – this over a period of 10 days visiting Beaulieu and Lymington as we went and finally to Milford on Sea. It was a great adventure only marred by the abundance of mosquitoes and the time (30 minutes) we had to boil the stream water, when no drinking water was available!

The Woodling Hike – Summer 1935.

The Author pushing the Trek Cart.

The Sea at last.

Cultivating a garden was encouraged and in my letters home I make frequent reference to crops and flowers grown. I mention making a pond, nasturtiums, tulips, lettuces, sweetpeas, irises, and radishes. Strangely enough my family and I now live in the school house and the garden I cultivate is where I had my original garden in those far-off Forest School days.

In the Autumn of 1936 both housemothers were expecting babies. Nelly, now married to Ron Brand, (Beefy), housemother at Meerhay, and Dorothea at Woodcot, married to Leslie England. Joycie and I, residing at Meerhay, watched anxiously whenever Nelly entered an earth closet in case the baby fell out – luckily this did not happen! I announced the arrival of both babies, (it appears they were born on the same day) in a letter home. I include it here as it gives a picture of our many activities at Forest School and how we were entrusted to light a fire in our bedroom when the weather was cold.

'Grandpa' kept the Camp store at the entrance to Sandy Balls. It was a converted cattle byre or stable – it was very primitive inside with a stable door and a window at each end. I remember a candle lighting the dark interior on a Winter morning, Grandpa with mittens on his hands, enveloped in a large white apron stamping his feet to keep warm; the smell of paraffin and candles, homely but overpowering. Here we spent our pocket money, one penny for every year, so I received 9 pennies a week.

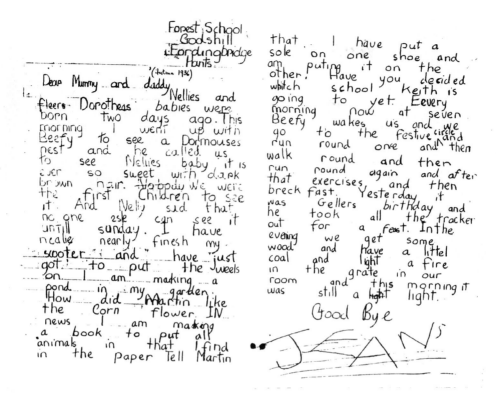

There was a craze for buying tiny tins of Nestle's sweetened condensed milk at 2d a tin. Grandpa kindly made two holes for us with a nail and we sucked the delicious sweetness through until all had gone – no thought of rotting teeth in those days! Large marshmallows, commonly called 'doorsteps' were another delicacy we all enjoyed. Other choice there certainly was but not remembered by me.

Food was plentiful and good. Muesli – Bircher Benner inspired – was a favourite summer dish. We all did our turn at helping in the kitchen and I remember making Yorkshire pudding to accompany the Sunday joint: cracking the eggs into the flour and when mixing trying to keep the yolk whole for as long as possible, then adding the milk and slowly and carefully beating the mixture until smooth and bubbly. At the end of breakfast and tea the obligatory mug of milk was poured out for us and not before. This left a milky slime in the mouth – word got round that Father as school doctor was responsible and the blame was somehow transferred to me. This made me very uneasy and perhaps I said something to Father, I do not remember, but the practice was discontinued.

The Craft Hut was a great source of delight to us and Margery Large 'Largery', a talented artist in her own right, was an inspiring teacher. I made a stool, wove a

The Farm buildings and Camp Store at the entrance to Sandy Balls.

'Grandpa' Harrod – outside the Camp Store.

belt, slippers with knitted tops and leather soles, an engine shed, a papier maché bowl, a bird table, a scooter, a lino cut for Christmas cards and an embroidered cover for the diary of the hike. Long hours were spent there happily occupied with items for our own use or as presents. We did weaving on simple looms while the older children did more complicated designs on full size looms, and leatherwork helped by one of the houseparents in Meerhay, Mary Roberts. She too was responsible for a production of Shakespeare's 'A Midsummer Night's Dream' and helped by Norman Keats the music teacher, Gilbert and Sullivan's 'Mikado'. There was plenty of work for everyone and the Mikado was performed in Godshill Village Hall to much applause.

Keith was always happily occupied at Forest School for there was great scope for his many talents. Trails, trials, treasure hunts, fireworks and wireless and indeed anything that needed a little concentration and initiative were his province. A contemporary, Edward (Teddy) Lewis, writing in the Forest School Camps Magazine in 1985 under the title 'Recollection of Forest School': wrote 'In the first dormitory Keith Westlake was the intellectual leader. I remember his study of the radio. He learned a lot about it and built a small receiver. He was 10 or 11 years at the time'.

There was an enthusiastic letter home from Keith in February 1935 about a treasure hunt …'We found the treasure there was lots of oranges and apples and sweets then we went up and they put us in a hot bath because we had all our clothes wet through and then there was a lovely fire and then there was plums and soup for tea.
Love and kisses from Keith'.

A Midsummer Night's Dream.

The whole cast in Meerhay.

Scene with Bottom the weaver, Puck, Titania and the fairies (Author, fairy in the centre).

In those days everything needed for making fireworks could be brought from the local chemist in Fordingbridge and on the 16th November I asked for more pocket money for Keith because he had spent it all in this way!

Then there were the Woodling afternoons when we passed trials. I remember vividly swimming across the river holding a lighted candle.

Jean (9), Father, Keith (10), Mother with Carol, Martin,
The Westlake Family in 1935.

So ended two years at Forest School and I look back with nostalgia to those close-packed carefree days and my first experience of so many things. I had my second experience of growing in quite a different environment. Back in Bermondsey for the next eighteen months, the Nature Study teacher enthused her pupils to grow a broad bean in blotting paper and record their observations. I have my record still. How many of us I wonder have observed the miracle of growth in such a way?

Chapter 6
Sandy Balls – 1923 - 1938

By 1922, Ernest Westlake had already established Sandy Balls as a centre for Woodcraft activities – but after his death, Father, with a busy medical practice in Bermondsey, was unable to supervise it himself. So, when in 1923 his father-in-law, Ernest Harrod, retired on grounds of ill-health at the age of 51 years, Father offered him the position as steward. My Grandparents were given a two-acre plot of land adjacent to Sandy Balls on which they erected a bungalow, calling it 'Woodcraft Lodge' – for they were keen members of the O.W.C. Indeed Ernest acted as Recorder (Secretary) of the organisation and Editor of their magazine 'Pine Cone' for many years.

Woodcraft Lodge newly built 1924.

Ida & Ernest Harrod outside Woodcraft Lodge 1929.

Grandfather supervised all Estate business, sale of wood, collection of water rates and campsite dues; he employed a woodman and when Ernest Westlake's other inspirational ideas were realised in Sandy Balls – Forest School in 1928 and Grith Fyrd in 1932 – he kept an eye on the Forest School children and the occupants of the camp as well. It was a very satisfactory arrangement, Grandfather regained his health and Father had peace of mind.

Grith Fyrd was adapted from the Ephebia scheme of ancient Greece for the training of 18 – 21 year olds in citizenship and was something much needed in the country at this time.

*"The early 'thirties and the great depression were upon them and problems needing a practical solution were making themselves felt. A vast army of unemployed, and more particularly unemployable, men were hanging round the streets with nothing to do. Here was a great social problem and the Order were well equipped to deal with it. Some of these men were so long out of work that they had become useless to society and themselves. A plan was worked out and advertised in the national Press and gradually men began to arrive at the site from many parts of the country. The project was given the name Grith Fyrd (from the Anglo-Saxon meaning Positive Constructive Peace). When the first of these men arrived they were given the task of getting a roof over their heads. Many of the men had only limited skills and were heavily depressed, but under careful guidance the buildings got underway'.

Grith Fyrd – Sandy Balls as a haven for victims of Depression – Extract from article in "Hampshire" by John Cheesman. 1966

Tree Felling.

Building the First Bunk House.

LIFE AT GRITH FYRD
1932 - 1937

Washing and bathing place.

Tea Time in the Dining Shelter.

Preparing site for Craft Room.

I remember Father telling me of the care with which the site was chosen, in the bottom of the wood, close to a spring with the river not too far distant: It was an ideal position for a pioneering venture and the camp accommodated groups of between 30 and 40 men. The initial group were told ' These are the trees you can cut down, if you want to be housed before winter sets in, you had better start building'.

'Originally plans had been made to construct dwellings using the age old Forest system of cob walling. They quickly discovered this to be impractical as the men were not capable of sustained effort and the plan was revised. They reverted to timber construction and soon the clearing they had made by the banks of the Avon rang to the shouts and sound of men at work again. Nor did it stop at hut building. The men were taught new skills. Many of them worked on the small farm that existed on the site at that time, and others were engaged in handicrafts like pottery

Making a Canoe.

and chair making etc. Most of them quickly adapted to their new life, doing work they would not have dreamt themselves capable of a few weeks prior to their arrival. The Order managed to persuade the Government of the day to pay the unemployment in one lump sum instead of the individual amounts, an unprecedented measure, and this money was used to purchase the essentials needed for all the men. The men came in relays and usually stayed in the camp for about eighteen months, some needed a little longer. When they came to the end of their term at Sandy Balls they left with renewed hope for their future and were prepared to tackle anything. Today some of those men still return to the site to recall those far off days that had meant so much to them. The children were not forgotten either. The principles laid down by the founder were followed and the Forest School was run on the estate, using his method of education, for over 10 years.

Weaving cloth for lumber jackets.

★ As reported – the men in the camp at Godshill have felled trees and built them into sleeping and dining shelters; made roads, bridges, wash and bathing places, goat house, chicken house and pig sties, as well as stools, tables, workbenches, cloth, socks and sandals; they have taken turf off a field and got it under cultivation – all these for their own use and advantage. Some of them have tramped as far as Derbyshire and back, exchanging experiences with unemployed men in many places on their way; they produce plays, give concerts and entertainments, play cricket and football, sometimes as a team, sometimes for Godshill Village. They have asked for and made good use of three courses of W.E.A lectures, as well as instruction in First Aid. They are just completing a semi-permanent craft house, and the first of the W.E.A classes for the Winter 1933-34 on 'Some Problems of Today' has just commenced.'

Camping Huts on the bracken covered hillside.

All roads lead to Godshill.

Alongside these educational schemes, throughout this period, Sandy Balls continued to develop as a holiday centre. In 1934, 12 furnished camping huts, several with annexes attached for children, were sited along the 200 ft contour line. My Grandparents supervised their letting. The first brochure entitled 'Sandy Balls for the Beauty Spot Holiday' was brought out in 1935. It was a lovely production highlighting the unique beauty of the site and what Sandy Balls could offer the discerning holidaymaker.

★ An essay by Norman Glaister in 'The Grith Fyrd Idea' by Prof. John Macmurray and others.

Gradually however, the different interests represented within, brought increasing tensions and problems. Following a leadership crisis in the O.W.C which came to a head at the Folkmoot of 1934, Father, who had held the chief offices, those of British Chieftain and Grand Marshal from 1923 – 1933, took no further active part in Order affairs. *Many of those associated with him dropped out at the same time. The British Order (and there were groups in other countries) met the next year for its first Folkmoot away from Sandy Balls.

After this we had little contact with the Order and our lives were busy in other ways — I feel though, that it was a great loss to us as children. It wasn't until 1956, when the Centenary Camp was held in Sandy Balls to honour the birth of the founder, that I was, once again, able to glimpse the mystery and magic of those early years. In 1963 the O.W.C leased Greenwood Camp (formerly Grith Fyrd) as a base for their activities and I became Warden, supervising the arrival and departure of visiting groups. In 1968 my two sons and I attended our first camp and Folkmoot and subsequently many others with my nieces and nephews in many parts of the country. Indeed, as far as my gardening activities allowed, I began to take an active role and to feel that I had returned to something that was long part of me.

FOREST SCHOOL
WHITWELL   REEPHAM   NORFOLK

*A fully researched account of this time can be found in 'The Order of Woodcraft Chivalry 1916-1949 as a New Age Alternative to the Boy Scouts' by Derek Edgell - Published by the Edwin Mellen Press.

Forest School Camps

Prospectus for Forest School 1938. Cuthbert with a group of boys Camping in the grounds of Whitwell Hall.

But to return to pre-war years – Grith Fyrd and Forest School also decided to leave Sandy Balls. In 1937, Grith Fyrd, now known as Grith Pioneers moved to Shining Cliff in Derbyshire where a second camp had opened at the end of 1933. Forest School found a new home at Whitwell Hall at Reepham in Norfolk. Here in 1939 the school building was requisitioned by the Army for the duration of the war years. The school never re-opened, instead a group of teachers and former pupils initiated a new company 'Forest School Camps (1938) Ltd'. This continues as a successful and expanding adventure camping organisation for children from 6^1/$_2$ - 17 years old, both at home and abroad. In this way Ernest Westlake's inspiration and ideas on education live on and the spirit of Forest School continues.

In the years between 1923 and 1938 'Grandpa' Harrod – as he was known to all – was a loyal and faithful steward of Sandy Balls, husbanding the property and supervising the enterprises introduced by Father to make it viable. By his honest endeavour, meticulous accounts and shrewd business acumen, he made it possible for us as a family to leave a safe medical practice in Bermondsey and, when Forest School decided to move to Norfolk in the Winter of 1937/38, to make Sandy Balls our new home.

Entrance to Sandy Balls Estate

'Grandpa' Harrod, Steward of Sandy Balls.

At the Seat of Custom enjoying a quiet game of draughts (see original).

Chapter 7

Early Days –

A Sanitation System for a Holiday Centre

...And so, on 1st January 1938 with the church bells ringing to welcome us, we arrived in Godshill! Mother said: 'It is a good omen'. The car contained the whole family, five children and my parents. My youngest brother, Richard, just 9 months old, sat on Mother's knee and Linda, our tabby cat, lay in a basket beneath our feet complete with new-born kittens presented to Mother the previous day.

'Woodcot', (one of the former Forest School houses), was not ready for us to move into until Autumn, and workmen, and then Mother spent long hours making it into a home. In the meantime we made do with our little holiday bungalow – the 'Eyrie'. Sleeping arrangements were made easier because I had elected to stay in Bermondsey to finish out the school year at the Secondary school I was so happy at – lodging with the Mother of my best friends, Dilys and Gwyneth Walder, just off the Old Kent Road; and Keith, who was by now at Kingsmore, a Boarding School in the Peak District, was only at home for holidays.

The Eyrie – Our Holiday Home with Gipsy Caravan alongside.

A camping ground since 1920, Sandy Balls now had a small but increasing resident population and during the summer months several hundred holiday makers stayed in the camping huts or tents. In fact the development of Sandy Balls and a rising interest in alternative medicine and organic husbandry were to be Father's chief concerns for the next 45 years. With a 100% mortgage on the property, five children to educate and the knowledge that it was difficult to make a livelihood from a piece of woodland however lovely, it was a daunting task.

An efficient sanitation system was a priority for a holiday centre, but latrines were not the answer. Sanitation in the countryside in those days, except for a few septic tanks, was the outside privy, and even in towns, e.g Fordingbridge, there was still a regular collection by the Rural District Council of 'night soil' from them. So it was natural that Father should wonder whether it was possible to devise a rural sanitation scheme for Sandy Balls.

Our 1¹/2 acre garden where the composting was carried out.

(above) Father turning the compost. (below) Standing by the 'honey wagon'.

Fortunately, in the Autumn of 1938, he came in contact with the work of Sir Albert Howard in regard to composting (tried out with great success in Indore, India). The necessary vegetable matter was obtained from any green waste, together with food refuse from the clearly labelled 'food refuse only' bins.

The actual collection was done by going round the earth closets as required with a motor and trailer, 'the honey wagon', pouring urine into a churn and the earth-covered solid matter transported to the compost yard, clean empty buckets replacing the full ones.

In this way large compost heaps were gradually built up, personally supervised by Father, as the process had to be done correctly according to precise instructions.

They usually heated up rapidly to a temperature of 120-130°F, high enough to deal with any pathogenic bacteria, were turned twice and left to mature. The result was a first class organic fertiliser.

Grith Fyrd (the camp for unemployed men) also left Sandy Balls in 1937 and we inherited not only the hutments, which Father planned to let to organisations, e.g The School Journey Association, but also their $1^1/2$ acre garden. This was the site of the composting operation and we gradually cultivated the garden learning all the while.

At first the compost was used on this kitchen garden, but on further study Father came into contact with the Bio-Dynamic view that food for human consumption must have the introduction of an animal cycle intervening; so it was spread instead on agricultural land. As animal manure became increasingly available this was used for garden crops.

Lady Eve Balfour, in her book, 'The Living Soil', published in 1943 by Faber and Faber, summarised this experiment as a Technical Reference under the title 'A Sanitation Problem and its Solution'.

Quoting from Father's unpublished autobiography...'I feel that this has been a most successful and useful experiment. It has solved in a very simple, practical and efficient way, and I might add cheap, what might have been an extremely difficult sanitation problem, as I might have in the pre-war years a large number of people using the holiday centre during the season, and even under war conditions, I had a resident population between 40 and 50.

It has demonstrated that it is perfectly practical to deal with 'night soil' on the scale I have to deal with it, and there has been no suggestion of any nuisance. Indeed the compost heaps are completely inoffensive, not even flies or other nuisances. It is a complete vindication of the composting method advocated by Sir Albert Howard and shows it can be used for any camping ground. Above all it is a constant source of satisfaction that one is doing one's small share in increasing the fertility of the countryside, important now in wartime and even more in days to come, and in restoring the natural biological cycle from man to earth and back again, so adding to the actual and potential health of all who come within the range of this experiment'.

Indeed, Father had the greatest pride in his heaps and in the resulting compost and being garden-minded we were equally enthused. Over the years we saw a marked improvement in the texture of our light sandy soil. As children we were expected to help in the garden and long Summer evenings were spent weeding, hoeing and picking and none of us were daunted by hard work.

Chapter 8

The War Years

All my teenage years were during the war (1939-46) and although Britain was filled with a sense of dread and foreboding, to us children (aged 14,13,11,4 and 2) the conflict was distant and unreal. However, I well remember 3rd September 1939 - we gathered as a family at 11 o'clock round the battery-charged wireless set to hear the declaration of war! A heightened sense of awareness followed; the seriousness of the situation contrasting strangely with our idyllic surroundings and the fact that Sandy Balls had emptied rapidly of holiday makers and we were completely on our own. Then followed an Indian Summer. Perfect weather continued day after day with heavy dews, blue skies and hot sun. We spent our days by the river (Hampshire Avon), swimming, sunbathing and picnicking with the strict warning that if we heard an aeroplane we should run into the wood.

My parents, fearing the worst, gave us the option to go to America under a Quaker Scheme. I was the only one keen to go and was spoken for by a doctor and his wife living in Maryland. However, this traumatic adventure was never to be, for the vessel before mine was torpedoed and the scheme abandoned.

Our close-knit, somewhat isolated, family life in Sandy Balls continued, but wartime obviously brought many restrictions – food rationing, blackout and lack of mobility and an added emphasis towards self-sufficiency, for there was no safety net of Social Security or Family Allowance in those days and money was scarce. It may be interesting to note our financial position at the end of 1939.

Total Income	£1463	Total Expenditure	£1597
(£1293 from Estate & Holiday Centre)		(£1042 on Estate & Holiday Centre)	
(£180 - medical income)		(£555 - family expenditure)	
Deficit of £134 covered by Bank Overdraft			
	£1597		£1597

We cultivated a large (1½ acre) kitchen garden, kept goats for milk, ducks and chickens for eggs and a sow affectionately known as 'Mary Westlake'. We picked up acorns and chestnuts for her from the New Forest Inclosures and joined a Pig Club, but pig-meal coupons were only allocated for fattening pigs, not an in-pig sow. Although we did our best, Mary was hungry and kept on breaking out of her sty. When she eventually farrowed she ate the lot, developed milk fever and had to be sent for slaughter. Coupons then arrived in abundance! Father wrote a strong letter to the powers in Whitehall saying how ludicrous the system was.

We earned pocket money in many ways. Sphagnum moss, abundant in boggy areas, was gathered for the Red Cross for sterile wound dressings and one Autumn we learnt our first lesson in the law of supply and demand. Mushrooms were fetching 4d/lb in Southampton Market (my Uncle, a carrier, took them in). One morning we picked 54lbs and thought our fortunes made - but everybody else had mushrooms and we received only 1/3d. We were bitterly disappointed.

Vehicles were laid up for the duration so, when the goat or pig needed to be taken for service, they had to be walked. We drove the sow to another village about 2½ miles away, where the boar resided, tempting her with chopped vegetables and all our lunchtime sandwiches prepared by Mother. About halfway she lay down to sleep outside a village shop, in the warm sun, much to the consternation of the irate shopkeeper. Keith was sent home to get more food for her and she finally moved on. We had more help bringing her back a few days later, and a lesson from a cottager who saw us in difficulties and said 'this is the way to move a pig' – and indeed it was but not the way intended at all. She shot off uphill the way we had come with our 'helper' hanging on to her tail. It was an hilarious sight.

The goat was equally embarrassing for she bleated continually as we took her to the Billy on the other side of Fordingbridge and smelt obnoxious all the way back.

We had few outings or treats but one school holiday we went as a family, Grandpa and Grandma as well, to the tiny cinema in Fordingbridge to see 'Gone with the Wind'. It was a very long film with a break in the middle for changing the reel, so we took refreshments and later walked home, arm in arm in the centre of the empty road. It was a bright moonlit night and bitterly cold.

We gave lodgings to a young officer employed on the experimental Bombing Range close by on the New Forest. When the rumour of the proposed range was confirmed, the Commoners were up in arms about the infringement of their Common Rights, and even under war conditions it was felt wise to negotiate. Father, as Chairman of the Godshill Village Hall Committee, was one of those chosen to meet the personal representative of the Minister of Air, Sir Kingsley Wood, and a compromise was reached. 'There would be no closure of our main link with Southampton, the B3078 and the fence would be removed when hostilities ceased'. Five thousand acres were enclosed with a high perimeter fence and all the bombs, including the devastating block busters, were tried out within.

'*Uncle Wal*'
Our Wartime
Helper.

Godshill was fortunate to escape all blast effect but villages farther away were not so lucky and had their windows shattered.

Our main helper on the Estate was a young conscientious objector known affectionately as 'Uncle Wal' who, after his term of imprisonment, worked for us for the duration. Mother had, as au pair, a 16 year old Jewess, Ilse Kahn, who had fled Germany when her father, a provincial butcher, was thrown into a concentration camp. She stayed with us for a couple of years, later marrying a British airman. After the war we heard that all her family remaining in Germany had been exterminated.

As the war intensified, Southampton was bombed heavily and evacuees appeared for short periods but the unlined camping huts were unsuitable during the winter months and they were soon rehoused. Our other accommodation, a cottage and two wooden bungalows, were occupied by young families whose breadwinner was on active service. A large air raid shelter was built on the site of the sand pit and a Red Cross Post established with Father in charge. The shelter was fitted out with bunks and was substantially made. Early on in the war we all made our way down when the siren sounded, but soon realised that there was little chance of bombs falling on Sandy Balls. At the end of the war, however, two small ones fell, one narrowly missing one of the huts which was occupied at the time. On reflection we felt that it was an enemy bomber unloading his remaining bombs before he sped for home.

DIG FOR VICTORY   LEAFLET No. 15

POTATO GROWING IN ALLOTMENTS AND GARDENS

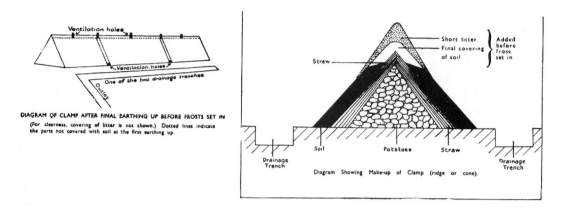

Issued by the Ministry of Agriculture and Fisheries,
Berri Court Hotel, St. Annes—Lytham St. Annes—Lancs.

A Home Guard unit was formed in Godshill and on our beautiful view point, Good Friday Hill, when invasion was thought to be imminent, a rota of fire watchers kept a nightly watch from a tiny look-out hut. On one brilliant moonlit night in November 1940 we watched as wave upon wave of enemy bombers flew over on their way to Coventry. Once a Junkers 88 crashed in the Forest and we all went up to see it.

Lord Woolton, Minister of Food, guided the nation's eating habits with the National Loaf (75% extraction), and gave recipes for the ingenious use of the foods available. The Ministry of Agriculture produced its celebrated 'Dig for Victory' Campaign and their easy to follow 'Grow More' leaflets inspired the nation to dig up their lawns and all farmland was put under the plough to make Britain 'self sufficient'. There was a close community spirit in the land and we in Sandy Balls were a microcosm of the whole. Whist and Beetle Drives were organised and many other activities took place in our communal hall known as the Folk House. A highlight of my war years was winning 1st prize at a beetle drive, a Japanese cup and saucer which I greatly prized.

Sidcot School – Quaker Co-Educational Boarding School.

Despite financial hardship, we children all went to boarding school, traditional in many Quaker families, as in ours. Help was obtained from the Friends Education Committee in the form of scholarships and grants. Keith, my elder brother, was at school in the Peak District, a brilliant pupil receiving many scholarships over the years. At this time however, I was at the South Wilts Secondary School for girls; Martin, my younger brother, was at Sidcot, a Quaker School. I had sat the scholarship at the age of 12 years and one of the compulsory questions was to write about any woman in the Bible. Perhaps our teaching at Forest School did not include the Bible; the fact is I was unable to write about anyone. For entry to a Quaker School this was a serious omission. As Mother remarked 'surely Jesus had a mother!'

Each morning I left early, cycling to Fordingbridge to catch the bus for Salisbury, complete with gas mask, identity card, school books and lunch packet, returning home at 5.45pm to homework by lamp or candlelight during the Winter months. As the war continued, another school was evacuated from Portsmouth and took possession in the afternoon. For that reason, in May 1941, I too went to Sidcot sponsored by Mother's Aunt Ethel. (She had married late, a wealthy Quaker, Alfred Moorland, and was childless). Sidcot was a co-educational boarding school dating from 1808 and run by the Society of Friends – both my maternal Grandmother and my Father had been there. The school lay in the heart of the Mendip Hills in Somerset; Cheddar Gorge only five miles away and the sea within cycling distance. The lovely limestone countryside had an abundance of wild flowers, meadows full of cowslips, snowdrops and many orchids; valleys of wild daffodils, woods starred with wild garlic and many rare ones not seen before or

Amberley.

Amberley in the Cotswolds.

since. It was a paradise to someone whose absorbing hobby was painting flowers and all my spare time was spent in this way. I was fortunate to have the help of a maiden lady living in the nearby village of Winscombe, an 'old fogey' mad about botany and plant identification! She taught me to use a Flora and gradually I filled a book with my paintings, improving all the while. School gardens were available for pupils, but only pocket handkerchief size ones and I was never really interested.

The extensive school gardens grew fruit, flowers and vegetables intermingled. I comment in my first letter home on 5th May 1941, ' The gardens are very well kept, everything seems to be in advance of ours. The curly kale has been absolutely wasted because of the holidays. Also there is a greenhouse filled with flowers of indescribable colours, red, oranges, deep blues, purples and whites'. The head gardener, Mr Lindsey, had known Father when he was Headboy in 1911 and was full of admiration for him, so allowed me to paint in the greenhouse (normally out of bounds) whenever I wished.

Although pocket money and sweet coupons were short, postage must have been cheap and delivery certain for I sent many parcels of wild flowers to my Great Aunt Ethel, living in Purley, London; all the spring flowers and even once, horror of horrors, a green winged orchid. ('They last so long and look so lovely'). During my second term domestic staff left to do war work, so a rota system was arranged for pupils to participate in these menial tasks. This was a revolutionary step forward for a Quaker School but part of the usual curriculum at Forest School. The heavy washing-up and vegetable preparation was reserved for the boys, who got on good terms with the cooks and were suitably rewarded, while the girls swept, dusted, laid tables, dried up cutlery and did other lighter jobs. Blackberries were picked, rosehips gathered and those joining the Voluntary Labour Squad (compulsory for the boys) helped with the harvest.

During my last term I considered my future career and I chose horticulture mainly because I preferred an outdoor life. I was equally fond of art and domestic science. Not being academic I did not take Higher School Certificate, equivalent to A-level but spent a cultural year in the 6th form studying Art and English. On applying to Reading University, considered the best at the time, I was told they had no vacancies for the coming Autumn. Disappointed, I wondered whether to return home but the Headmaster had a job in mind and I spent a happy year at Amberley, high up in the Cotswolds.

The Mount School, Mill Hill, London, a minor public school, was evacuated for the duration and needed somebody to look after a herd of goats, two ponies and to help the odd job man with a vegetable garden. I well remember my arrival. The

On the Common at Amberley, Herd of goats and helpers.

goats, seven of them, were tethered on the extensive common. They browsed on bramble patches and other vegetation, being moved twice daily and milked in situ. They were moved on and on, and only under exceptional conditions during the summer were they housed. The large goat house was reserved for their winter quarters, hay, roots and cake being fed during this time. The Headmistress, Miss MacGregor, was a massive lady, ruling her school with a gentle glove of iron. She considered goat's milk best for her 'gels': so on the first day, complete with milking bucket, I sallied forth to milk but I was a stranger and they ran round me in circles and butted me with their horns. In despair, I spied a young girl in the distance who came to assist me and later became my most devoted helper.

I learnt to handle and harness the ponies and drive out over the common in trap or carriage with the children or to get fodder for the animals, once through a blinding snowstorm. We attended gymkhanas and I came first in a bending competition and experienced for the first time in my life the County influence. Mill Hill was a minor public school and the girls associated with others of a similar class. I rarely left the immediate environment, only twice taking the bus to Stroud to shop in the valley far below. I was paid £1.00 a week and managed to save £40.00 during my time there which I used as pocket money during my two years at Reading.

My job at the Mount School Amberley, taking children out in the carriage with Kitty.

Chapter 9

Preparation for life in a Post-War World

In the Autumn of 1944 I started a Diploma course in horticulture at Reading University, living in the Wessex Hall of Residence. Shinfield, the horticultural station, was 2^1/$_2$ miles away and half our time was spent there doing practical work. There was little traffic on the roads and bicycles were our only form of transport.

In a large field at the Horticultural Station of Reading University individual plots, all standard size allotments 30 x 90ft, were laid out. Every job was demonstrated to us and then attended to with meticulous care. It was an ingenious system, for the lines of identical produce stretched the entire field length and were harvested by the staff. We students became so keen to win the prize for the best plot that we cycled the two and half miles to work on them in our spare time.

There are many practical guides to vegetable growing but the first edition of the 'Vegetable Garden Displayed' published by the Royal Horticultural Society in 1941* and used by us at this time, remains my firm favourite. It is simple, straightforward and the photographs easy to follow. There is nothing better than learning by doing – the 'Woodcraft way'– and over the two-year period we kept careful notes and developed quite an eye for what to do at any particular time; in fact it was a useful introduction to kitchen gardening. We were taught by gardeners who still retained the instinctive wisdom passed on from father to son. This is no longer the case and we must now make a conscious effort to understand why we do this or that in our gardens today.

Other training with flowers, fruit, greenhouse and lawns, planting and pruning, care of tools and work in the potting shed was equally thorough, although the few young men on the course (rejects from the services) complained about the lack of machinery. It was mostly hand work which suited me down to the ground. We even did woodwork and I made a nice little cabinet to house my collection of insect pests. Most fine lunch hours were spent noting down and learning the names of plants for the weekly identification test and even today the names are as clear to me as they were then.

Professor Stoughton was Head of Department; he was carrying out research into hydroponics and the greenhouses were filled with his tomato experiments. Our course did not go into anything quite as advanced but we were given a sound grounding, both practical and theoretical, of the subject. Everything now fell into place and I found I was one of the better students.
Nevertheless, chemistry defeated me so I wrote to my brother, Keith, now a

A fully revised 1981 edition available today.

medical student at Cambridge, for help. A wad of meticulously written notes on organic chemistry and formulae appeared which I carefully put on one side and hoped for the best. It is interesting to note that equal emphasis was placed on the use of farmyard and other organic manures as on basic mineral fertilisers, whilst crop protection was portrayed as mainly cultural, preventative or the good old-fashioned standbys of nicotine, Bordeaux mixture, lime sulphur or soft soap.

The surrounding countryside was a constant delight and at weekends, when we weren't busy on our vegetable plots, we explored the Thameside and Chiltern villages, found meadows full of snowdrops and the wild fritillary or snakeshead and attended church in many places. We were allowed one weekend a term away from our Hall of Residence so there was plenty of companionship. Sunday tea was not provided and only buffet supper, so the shops were combed for anything edible not requiring ration books or bread units to share with our friends. In fact the food in Hall was meagre and inadequate but nobody dared complain for the war was entering a critical phase.

…And so the war ended. V.E followed by V.J Day and I must have been so busy with my finals that the actual celebrations at the University are a hazy blur with no clear memories remaining. Near the end of my course I was interviewed by the Appointments Board and this is the letter I wrote in answer to an advertisement.

'Dear Sir,

The assistant of the Appointments Board at Reading University has given me your letter and has advised me to apply to you. I am just 20 years and am taking my final examination for a Diploma in Horticulture in June.

I went to school for two years at the Forest School, Godshill, Hampshire, which was the result of the ideals of my Grandfather, Ernest Westlake. This was a school of the New Education Movement, putting into practice the principles of education of the Order of Woodcraft Chivalry. Here I gained my love of animals, gardening and the study of nature.

After being at two secondary schools in Bermondsey and Salisbury, I went to the Friends' School, Sidcot, where I took School Certificate. For a year before I entered Reading I had a post at a small boarding school in Gloucestershire where I was completely responsible for a herd of goats, two ponies and a small vegetable garden.

This term I am taking an elementary course in bee-keeping and during the holidays hope to stay with friends in Gloucestershire who keep about 200 beehives and gain a thorough knowledge of bee-keeping. I have had no experience of teaching but considerable experience with small children. It is only fair to say that when I am nervous I tend to develop a slight stammer but am making arrangements to see a speech therapist as soon as possible.

Yours sincerely,

Jean Westlake'.

At the subsequent interview with the Headmaster and his wife, Mr and Mrs Lyn Harris of St Christopher School, Letchworth, Hertfordshire, I was very nervous and thought I had done badly, but later, back home, I had the triple excitement of receiving my results – a 1st class Diploma and the Noel Sutton Prize for the best student, also the news that I had been offered the job starting in early September.

It was almost too good to be true. I know now that my parents were disappointed that I did not want to work at home, but at the time I saw little sign of this and was helped in every way to prepare for my new life in a post-war world full of promise.

A Post-War world full of promise – The Westlake Family in 1946.

Chapter 10

Three Idyllic Years

My first job after leaving University was one of reclaiming a school flower garden neglected during the war years, rejuvenating a Young Farmers' Club and teaching Nature Study to 5-12 year olds. St Christopher was a progressive vegetarian, co-educational boarding school on the outskirts of Letchworth Garden City in Hertfordshire and I was young, keen and enthusiastic.

With the return of mobility of labour there was an influx of new young staff to the school and I found there were several there about my own age. Three became my special friends, Iris and Elizabeth were Oxford graduates and taught French and English, while Rachel taught music. I remember she was the daughter of a Bishop.

Three full-time gardeners were employed on the land to produce an abundance of fruit and vegetables for the school and, I guess, had little time or inclination for rejuvenating the flower beds round the school buildings. They had been working there for many years and in comparison I felt very young and vulnerable in my inexperience. However, they were always friendly and helpful when our paths crossed. One Easter holiday a large area of cauliflower hearted early and were over before the children returned for the Summer term. The difficulty in producing crops for term time consumption must have been considerable; few were needed

Young Staff at St Christopher School outside the Staff Room.

during the holidays as only a skeleton staff remained of which I was one. I admired the leisurely paced work pattern of these landworkers – starting at 7.30, a full hour for lunch, brewing up tea, reading the paper, finishing at 5pm, but devoting plenty of time to cleaning their tools and leaving everything in apple-pie order for the following day.

My pattern was completely different: the Young Farmers and I milked early before breakfast and when I helped with evening staff duties it was well after 10pm before I finished. Something I was happy to volunteer for was to accompany a group of the older children Youth Hostelling during the Summer and Autumn terms. We visited Cambridge, Saffron Walden, High Roding, Thaxsted and many other hostels, leaving after school on a Friday, returning on Sunday evening. One half-term we cycled to Oxford. Most of our food had to be carried, for rationing continued, and the boys slung quartern loaves under the cross bars of their bicycles. A strange sight!

It was a job after my own heart combining everything I enjoyed doing. I had no one above me – the headmistress suggested this or that but on the whole I was responsible for my own time and work. For this I was paid a monthly salary of £3 a week plus board and lodgings. I felt very privileged indeed.

My group of children with the Warden outside the Hostel.

Sketch of High Roding Youth Hostel.

Evening High Roding May 24th 1947

The Main School House at St Christopher's.

Anyone able to remember the Autumn, Spring and Summer of 1946/47 will sympathise with me weatherwise for my first year was a testing one. The heavy clay soil was demanding – sticky during the wet Autumn of 1946, frozen solid and snow-covered during the Spring of '47 and cracked open during the long hot Summer. Unable to work the land for several months I made plans for the garden, and the expansion of the Y.F.C, and many were the nature walks I took with my pupils through the snow-covered countryside.

But to return to the Autumn term. My father, Dr A.T Westlake, came to give the first Open Meeting to the club entitled 'Soil Fertility and Composting'. He emphasised how important it was to maintain the natural balance and gave a very precise account of methods to use on a farm and garden scale. He outlined the way to make a compost heap using Sir Albert Howard's Indore System, briefly described the New Zealand Box method, and finished by again stressing the importance of keeping to the natural cycle and by so doing maintaining soil fertility. Indeed I found that top dressing with well-matured compost proved to be the key to my 'difficult-to-work' clay soil.

The lecture was followed with a demonstration by the Club Leader (myself) of how to make a compost heap. It was well attended by members and several staff, who later made heaps in their own gardens. All ingredients were to hand – vegetable waste from the school kitchen, goat and duck manure together with weeds, leaves and organic material. This heap heated to a very high temperature within a few days, was turned twice and when mature found its way onto the Young Farmers' garden.

Young Farmers with their pets.

In my account for a National Efficiency Competition I covered the gradual rise in membership (from 21 – 57) and emphasised the active participation of all in the practical work of the club. Indeed I had such good members that I could spend a day in London occasionally and go Youth Hostelling with no anxiety that anything would be forgotten or neglected. The day-to-day practical work included goat-keeping, kid-rearing, milking, bottling and sale of milk at 6p a pint, care of ducks, chickens, rabbits and other small pets. Other work included the formation of an apiary and bee garden, honey extraction; bottling and sale of honey (at the controlled price of 2/9d a lb) and the cultivation of a small kitchen garden (12 x 36ft) from which compost-grown vegetables were sold to members of staff who lived locally. The older boys were keen to keep pigs but in a vegetarian school this was not acceptable.

I well remember the school Open Day when staff and parents came to visit Pets' Corner and with what pride the children answered questions about their compost heaps and the cultivation of <u>their</u> garden.

Later a village survey was undertaken, inspired by Mr Vosey, Education Officer of the National Federation of Young Farmers' Clubs. Many pleasant afternoons were spent surveying, photographing and making notes about Old Letchworth, the village of our choice. This encouraged members who were artistically or historically orientated, and I still possess hand-written notes and meticulous maps and drawings from this time. Contact was made with local farmers, and the older boys, bored with goats, helped at weekends on real farms and milked real cows. The local historian was of considerable help and later gave a fascinating talk on 'Old Inns of Hertfordshire'.

During the summer term we were privileged to hear Lady Eve Balfour, founder of the Soil Association, speaking on 'Soil Fertility in Relation to Health'. I quote from my report: 'Young Farmers felt that this talk admirably linked Dr Westlake's lecture, their own efforts at compost-making and its use on a small vegetable garden'. I wonder now, 50 years later, if this early introduction to such an important subject had a lasting affect on my young members. I hope so. It certainly did on me!

A Young Farmers' Camp was organised for the last week of the summer holidays in the spacious grounds of a recently acquired property, where we prepared our meals and had an enjoyable time. Many jobs were undertaken including haymaking and scything a large orchard. Several boys and one girl became proficient at sharpening and cutting and, despite staff fears that Young Farmers would cut themselves, no accidents occurred. A small haystack was built and a local farmer came to demonstrate the art of thatching.

The idyll of three busy years spent at St Christopher's ended when I contracted severe glandular fever and returned home to recover my health. They were good years, natural and unspoilt, a time of innocence of which I was part, a time of culture in which I participated. Neither Television nor Radio stole our time, and over the years I had a willing band of helpers and made many friends. The school gardens regained their former glory and I was congratulated by the Headmaster for my work with the Young Farmers and Nature teaching. I left with the greatest regret but also a feeling of satisfaction that I had done a good job, learnt a great deal and passed on in a practical form much of lasting value.

My three friends – Heather, Iris and Rachel in 'As You Like It'.

Chapter 11

St Christopher School Young Farmers' Club

National Efficiency Contest

October 1946 – September 1947

This report will be divided into two main sections; firstly Club Activities, and secondly Club Records: together with photographs and diagrams illustrating points of interest.

Business Meetings

The St Christopher School Young Farmers' Club came under new leadership in September 1946. From the previous minute book of the Club, it was seen that no meetings had been recorded since May of the previous year. At the first business meeting, which was held soon after the beginning of term, it was decided to begin completely afresh. Officers were elected, those of Chairman, Secretary, Treasurer, Goat-keeper, Duck-keeper and Bee-keeper, and rotas soon made out for the care of the livestock. It was also decided that the frequency of business meetings should be in the hands of this committee, but should take place whenever there was business to discuss. As a school society we were entitled to three Open Friday evening meetings in the Autumn Term which were open to the whole school, two in the spring term, the summer term being devoted to outside work hours.

During the rest of the term rules of the club were discussed, the only one considered suitable from previous years being one that read "Members will be under a definite obligation to take a responsible share in the club, care of livestock, maintenance and improvement of club-buildings and equipment and clerical work in keeping accounts, arranging meetings, visits and demonstrations". All the others were rescinded as they dealt with Associate Members whom we had done away with, the club feeling very strongly that all members should be active members. A subscription rate of 6d per term was made and at a further meeting the year's honey was given out to members who had ordered it. Only 36lbs had been extracted, the season being very wet and unfavourable.

During the Spring Term of 1947 many items of business were discussed. On February 12th Mr Vosey, Educational Officer of the N.F.Y.F.C., came down to visit the St Christopher School Club. He told us a little about the Young Farmers' Club Movement in the country and about the National Competitions. We were very taken with the idea of the Village Survey. During the term the subject of the survey came up for much discussion and by the end of the term we had formed ourselves into groups, ready to advance on the village we had chosen; that of Old Letchworth, early the next term.

Business during the summer mainly consisted of items of interest from the National Federation, suggestions and proposals for speakers and excursions; plans for a Y.F.C. Camp to be held during the holidays, giving out the season's honey; statement of accounts, not forgetting the termly elections, and the gathering in of subscriptions.

Meetings Open to the School

During the Autumn Term the young Y.F.C was able to arrange for one outside speaker to come down, other societies having arranged meetings on the other evenings available. On this occasion Dr.A.T.Westlake gave a most interesting and instructive lecture to a large audience on "Soil Fertility and Composting". He told us how important it was to maintain the natural balance, and gave us a very concise account of methods to use on a farm and gardens scale. He outlined the way to make a Compost Heap by the Indore System, briefly describing the New Zealand Box method, finishing by again stressing the importance of keeping to the natural cycle, and by so doing maintaining Soil Fertility.

At the beginning of the Spring Term Mr C.A.Day, J.P.,Secretary of the North Herts. Bee Association, gave a Lantern Slide Lecture on "The Life and Habits of the Bee". He told us something about the history of keeping Bees, the life histories of the Queen, the drone and the worker, and various methods of Beekeeping. This was most instructive to Young Beekeepers who wished to have hives of their own.

In the summer the school was very lucky to hear Lady Eve Balfour speaking on "Soil Fertility in relation to Health". Young Farmers felt that this talk linked up Dr Westlake's lecture, their own efforts at compost-making, and its use on a small vegetable garden.

Excursions and Demonstrations

On one wintry morning several of the younger members paid a visit to the Co-operative Creamery at Letchworth Gate, where they saw the whole process of Pasteurisation. Enthusiastic Beekeepers also paid a visit to Taylor's Ltd of Welwyn, where they saw hives being made, an excellent Observation Hive, and a demonstration of how to take a nucleus.

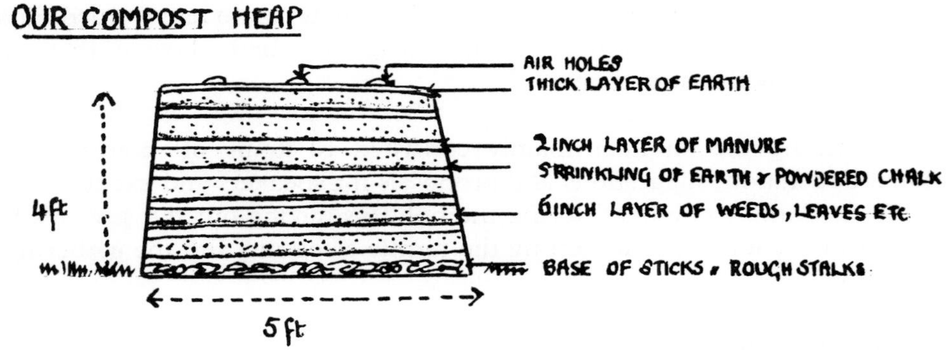

OUR COMPOST HEAP

AIR HOLES
THICK LAYER OF EARTH

2 INCH LAYER OF MANURE
SPRINKLING OF EARTH & POWDERED CHALK
6 INCH LAYER OF WEEDS, LEAVES ETC.

BASE OF STICKS & ROUGH STALKS

4 ft

5 ft

One evening a stray swarm was sighted flying across the school field. In no time Young Farmers were clustering round it and early in the evening the Head-Beekeeper demonstrated the art of taking a swarm. A spare hive was made ready and later on we had the pleasure of tipping our catch onto a white cloth and seeing them walk up into their new home. This swarm was never claimed and became part of the Y.F.C. stock. Following the visit to Welwyn, one keen beekeeper made a two-frame observation hive and many otherwise frightened members were able to observe these fascinating creatures in complete safety.

Dr Westlake's Lecture on composting was followed up by a demonstration given by the Club Leader on: – How to make a Compost Heap. Goat and Duck manure were used, together with weeds, leaves and rubbish. Several staff attended this demonstration, and later made heaps in their own gardens. This heap heated up to a very high temperature within a few days, was turned twice and in due course found its way onto the Young Farmers' Garden. Above is a diagram of the method we used; and owing to the wet season no water had to be added.

Stock: Goats, Bees, Ducks and Rabbits

To begin with the Bees: the policy we have adopted is to keep not more than three Club hives, and to encourage individuals to look after hives of their own. We have found that this personal interest encourages them to learn a great deal more than they would otherwise do. During the summer, with the stray swarm, the club looked after three hives, individuals owning 9, making a total of 12 hives. As soon as the mild winter came, Spring Cleaning was done, and the bees settled down to a long sunny season.

Plans were already in progress for the making of an Apiary. In the early Autumn the following appeared on the notice board:

WORK TO BE DONE DURING THE WINTER ON THE FORMATION OF AN APIARY

It is proposed we lay out an Apiary. The plan of which will be something like this.

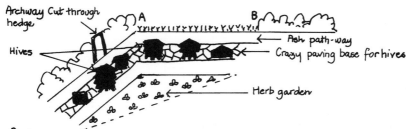

Autumn Work

① The whole area must be scythed, the rubbish raked up and burnt

② A trench must be dug across the wind gap A–B and cuttings of lonicera (evergreen honey-suckle) planted.

③ With the aid of saw and secateurs an Archway is to be cut in the hedge, to serve as a suitable entrance to the Apiary.

④ Ash pathways are to be made and a crazy-paving base made for the hives

This work can be done in games or free time

Jean Westlate
(Leader Y.F.C.)

By the time the bees were flying all this work had been done except for the planting of the herb garden. It was considered that the ground should be left fallow for one season, and not planted up until the weeds were under control.

The season was excellent in all respects, first the flow from the Spring Blossom and just before extracting there was a large flow from the lime trees which are one of the most prominent road-side trees in Letchworth.

The honey was extracted over a weekend, Y.F.C. hives being done first, followed by those of individual members. An extractor was borrowed and many willing hands sliced off the wax, steadied the extractor and filled up the jars. Total honey sales amounted to £14 6s 0d at the controlled price of 2/9d per lb. Complimentary jars were presented to the best helper in the Y.F.C. for the summer term. Her termly record looked like this.

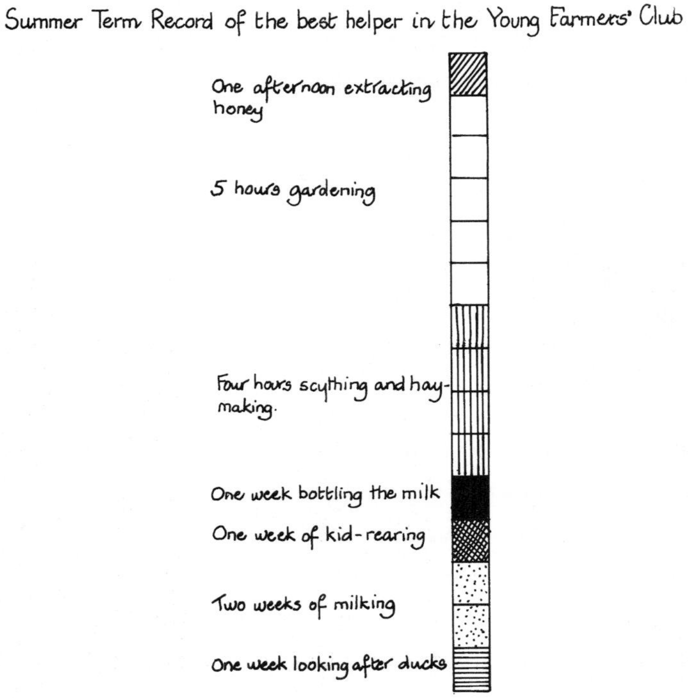

Summer Term Record of the best helper in the Young Farmers' Club

One afternoon extracting honey

5 hours gardening

Four hours scything and hay-making.

One week bottling the milk

One week of kid-rearing

Two weeks of milking

One week looking after ducks

Two jars to members for their work with the bees and 4 jars to the Principals of the school. Following the summer holiday the hives were prepared for the winter, a considerable amount of honey being left for them, many Beekeepers being advocates of Natural Feeding whenever possible.

In the Autumn of 1946, the Club owned two goats and a goatling all white, hornless British Saanens. During the Spring and Summer Pet's Corner became a very popular place as two of the three goats were in kid, both having been mated to Welwyn Littlejohn BSR903, owned by Mrs Hughes of Ashwell nr. Baldock.

Early in March "Regus", our largest goat, born in 1942, had four kids. Unfortunately they were all Billies and a keen biologist chloroformed three of them for us – immediately they were born. Being a little unskilled, I'm afraid it was a rather long process. A little light brown one was kept for a time, and was hand-reared with a bottle by the younger members until the holidays.

At the end of April 'Rina' our goatling kidded. She had one little white hornless nanny whom we called 'Amberley'. Rina would have nothing to do with her, so that she was taken away and completely hand-reared. She was fed for six weeks on whole milk; gradually a calf-food called 'Lactifer' was introduced, until she was weaned at the age of 4½ months. Soon after her birth Rina accidentally strangled herself by twisting round her tethering stake. Although this was a great loss to the club, it completely relieved a Goat situation which had arisen. Rina had been reared by the Y.F.C. but had never been properly weaned, she consistently milked the other two goats whenever she had a chance, and also drank all her own milk.

Pet's corner – Goats and a Young Farmer.

Amberley aged 3 weeks in Pet's Corner.

Regas gave up to 12 pints a day for a considerable time, the maximum ever being sold on a single day being 14 pints. The kid at that time was having 3 pints a day.

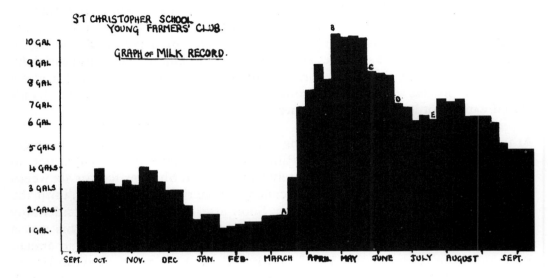

The routine-work rotas were arranged so that members who wished to could milk for a week and sometimes a fortnight a term.

This lino-cut shows the method of tethering used.

The six Khaki Campbell ducks on the other hand, did not respond to this co-operative effort. Although they started laying as soon as could be expected after the long winter, they developed rheumatism and did not properly recover through the warm summer months. Several members welcomed the idea of hatching ducklings. A Broody hen was acquired with some difficulty, but after a week she started eating her eggs and then began to lay herself. During the summer months while the Club-Leader was away on holiday, the duck's pond dried up, they became very neglected and as a result stopped laying.

Club Activities

A Young Farmers' Camp was organised for the last week of the summer holidays. The work to be done was to move the Club Livestock from their present cramped quarters, to a more spacious home in the grounds of a new house recently acquired by the school. Members camped in tents, prepared their own meals and altogether had a very enjoyable time. During the day, a new enclosure was made for the ducks, their house was scrubbed and creosoted. The goats were installed in their new quarters, the shed being whitewashed, creosoted and thoroughly overhauled. A small hay-stack was made. Many of the school staff feared that the Young Farmers would injure themselves while scything, but no accidents occurred and several boys and one girl became very skilled at sharpening and cutting. A small piece of ground was put at our disposal and ultimately a Young Farmers' Garden came into being. As soon as the heavy clay soil had lost its stickiness two double rows of runner beans were planted, followed by peas, carrots, radishes, marrows, sweetcorn, tomatoes and swedes. Home-made compost was used in huge quantities, and although a great deal of watering had to be done, some good produce was marketed or fed to the members' rabbits.

This is the plan of the Garden at the end of July.

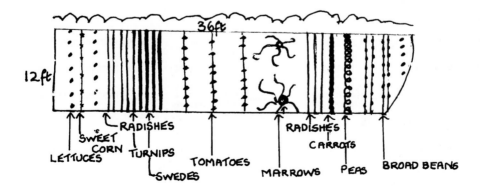

The Village Survey comprised the other free-time work done by members not already catered for by the Apiary or Gardening. Several groups were formed, and many pleasant afternoons were spent surveying the disused Letchworth Hall Farm, the Old Manor House, the Old Houses and the Old Letchworth Church, dating back to the 12th Century. Several good photographs were taken, and copious notes made of its history from very early times to the present day – sketches of the Church and individual windows of interest as well as many excellent maps showing the development of the Letchworth district including the growth of the Garden City from 1903. Unfortunately this survey has never been finished, but we hope that more work will be done on it in future years.

In connection with the survey two members became very friendly with workers at the Manor Hall Farm at Willian, and, becoming a little tired of the goats, they spent subsequent weekends helping to milk the farm cows. Also in connection with this survey we made the acquaintance of Mr Reginald Hine F.S.A. We borrowed from him a folder containing newspaper cuttings, notes and photographs of Old Letchworth. A great deal of knowledge was gained, and this culminated in Mr Hine coming to speak at an Open meeting early in September on the "Romance of Hertfordshire Inns".

Financial Records

At the beginning of the year several debts had to be paid – so we only began with £2 7s 4½d in hand. By the end of Spring term we were a few pounds in debt, but with increased milk sale our Credit Balance mounted until in September 1947 we had £9 17s 7½.

Balance Sheet for Aut. 1946.								Balance Sheet for Spring 1947.							
CASH IN HAND	£2	7	4½	GOATFOOD	£5	11	8	CASH IN HAND	£1	7	5½	SEEDS	6	-	
MILK SALES	5	10	11	STUD FEES	1	-	-	MILK SALES	7	6	9½	RABBIT & KID TO VET	10	-	
SUBSCRIPTIONS		5	-	POSTAGE		2	2	SUBSCRIPTIONS	1	2	6	POSTAGE	2	6	
				CREDIT BALANCE CARRIED FORWARD.	1	7	5½	DEBIT BALANCE CARRIED FORWARD.	1	12	5½	MILK TOPS & GOAT-FOOD	10	8	2
	£8	3	3½		£8	3	3½		£9	16	8½		11	9	2

During the summer many more things were bought for the use of the club and for the livestock. The buying of several new goat chains, milk buckets, and garden tools being a rather heavy expense, as can be seen from the Balance Sheet for the Summer Term 1947.

Balance Sheet for Summer Term 1947				
			Debit Balance b/fd	1 12 5½
SUBSCRIPTIONS	5 -		Flit Spray & Sprayer	5 6
PRODUCE FROM GARDEN	10 -		(Milk Tops, Filter Pads, Rubber Teats & Salt Lick	16 2
MILK SALES	21 18 11		(YFC Badges Postage & Stationary	12 6
			(Scythe stones, Ropes and Garden Tools	1 7 6
			Tomato Plants & Seeds	4 11
			(Chains, Collar, Milking Buckets	3 3 6
			Goat & Duck Food	4 13 9
			CREDIT BALANCE CARRIED FORWARD	9 17 7½
	£23 13 11			£23 13 11

Membership Record

	11-14yrs	14-18yrs	New members	Members who resigned	Left school
AUTUMN TERM 1946	21	12	9	16	1	—
SPRING TERM 1947	36	22	14	15	3	—
SUMMER TERM 1947	48	36	14	21	3	7
AUTUMN TERM 1947	57	38	19			

The table above shows the gradual increase of membership throughout the year. It should also be mentioned that the St Christopher School Young Farmers make full use of the facilities for Folk-Dancing, Play Acting, Art and Craft work and Youth Hostelling which are all part of the school activities. An article was written by those at the Young Farmers' Camp for the County Federation Booklet "Gleanings", but before this we had no contact with the Country, as the Organising Secretary did not contact us in any way. Although up to this stage the club has existed in almost complete isolation, we hope next year's report will show contacts with the county, other School Clubs, Local Farmers, and other places of interest in the surrounding countryside.

Beekeepers and Honey, July 1947.

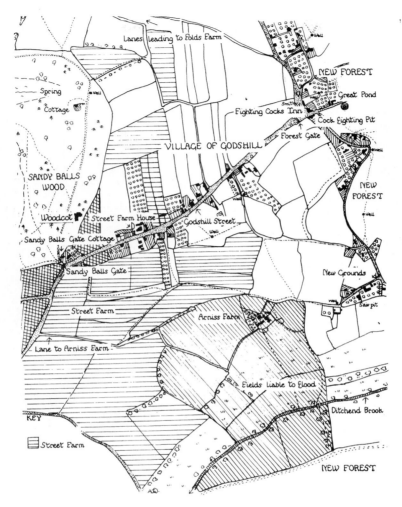

Street Farm Godshill, 62 acres.

Chapter 12

Cottage Practice

Martin left school two years after me in 1946 and my elder brother, Keith, still a medical student, knowing he wished to take up farming, suggested a course at Cambridge! Inviting him for a visit, Martin decided quite definitely that the study involved was not for him and instead spent two years as a trainee on a farm, close to home, in Godshill under the boss, Jimmy Witt. During the bitter winter of 1946/47 he was in charge of sheep, moving hurdles daily, often hacking these out of frozen ground. It was a testing time for him as well.

The Boss – Jimmy Witt.

Mr Witt – senior
with his Grand-daughter on Prince.

Street Farm was 62 acres in extent mostly on the plateau gravel with pond in farmyard and spring not too far distant. Three cart horses were kept, Prince (with two speeds, dead slow and stop!) Duke and Molly: there was a milking herd of mixed Shorthorn cattle, pigs, sheep, ducks, chickens and geese.

In fact, a mixed farm typical of a small acreage in the 1940's.

During his time there he got to know the local villagers and other farmers, the ins and outs of markets, local customs and practice, the idiosyncrasies of animals, fields and crops which stood him in good stead in the years to come. Long hours and hard work were good experience for an embryo farmer and an excellent relationship developed between Martin and his boss and Bob, the farm worker. Jimmy Witt's sudden death in 1959, necessitating the sale of the farm, came as a shock to all who knew him.

At this time there were four other working farms in Godshill – that is, they were making a living solely from farming. Today, in the 1990s, there may be one. But Godshill was never a typical village, lying on the edge of the New Forest – it had a character of its own. Most of the villagers had common rights and kept a variety of animals, putting them out on the open Forest; renting a field or two, they grew a number of crops, beans, peas, roots, etc., which they sold in Ringwood market eight miles away. I well remember little Henry or Jacky Chalk, with cart piled high with rhubarb, gently jogging by. The pace of life was slow then, governed by the seasons; the able-bodied practised a way of life, close to nature subsistence farming, unchanged for centuries. This hardy cottager is now no more.

Martin tells a story which reflects this pace of life. 'Prince' in the shafts, he and the boss were bound for Fordingbridge. They called to Jacky Chalk, walking, obviously going there too: 'Do you want a lift?' 'No thank you,' he replies, 'I am in a hurry'. Another, which shows how close to nature they were:

(In a broad Hampshire Dialect) 'Doctor, I think I must have hurt my ear'. 'How did it happen?' 'Well you see, doctor, I was working late last night and a piece of corrugated roofing slipped so I went back home to bed. This morning I knew something must be wrong for I couldn't put my cap on'.

The ear was hanging off!

'You must go to hospital'.

But Charlie would not hear of it. 'You sew it back on, Doctor'.

So, cleaning the dirty wound as best he could, Father stitched back the ear through the tough cartilage with no anaesthetic or other medical conveniences and, not expecting much, told him to come back if it troubled him. A week later Father saw him in the village and was amazed to find the ear had healed by first intent – no sepsis, no discomfort, the threshold of pain as high as an animal and, as an animal, it had rapidly healed.

Farmers would back carts into the river to fill churns for watering their animals.

Water was the restricting factor to this type of husbandry. Wells and collection of rain water may have been adequate for thrifty household use, but watering a number of animals necessitated a daily visit to the river Avon below, and bringing home the precious liquid in churns or water carriers was a time-consuming task. Godshill was more fortunate than some villages in this respect for when Ernest Westlake (Grandfather) bought Sandy Balls in 1919, his first concern was a water supply. He bought army surplus piping and fitments from Sandhill Camp, Warminster for £143.7s.6d (a considerable investment) and installed a hydraulic ram which pumped spring water from its heart to a reservoir above, for Sandy Balls and later, part of Godshill. Those able to pay a water rate received the benefit of a standpipe and, for many years, it was a much needed source of Estate income. This limited supply was augmented in the 1930's when Father put in the 'new ram' on another spring, capable of pumping 2000 gallons a day. It was not until 1950 that mains water arrived and our 'pure' spring water became contaminated and was condemned.

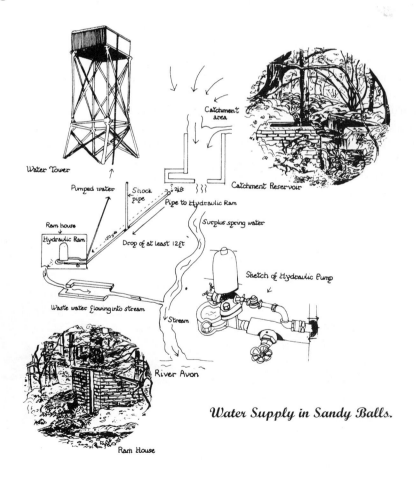

Water Supply in Sandy Balls.

Chapter 13

A Conservationist of Repute

THE MEN OF THE TREES

The Society for the Planting and Protection of Trees

Founder: Richard St. Barbe Baker

The year 1948/49 Martin spent as a forestry apprentice to Richard St Barbe Baker, founder of the <u>Men of the Trees</u> on an isolated farm in Dorset. Father knew and admired St Barbe Baker and felt that learning from such a remarkable man would prove useful in the future. He was not only a trained forester but an author and a conservationist and had earned for himself the reputation of being the greatest living authority on the supreme value of silviculture; vast tracts of land in many countries, including Africa, had been reclaimed and saved by his inspiration. Later his name was brought to national attention by his 'Peach Stone for the Sahara Campaign' and his book 'Sahara Conquest' was given a literary award as being <u>Book of the Year (1966)</u> most likely to advance the cause of humanitarianism.

The Gate Farm was near Abbotsbury on the Dorset coast, home of the famous swannery. The work involved planting out and tending 10,000 rooted cuttings, the study of forestry and ecology and general farmwork. On visiting him one Autumn afternoon we were impressed with the lie of the land, high up within smell and sound of the sea; the sweep of the hills masking the sea itself; the young wife who gave us hospitality, home baked bread and fresh honey; from St Barbe Baker's own hives, the secretary Mr Finlayson and Adam, the farm manager.

Adam was a giant of a man, a Lithuanian descended from peasant stock, incredibly strong, kind and gentle.

$2^1/2$ cwt bags of grain could be carried with ease up the granary ladder. He was the mainstay of the farm, for St Barbe Baker, now in his mid-50's, was often away lecturing or in foreign countries spreading the gospel of conservation, and seldom at home. As Martin writes in a letter home – 'Mr Baker is going off again Tuesday for 10 days. In fact, he spends more of his time away than he does at home which makes it very difficult for us as he takes the car and so we have no transport to fetch anything. He won't let anyone else drive the car and when he is here he is so busy writing and thinking that it is all we can do to get him to do the necessary running about for things such as going to the mill, getting petrol, paraffin, etc'. Indeed, it was a lonely life for an attractive young wife with tiny child and much later we heard she had married the farm manager!

Adam was a fund of information on peasant culture and practice. I remember being astonished to hear that, in Lithuania, fields of mangels and beets were transplanted from seed beds and not sown and singled as in England. A leguminous crop was widely grown for fodder so, at Martin's request, I wrote to Suttons, the Reading seed firm, and, in reply, received free samples of all they grew. These were planted in an experimental bed back home but whether they included the one we wanted I cannot remember. Inspired by Father, Martin was also a compost enthusiast. He wrote home – 'I am going to Gordon's this next weekend and I shall preach compost to his Father, who is like most Dorset farmers, hopelessly out of date and not farming scientifically" (A strange remark to equate compost and science!).

And so, in the Autumn of 1949, we both returned home, Martin to start up a small organic farm and I to regain my health and help him and the family meanwhile.

Later Henry Finlayson was to move to Sandy Balls where he was an invaluable help to Father, editing his first book 'The Pattern of Health' and then settled in Godshill, marrying Mother's best friend, Agnes, a widow.

Richard St. Barbe Baker

Chapter 14

The Saga of an Entrepreneur

It was at the end of my time at St. Christopher School that I met a young Cambridge undergraduate – I well remember our first meeting on a London train returning to Letchworth from Cambridge to buy clothes for my brother Keith's' wedding (July 1949). I was wearing a red dirndl skirt of the 'new look' (hemline 11 inches from ground level), a white peasant blouse, both home-made, and a green suede jacket, one of my earliest purchases from a wage of £3.00 a week. I felt attractive and obviously was attractive to this young man. Taking a degree in mathematics, he confided to me that, as he realised he was not the best student of his year, he had decided to change to English because a mediocre Arts degree did not matter so much. He had two more years to go and was 21 years old.

During the next few years I was concerned with and, indeed, took an active part, in shaping his future. After leaving Eastbourne College he had done national service in the Parachute Regiment for he loved danger. Then, excelling in mathematics, he got a place at Queens College, Cambridge. Finding it impossible to get on with his ex-Indian army Father, he lived in rooms during vacation, although he adored his Mother and had a filial affection for his brother.

Several times he visited the Common Cold Unit in Salisbury where he lived like a lord, studying hard and seldom succumbing to the virus infection. At my home, he was well received by the family, for he had great charm, but did not feel that the holiday centre, as it was then, had any potential for him. He was a budding entrepreneur of quite ruthless ambition.

His proposal of marriage and suggestion that we should emigrate to Canada came out of the blue. My first thought was, how could I possibly marry a man who pushed to the top of a queue? And, after further consideration, I doubted whether I could withstand such a dominant personality, however much he loved me, or I him. Bitterly disappointed and thwarted, but feeling that I would eventually consent and that his lack of income and prospects were the reason for my refusal, he looked afresh at his future and our friendship continued.

As a Cambridge graduate, there were plenty of interesting jobs to apply for but, instead, he decided to set up an ice cream business with a partner in London and wondered whether <u>my</u> savings of £200-0-0d from St. Christopher's could be <u>his</u> share of the required capital! He wrote me a persuasive 'matter of life or death' letter: I could hardly refuse.

"…Now this capital that I asked you if you could put up may make a difference of whether I can start at all, and it is partly because it means so much to me that I suggested so high an interest as 25%.

It may be practically life or death to me, but you must believe me that it would benefit you quite a bit too…This business can't really fail since we have the sales, the equipment is lined up and the materials are readily available. My partner has his share of half the starting capital and then, with mine, we can move the equipment into the premises I have obtained, and every box going to the wholesaler, who has agreed to take them, brings in the income. Actually, in London, the demand for lollies exceeds supply in summer and our machinery would, by about June, be working 24 hours a day. But, anyway, come what may, you would also have my word and bond and you would be quite and absolutely safe.

You can see I am very anxious about it and you can understand why. It is an opportunity of a lifetime, to start and build up a growing organisation that may lead who knows where. And, later, when it has been built up, I may be in a position to repay any help you could give me now more substantially.

…If you can, please, please help me with this".

The following summer I visited frequently to see how my money was doing, travelling to Covent Garden with my Uncle, the carrier, being delivered back there at 12 p.m midnight for the return journey home. The tiny factory was in Ladbroke Grove, not a part of London I knew, or would ever wish to know, for the side streets, even then, frightened me, but the cream lollies he produced and distributed over a wide area were the most delicious I have ever tasted.

What exactly happened to the business I do not know for, by the following Christmas, although it was still running, he had decided to join Shell – or was it B.P – location Singapore!

Out in an Outboard Motor Boat exploring islands 10 miles south of Singapore.

Tennis with the boss.

After an initial training, fitted out with tropical kit, he headed East and I received letters and photographs of his life there – the club, tennis with his boss, the beautiful Chinese girls – but it was not the life for him. There was no scope, no danger, nothing to pit himself against; even weekends exploring the islands with an outboard motor, the fantastic sight of coral reefs and tropical fish seen through sparkling water and his growing skill as a skin diver were insufficient compensation for a job that bored him. A period of silence followed, then news of his salvage enterprise raising sunken warships from Singapore Harbour. He writes "The men look like villains, but are wonderful workers. My labour force consists of one Irishman, five Malays, five Indians and one Chinese". He had fallen in love with the Far East and its people and was on his way to financial success, for every 100

*A beautiful
Chinese Girl
Friend.*

The Crane Barge – The men look like villains but are wonderful workers.

tons raised equalled £2000! My money was repaid plus the 25% interest he had promised. His word <u>was</u> his bond, as I knew it would be.

Little gifts now began to arrive – jade, silver and gold, but fewer letters and finally both petered out. In 1961 he returned to England, phoning me from London to suggest a reunion in a Park Lane Hotel but I was, by then, married and so declined.

Lifting a piece of ship's side = £2,000.

Raising the cargo of a sunken lighter for Shell Co. The outside boats are mine, the crane and centre lighter are hired.

Communication between us ceased, although rumours reached me of his string of hotels around the world and his marriage at 42 to a girl of 21 years. So I was more than surprised 25 years later, in 1986, by his reappearance: a knock on the door – another customer for vegetables?

I had the impression of a young man standing there. "Do you remember me?" he said, and, of course, I did, for he had not really changed and neither, he said, had I! I showed him round the family-run holiday centre which had changed considerably, for another entrepreneur had stamped his mark on it and he was suitably impressed.

He told me about his training for and love of marathon running, his daughter by a Chinese girl, his Mother, his brother, the divorce from his wife, her love of horses. He spoke vaguely about his holding companies and then, to help me clarify a legal problem, suggested his own lawyer in London. Feeling I should take his advice, so kindly offered, I went and was interested in the long, searching look at the 40-year old photograph I had taken with me – the young face of my 21-year old friend. What was the lawyer looking for so intently? He did not say.

Later I knew, for the whole story began to unfold. I was not really surprised and initially felt amused that, for so many years, he had coolly held the Stock Market to ransom, although the collapse of Milbury, with 2000 aggrieved shareholders, and of the Isle of Man Savings and Investment Bank, in which his companies were implicated, was no laughing matter.

The J.R Affair filled the financial papers. In a long-awaited Department of Trade and Industry Report (price £37.00), the disgraced former financier was described as "devious, dominating and unscrupulous", a man whose activities – milking public companies – were inadequately controlled. By flouting the City's authority, his motivation was out-and-out self-interest. The Report was also highly critical of the Stock Exchange itself and the self-regulation in the City. Senior members of the Exchange were marked out for strong censure. There were many red faces.

The High Court Judge at the Old Bailey, in gaoling him for a maximum of two years in his absence for contempt (he had fled the country), described it as the most 'deliberate and serious' contempt of court he had ever come across and hoped the sentence and warrant for his arrest would stop him from 'cocking a snook' at both the City and the courts in future. Life had helped him amass a huge fortune estimated at £50 million. For the last 25 years he had enjoyed the life style of a millionaire and had left in his wake a trail of bankruptcy and bitterness. He had now followed his vast wealth to an offshore tax haven (last heard of in the Philippines) – a £50m. fugitive from the law.

And so, forty years later, my saga ends. Beginning with a casual meeting, developing as a search for happiness and a satisfying career, and ending for J.R who knows how or where. And for me? Did Christmas cards encourage me to dream of Monte Carlo and Mediterranean cruises in a luxury yacht? Who can say!

Chapter 15

A Change is as good as a Holiday

Life at home was much quieter than I had been used to and I missed the companionship and cultural life of a community; and because I had been away for so many years – school, university and job, I had few friends or contacts in the village, unlike Martin who knew everyone. However, I joined the W.I and we (Mother, Martin and myself) went weekly to the Salisbury Folk Dance Club where Martin met Valerie, a beautiful dancer, who later became his wife. As a family, we took an increasing interest in the recently formed Soil Association, visiting other farms in the Wessex area, and, at the end of 1952, Father was elected to the Soil Association Council so we were in touch with the heart of the movement. Martin also joined the White Horse Morris Men and the Bodenham and Nunton Y.F.C., but it was an elite club, including the sons of large landowners, and I never really felt at ease.

Display of Organic Produce at a Soil Association Meeting in Sandy Balls, September 1952.

Later I was to spend the quiet Autumn period (October to Christmas) taking a part-time job away from home, gaining experience in many ways: au pair to a Russian Jewish family in Southall; home help to a publisher and his wife;

receptionist at a hair clinic in Nottingham; a long extended holiday in Paris helping a friend and, during the Autumn of the last great 'pea souper' in London, I was employed as a relief worker by the London County Council at 1/8d per hour. I went to a variety of schools whose workers were sick, all within walking distance of my room in Hampstead. The schools varied greatly, from newly-opened ones with light, airy classrooms and spotless kitchens to dirty Victorian buildings reminiscent of Dickens' time. In a letter home I give an account of one of the latter:–

186 Adelaide Road
Hampstead
Sunday November 30th 1952

'On Monday morning I was sent to a school at Brecknock. This school is in complete contrast to the other two I have been at – no electricity and very dirty and old-fashioned with mouse traps under the cupboards and dead cockroaches to be swept up each morning; the workers quite a different type, loud and coarse. The plates never get very clean because the Ascot heaters don't work very well and there is never sufficient hot water. No potato machine and doing small potatoes for 300 is no joke. The cook asked could I work 8.30 – 3.00 o'clock, which, as it is 40 minutes fast walk from here, really suits me better than starting at 8.00 o'clock. You can guess I felt pretty wretched by the end of the first day – but it's not as bad as all that.

Things were in rather a state at first as two of the four helpers were away. It is in many ways easier than the other two schools, they don't drive themselves and for all the rather common, rough exteriors of the women, they have hearts of gold and there is always time for laughter and teasing. So it's good fun really and I enjoy the longer walk in the morning, especially as it has become very cold.

When I first went to Brecknock the women smoked continuously although it is completely against all rules – the cook as well…. when after lunch who should walk noiselessly in but Miss Kirby, one of the L.C.C supervisors. The assistant cook was the only one at that moment smoking and she gave her a week's notice.

For the rest of the week the cook raised heaven and earth for her to stay on. They got in touch with their union and had a representative down and the upshot of it all was that she went down to headquarters to see Miss Kirby on the Thursday afternoon and was allowed to keep her job.

The person I was replacing came to tell us about her miscarriage – what the doctor said to her and what she said to the doctor.

On Friday they were all, including the cook, going to a variety show and all, without exception, washed, curled and set their hair, bought a plenteous supply of chocolates and cigarettes and arranged to meet an hour before the show began to have drinks and a car to take them home at 12.30 (dead drunk I expect!)'.

Back home for Christmas, with presents for the family and refreshed by my change of work and scene, I looked forward to a busy summer. According to my garden record book I was off to a good start for, on January 1st, I planted 9lb of shallots and January 3rd moved rhubarb in for forcing and planted Jerusalem artichokes.

Seeds ordered from Unwins and Toogoods had obviously arrived for, by the end of February, brassicas, carrots, onions and leeks had all been sown and the whole garden had been planned, as can be seen from the sketch below.

Plan of Market Garden.

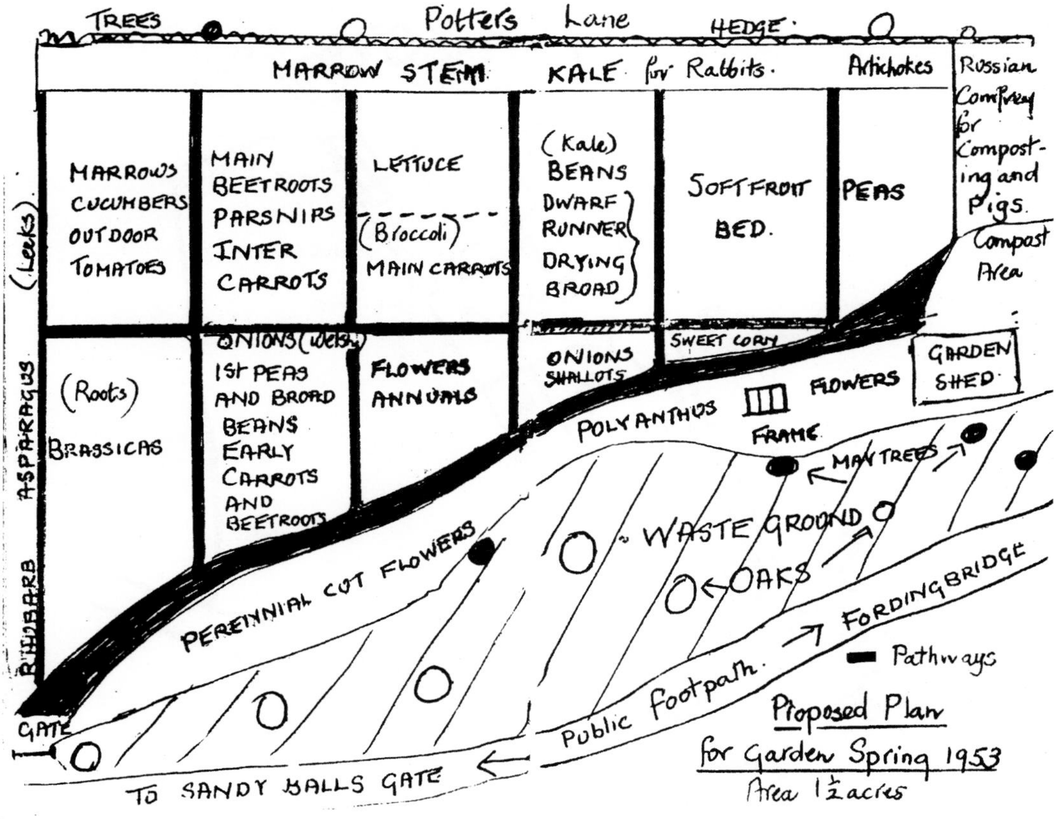

Chapter 16

The Organic Farm

At first, Martin's farm was little more than a smallholding, 16 acres on sand and plateau gravel, with access from the B3078 Cadnam to Southampton road. Most of the fields belonging to Sandy Balls had been rented out for many years to local farmers but, in preparation for Martin's return, they had been given notice to quit. Only a 4 acre field 'Meerhay' necessitated going on appeal to the Ministry of Agriculture and, fortunately, it was decided in our favour. So, in partnership with Father, 'Westlake and Son' came into being.

Sketch Map of Farm Layout.

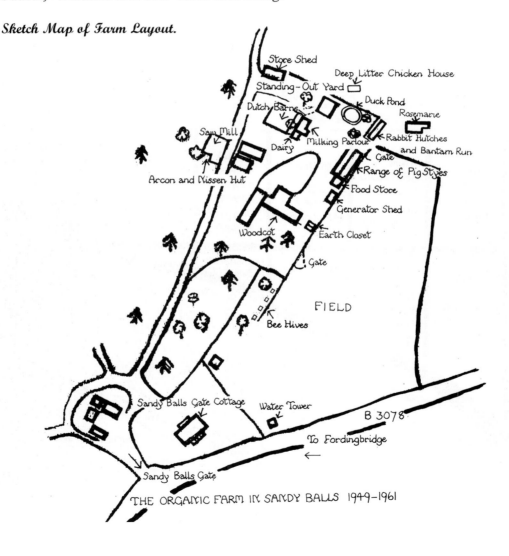

Store Shed

Deep Litter Chicken House

Standing-Out Yard

Dutch Barns

Duck Pond

Rosemarie

Saw Mill

Dairy

Milking Parlour

Rabbit Hutches and Bantam Run

Gate

Arcon and Nissen Hut

Range of Pig Styes

Food Store

Generator Shed

Woodcot

Earth Closet

Gate

FIELD

Bee Hives

Sandy Balls Gate Cottage

Water Tower

B 3078

To Fordingbridge

Sandy Balls Gate

THE ORGANIC FARM IN SANDY BALLS 1949-1961

A gaunt shorthorn cow, Bella, was bought from the boss – before we received a licence to sell milk, we were at our wit's end to know what to do with the gallons she produced. We made cottage cheese, clotted cream and butter and Mother and I thought quite seriously about taking a beauty bath!

Gradually, farm buildings were erected, a milking parlour for four cows with dairy attached, a barn, a range of pigsties with water laid on; a rat-proof food store and other sheds, all made with second-hand materials and all conveniently close to our home in Sandy Balls, 'Woodcot', where later (1981) the swimming pool was built. Little by little, a pedigree Jersey herd was established and I still remember the joy of being responsible for feeding the heifer calves, a promising bunch of youngsters, Sunshine, Shadow and Starlight.

Father had given me sole charge of the $1^1/2$ acre organic kitchen garden and I decided to build it up as an intensive unit growing crops for market as well as for ourselves and the holiday visitors. At first, however, it was thought necessary to put all monies received from it into the farm and this continued for several years.

My parents lost no time in advertising the changes in Sandy Balls and, in a friendly letter sent out to previous clientèle, dated January 1950, they mention a long list of improvements within the Holiday Centre, including the restaurant opened the previous season.

1950 - Aubrey and Marjorie Westlake welcome visitors to Sandy Balls.

SANDY BALLS HOLIDAY CENTRE
Tel. No.: FORDINGBRIDGE 3151

SANDY BALLS,
GODSHILL,
FORDINGBRIDGE.

January, 1950

You are probably already thinking about your summer holiday, so my wife and I feel you may like to hear the latest news about Sandy Balls, in case you would care to come here this year.

(1) We are very much alive and ready to welcome our old friends and visitors.

(2) This last season we started a restaurant in the Folkhouse (under the management of Mr Coleman) where morning coffee, lunch, afternoon tea, supper and snacks can be obtained from 10a.m. to 10p.m. every day. The prices are very reasonable – the lunch is 2/3 for adults and 1/6 for children.

This facility was much appreciated by our visitors this last season, in particular by the mother and housewife, as it gave full freedom and choice to cater or not for the family, as was desired.

The food, as far as maybe, is provided from our own garden (under the management of our daughter Jean), so as to make sure the food is fresh and of the best quality. This applies particularly to the vegetables, which are all compost-grown.

The estate store (still managed by 'Grandpa') is open as it always has been and visitors will be able to continue to shop there and cater for themselves if they so wish. It is hoped it may be possible to provide ample milk from our own attested cows (which form part of the estate farm, managed by our son Martin).

(3) The bathing place has been much improved. As visitors last year know, the bank has been concreted with three pairs of steps down to the water. There is a diving board, and it now forms the best bathing place on the Hampshire Avon. There is also a first class paddling pool with constantly running water, close by, where the younger children can disport themselves in complete safety.

It is hoped to have the creek in working order again, so as to provide a safe shallow bathing place for children.

(4) The Folkhouse, when meals are not being served, is available as a Social Centre, and there are various games provided, billiards, table tennis, darts, draughts, cards, etc. It has been fitted up with loudspeakers so that it can be used for dances, etc.; there is also electric light so that there is adequate lighting in the evening.

There are socials from time to time during the season and every effort has been made to provide a real social centre.

(5) There is now more accommodation for families, as four of the chalets have annexes attached; and the large bungalow "The Larches" is available for families and small parties. Children are just as welcome as they have been in the past.

(6) Remember we have ample room for caravans and they can be left safely on the site. Also there are many first-class camp sites.

(7) Prices of the Camping Huts have not been raised and remain at £1 7s 6d.per adult. The camping dues have been slightly raised to 7/- per week per adult.

All that has made Sandy Balls such a delightful holiday centre has been preserved, and our old visitors will find it just the same as ever it was – a place of real recreation. With the new facilities it can now claim to be and to provide everything that anyone, who likes a simple unsophisticated holiday, could possibly want.

May we book you for the coming season ? Remember June is the best holiday month – Sandy Balls is in its full glory and the days are the longest.

With our best wishes for 1950,
AUBREY AND MARJORIE WESTLAKE

SANDY BALLS HOLIDAY CENTRE 1950's

The Camp Store.

The Best Bathing Place on the Avon.

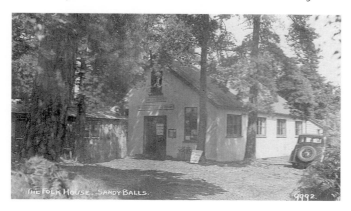

The Restaurant and Social Centre.

Mother with Dairy and Farm Buildings in the Background.

'Rosemarie' The tiny bungalow.

In 1954 I write to a friend, former French teacher at St.Christopher's – *"It was a surprise to hear from you again after so many years and, in the Autumn, when I can get away, I should love to come over and see your farm. (near Oxford).*

'I'm sorry I can't help you about a herdswoman because I don't know anybody around here suitable except myself! and I'm more than fully occupied with my market garden. Last year I did a great deal to help Martin on the farm and, during the two months he was ill, I managed our eight milking cows pretty well single-handed – but now Martin is married, his wife helps him and so I can concentrate on my garden and fruit and vegetable stall.

It's been a long hard grind for both the farm and garden since you were down (Autumn 1950) but at last the farm has turned the corner, so the money I earn goes to me at last.

I have a tiny three-roomed wooden bungalow which I am in the process of redecorating and furnishing, using the money I saved while I was at Chris (St.Christopher's). I hope to move in as soon as I have the bed-sitting room ready, leaving the kitchen and craft room and installation of electricity until the Autumn.

There is about $^1/_8 - ^1/_4$ acre of ground around the little house which I have cleared and it is now down to early potatoes. If I succeed in cleaning it of couchgrass, I'm going to have a lovely flower garden – lawns and herbaceous borders, a garden pool and rockery, flowering shrubs, etc. In my mind's eye I can see it now and it's going to be really beautiful.

We have one cow who is going to (we hope) get her C.M (Certificate of Merit). So far, in 100 days, she has given over 5,000lbs of milk with an average butterfat of 5.2%.

We have some young heifers who are very promising and, as our own bred animals calve down, we are selling off older cows we bought in to start with...'.

And, indeed, Martin's marriage made a great deal of difference to me. I no longer woke each morning with the prospect of milking or, even earlier, to single field root crops, but instead was able to concentrate on my own little enterprise, although I still continued to spend the late Autumn away from home on holiday or part-time job.

Photograph of the garden at 'Rosemarie'.

Chapter 17

The Story of a Most Remarkable Man

In the early 1950's, Father became interested in the work of Dr.S.Marian D.Sc. who, in the Soil Magazine, a small monthly publication, claimed to have discovered the true factor in soil fertility: a hexagonal carbon – which he called Actumus (active humus). He first isolated this substance in 1933, by a complicated chemical extraction from woody matter and found the resulting crystal of carbon, in hexagonal form, had a high capacity for absorbing oxygen – the very substance of life – and of releasing it in a continuous stream. On an average, each crystal contained at least 2000 carbon atoms and a soil crumb (that essential constituent of fertile soil, visible to the naked eye) consists of millions and millions of soil crystals with their accompanying hexagonal carbons, thus could be regarded as highly efficient oxygen donors.

An Austrian by birth, Dr Marian had come to England in 1938 as a refugee. He was an experienced analytical chemist and soil scientist and an expert in coal and charcoal formation. During World War Two the Government had put him in charge of all charcoal production in Britain – absolutely essential for the necessary alloys and precision tools for war purposes.

Timber supplies in various counties became exhausted but fortunately he found 1000 acres of scrub oak on the edge of Dartmoor managed by the Trustees of the Dartington Hall Estate. Oak was found to be the best raw material and this woodland, he estimated, would yield 10,000 tons of charcoal and take eight years to clear. So Fingle Bridge, neat the picturesque Devon Village of Drewsteignton, became his headquarters from then on.

After the war, when cheap charcoal could again be imported, the factory was adapted as a rural industry producing peats and composts and later, Actumus and related substances, e.g Cloudy Charcoal – a medical product, Exogen – a biological extract of oak, Formone – for conversion of hardwood, etc. From the first issue of Soil Magazine (March 1949), he had launched a surprisingly successful campaign for their use throughout the world.

Dr. Marian's passionate interest in soil fertility arose out of his remarkable piece of research undertaken at the Institute of Applied Chemistry in Vienna in 1926 and later published in the foremost scientific journals of the day. This showed quite conclusively that the acids formed by ammonia salts within the soil are far stronger than pure acids and, indeed, shatter the particles like an explosion and would eventually destroy the soil itself.

The industries producing these salts, used in peace and war as fertilisers and explosives, were in the hands of the world's most powerful multi-million pound concerns. So there could be no turning back.

He was a deeply sincere man; this shows in his writings, as does his complete mastery of the English language. From this time on, his whole personality and driving force, (and he appears to have worked ceaselessly) were fixed on one point and one point only – the key to soil fertility! For he had not only to warn mankind of the catastrophe that lay ahead but to find a solution to it and offer an alternative. Later Dr.Marian was to say, "I have worked for the elucidation of this great secret of nature and life not only with all my energy and power of body and brain but also from the depths of my heart". Stirring words indeed!

He now looked at the soil particle itself with a complicated X-ray technique and found the fertile skeleton of alumina-silica with carbon – probably the original life-promoting medium. He also observed how this kernel was enveloped by different protective shells, the greater the number of shells, the less fertile the soil. A micro-chemical analysis of these shells showed that they were formed by acidified humus alternating with a shell of metal salts and then one he called the fertiliser shell, and so on.

So he extended his research to find answers to two questions: firstly, was it possible to stop the deposition of further shells and secondly, were the ones already formed able to be removed so that the original fertile kernel could again function by a living interplay between soil and plant? Exploring many possibilities, he found the same simple answer to both. By watering with a solution of plant ash, most infertile soils could be brought back to full potential (dependant on the original parent rock) and the factor responsible for this phenomenon was a soluble carbon compound. He called it Carbon X and later "Actumus". But where was there sufficient organic matter which could be burned to get the amount of ash needed? And the answer again proved simple. Other sources aside, where else but within the soil itself? So, experimentally, he burnt many acres of topsoil with sawdust and found that Actumus was released and fertility restored.

Thinking that in this burning process, he had made a fundamental discovery, he was surprised to learn upon his arrival in England in 1938 that, in several counties, i.e Norfolk, Suffolk and Essex, this had been common practice for centuries. Although, by this date, farmers had been tempted away from such a time-consuming practice to the use of artificial fertilisers, little realising the potential harm to their soils.

Now, fully convinced he had the answer to soil fertility and that the method had a sound scientific basis, he launched a campaign which cut right across the inorganic and organic schools. He stressed the destructive forces of fertility "out of a bag" <u>and</u>

the use of cellulose and other rotting organic matter with the accompanying build-up of humic acid shells…human and animal manure, which had already been subjected to a similar burning process within the body, could be safely composted with soil to make a soil compost; <u>all</u> other organic waste matter he recommended should be consigned to a slow-burning bonfire and the resulting ash carefully collected and used later. The Actumus method ensured the complete functioning of the life system. All other methods, acid-forming chemical and rotting matter, interfered with this action.

It was a very simple method and it is no wonder then, that Father, who had carefully studied Dr Marian's work from the beginning, should be keen to try it out on our own land and Martin and I were willing to co-operate on farm and garden scale, as the following account written after Dr Marian's sudden death in the Spring of 1952 makes clear.

Trying Out the Actumus Technique
by A.T.Westlake, M.B, M.R.C.S, L.R.C.P, ETC

I feel that the tragic death of Dr Marian, in these crucial times, makes it the more incumbent on those of us who have understood in some degree what he was driving at, to do all in our power to carry on his work. If Dr Marian was right in his fundamental conceptions, then it is essential that this truth shall not be overlooked or forgotten with his passing.

For soil fertility – or, as he preferred to call it, soil productivity – is the great problem of the future. How is the world to be fed and to be fed healthily? Can the soils of the world sustain an ever-increasing population without becoming exhausted, with consequent famine and disease on a world scale? The statistics are ominous – the present annual average increase of world population is 1.25 per cent; the annual average increase of world agricultural production, 1937-50, is only .3 percent. The position of this country is even more critical than this, for relying as we have, and still are, on "cheap food" from abroad to feed our 50m population, we have neglected our agricultural possibilities for the last 100 years; and even today we take and use first-class productive land for every other purpose than the growing of essential food.

But I am also certain that the current "scientific" attitude and outlook on agricultural fertilisers, poison sprays and all the rest of the rake's progress, does not provide the answers. On this I am sure the organic school of thought is essentially right – but even this school does not go far or deep enough. If we are to get the answer to our problem we require a new and penetrating science of the soil and its cultivation, and this I am convinced Dr Marian had started to give us in what he called "Biogenic Soil Hygiene", particularly the method of operation through hexagonal carbon and the formation of the soil crumb and the physical, chemical and biological reactions which resulted therefrom.

For make no mistake about it, Dr Marian's ideas, if true, are revolutionary and cut right across both the orthodox and unorthodox schools of agricultural thought, across the advocates of artificial fertilisers and the advocates of compost.

I am sure myself that Dr Marian went far enough to establish an a priori case and that the time has come when his work should, in the national interest, be thoroughly investigated and tried out on a large and convincing scale. If his contentions are true – then, in Sir Albert Howard's famous phrase, "the answer will be writ on the land".

Do Actumus, Formone and the other products give the results Dr Marian claimed? Are his theoretical conceptions correct in practice? We ought to know quite definitely; for if they do and are, then their neglect is criminal in view of the primary national need for healthy food. Incidentally, it is to my mind a most strange thing that whereas an American product like Krilium can be tested out, our prior English product, Actumus is completely cold-shouldered. And this is the more serious for, according to Dr Marian, their resemblance is only superficial, and Krilium as a fuel carbon cannot, by its very nature, produce a true crumb structure.

In my limited way I am endeavouring to practise what I have preached above, and it may be of interest to readers of Soil Magazine to recount very briefly how I came to be interested in this whole subject and what, up to date, I have managed to do.

The question of soil fertility has interested me, as a medical man, for many years. Even when I was in general practice, between the two wars, in a congested industrial area of South-East London, I felt the problem of human health and disease was largely bound up with the health of the soil – in fact, that Agriculture should, and indeed someday must, be the primary health service.

When in 1938 I had the opportunity to leave London and come down to my estate on the edge of the New Forest I determined medically to come right down to earth. At that time I knew little about the whole matter, but it was clear to me that the institution of water-borne sewerage was one reason at least for the fall in soil fertility, as with the growth of the large towns human wastes were being largely lost to the land. Accordingly I decided to run the sanitation of my Holiday Centre on conservation lines.
Starting with Dr Poore's methods as advocated in his eminently sane and practical but little known book Rural Hygiene, I soon came across Sir Albert Howard's work and was immediately impressed by his ideas, and when later I had the privilege of meeting him on several occasions and of having his generously given expert advice on my soil problems, I knew I was on the right road.

For the next 11 years I composted all the night soil and vegetable wastes, etc., by the Indore system, and most religiously observed the "law of return", returning everything that came out of the soil – and a great deal more – back to the soil.

In this way I manufactured tons of compost a year and it was chiefly used in our kitchen garden of about 1 acre. It transformed it from an unproductive tract of sand into a fertile healthy garden, without the addition of one ounce of artificial fertiliser. I became a firm believer and outspoken exponent. I joined the ranks of the organic gardeners and farmers and was a foundation member of the Soil Association.

But some doubts remained. The compost methods I was using gave splendid results up to a point; beyond that point it seemed impossible, indeed I had largely ceased to bother about it, but it was still there. For example, it seemed impossible to get rid of the virus infection in the potatoes and strawberries, though I did everything possible according to the tenets of composting.

It was at this point that I came across Dr Marian's ideas and work.. At first I was not impressed, indeed I thought he was just another stunt-merchant trying to sell me something in a bag made more attractive by being labelled "organic". Later I was more interested but did nothing about it until I heard him lecture on "The role of Hexagonal Carbon in Soil", when his ideas suddenly became alive for me and I began to see what he was driving at.

From then on I became more and more interested and began to grasp the far-reaching and long-term implications of his fundamental researches and discoveries. I started myself to experiment with Actumus and his other products.

About this time, with my son's help, we started to farm all our agricultural land for ourselves, and I took the opportunity to get Dr Marian to take soil samples and to advise us on their cultivation. In addition I had the privilege and good fortune of a personal visit from him so that he could advise me on the spot, and he was unstinting in giving me the full benefit of his fund of soil wisdom and scientific experience.

As a result I started to modify our organic methods and procedure in regard both to our horticultural and agricultural holdings. Instead of composting by the Indore method with vegetable waste, I did Marian's soil composting both with the night soil and the farmyard manure, and found that it was not only much simpler but appeared to give better results. All burnable refuse we now burnt, in fact we re-introduced the garden bonfire on a bigger scale than ever, and all the ash was carefully collected and stored, being used with the soil compost or direct on the land according to requirements.

In the garden, on Dr Marian's advice, we put no compost for a year. According to him it already had enough, if too much, humus. What was required was to make it available, which could be done by intensive working of the soil. Accordingly we cultivated and re-cultivated over and over again any land free of crops with our Clifford Rotary Cultivator, and hoed intensively during the whole season. In the agricultural fields we have also gone in for intensive cultivation, as well as using hard-wood sawdust activated with Formone and the wood ash from our bonfires.

It is too early to say what the results will be; but so far they have been encouraging in the fields and excellent in the garden. Indeed in the garden we have never had such consistently good crops nor been so free of disease. I should perhaps add, to be quite fair, that the garden has never had such devoted and expert care as my daughter, who manages it, has given this year.

I am well aware of the small scale and inadequacy of my experiments, but I am hoping that, in trying to carry into practice Dr Marian's ideas and conceptions, I shall arrive at maximum health and productivity both of my land, the crops and the animals, and consequently of the humans fed thereon; and if so it will, at least, be some contribution to the solution of the problem which, as I said at the beginning, is the greatest now confronting mankind – not excepting the atomic bomb.

In the summer of 1952, Dr Marian's wife, wishing to continue the magazine on a quarterly basis, appointed as assistant editor, Dion Byngham. Because he knew Father, from Woodcraft days, I was asked to supply a practical gardening article. I felt honoured to contribute but was nervous, too, for I had never done anything like it before. So Father suggested that the use of his special writing room on Prospect Point in Sandy Balls would give me confidence and inspiration.

I still remember this little thatched hut (pulled down in 1962 to make way for Sandy Balls House); regularly supplied with a vase of flowers arranged by a grateful patient, the soft call of pigeons evocative of childhood, the heavy scent of pine intermingling with the fragrance of heather, gorse and bracken. Through its picture window a pristine loveliness enclosed me, a veritable Eden garden untouched by man. I sat in this lovely environment waiting for inspiration.....and here is the result: a Winter Work Programme. There were ten articles in all.

Two years later, publication of the magazine ceased (we never really knew why) – and the story ends here. Father however, kept a bag of Actumus – the dark brown powder just as I remember it – which, after his death in 1985, I found hidden in a cupboard and then sprinkled it over my garden.

There is no doubt in my mind that Dr Marian was a <u>most</u> remarkable man, that his message was just as remarkable and as important today, or even more so, than it was then. Yet how many people remember anything about him or his work?

His thought-provoking essay 'For Peace' was published after his death. It contains one of his most important findings: that the special property of hexagonal carbon is to act as an accumulator and transmitter of cosmic energy in a never-ending supply. That this freely given cosmic radiation is so great that we could grow dynamic, sustaining, healthy food for many times the world's present population. All that is necessary is to install within our soils the mechanism by which to catch and transmit to the growing

The Late S. Marian, D.Sc.

plants the peculiar energy pattern of Hexagonal Carbon. He ends by saying: if the same amount of money were spent on producing this substance from freely existing raw materials as on artificial fertilisers, there would be no hunger in the world, living nourishment would be available for all – <u>and peace would reign!</u>

An oak tree was planted, close to Fingle Bridge, the home of Actumus, as a living memorial to a man who gave his life for his belief in order to benefit mankind.

SIEGFRIED MARIAN, D.Sc.
Born in Austria 14th September, 1898
Died in London 17th April, 1952

THIS OAK TREE WAS PLANTED ON 11th DECEMBER, 1952 BY HIS ADMIRERS AND SUPPORTERS IN MEMORY OF HIS PIONEER DISCOVERIES IN SOIL SCIENCE

And he shall be like a tree planted by the rivers of water, that bringeth forth his fruit in his season; his leaf also shall not wither: and whatsoever he doeth shall prosper. – Ps. I, v. 3.

Chapter 18

Practical Actumus Gardening
Winter Work Programme

Winter, with its short days, hard frosts, cold rain and keen winds, is the time of year when some of your gardening may be done by the fireside. Planning your cropping and manurial programmes, ordering seeds, overhauling tools and machines are all jobs for the long evenings, and rainy days. But when the days are bright and the soil workable there is digging and pruning to be done, not forgetting the late planting of Shallots and Artichokes and the early sowing of Peas and Broadbeans and other hardy vegetables.

Those who have greenhouses will make early sowing in heat, and start taking their Chrysanthemum cuttings, for even in Winter there is plenty to be done, and the part Actumus plays in your work programme is important. The weathering affect of frosts will do much for the crumb structure of the soil, but to secure consistent growth during the Spring and Summer, watering with an Actumus solution should begin as early as February, before the growing season begins. Strawberries, soft and hard fruit, Spring Cabbage, Winter Lettuce, and all the crops over-wintering in your garden, will benefit from a very weak dilution of Actumus and constant hoeing during mild spells.

Shallots may be planted on the shortest day, or as soon afterwards as possible. Put the sets (your own saving, I hope) 6 inches apart in rows 12-18 ins. apart and just press lightly into the soil. Last year I experimented with three separate plantings, the first in November, the second on the shortest day, and again in the early Spring. The planting on the shortest day gave the earliest ripening, combined with the greatest weight of usable bulbs. A great number of the November planting ran to flower, while those planted in the Spring never grew very large.

Jerusalem Artichokes should also be planted at this time, for they need a long season of growth. Select nicely rounded, medium-sized tubers and plant in rows 2ft. apart, leaving 18ins. between each tuber. Remember, as always, to plant with Actumus.

In between hard frosts from leaf fall until bud burst is pruning time. I shall deal very simply with the pruning of fruit trees, because it is specialised work and a tree may be more spoilt by wrong pruning than by none at all. If in doubt call in an expert to advise you, but for those wishing to try for themselves here are a few basic hints to remember. There are three stages in the life of a fruit tree. Firstly, by hard pruning of the young tree you aim to build up the branch framework; secondly, by light pruning to encourage the tree to come into bearing; and thirdly, to keep the tree in a balanced state of healthy growth combined with regular cropping, by hard or light pruning according to circumstances. Thus no hard and fast rules can be laid down, each tree is an individual and should be treated as such. Knowing your varieties is invaluable, so label the trees clearly at planting time, or use one of the many fruit-naming services for finding out the varieties you have forgotten.

In general, however, a tree will bear fruit if it is healthy. This implies that the roots must be properly nourished and the branches and twigs must receive plenty of light. So keep the centre of the tree open, remove any crossing or rubbing branches so that each branch has at least 12ins. between it and its neighbour, and dress yearly with Actumus and mulch young trees with Soil Compost. In early Spring, after rain, a dressing of dry Actumus sprinkled to the circumference of the branch formation will do a great deal in providing ideal conditions for healthy growth and the formation of fruit buds in the year to come.

There are many schools of thought on the subject of "How to Dig", or whether to dig at all ! – but I believe in thoroughly aerating the soil. On our light, sandy soil we use a Clifford Rotary Hoe. As soon as a plot is cleared it is Clifforded. This leaves the soil in an aerated condition rather like an eiderdown. During the Winter each vacant plot is Clifforded three or even more times, and in the early Spring a liberal dressing of Soil Compost is spread and this is turned in, in readiness for the Spring sowing. The amount each bed receives depends on the crop and its performance in the previous year, e.g., the brassica patch receives a heavier dressing than the root bed. Bonfire Ash and Actumus are applied later with the seed or seedlings.

Trenches filled with compost are made for the Peas and Beans, covered with soil and firmed. The Peas are put in 3 rows per trench with the seed 2ins. apart in the rows, covered with an inch or so of soil and pressed down. Broadbeans can be sown in single rows 18ins. apart, with the beans 9ins. apart in the rows, or double rows 10ins. apart with 15ins. between the double rows.

Our soil, being light, warms up quickly, and by the end of February, besides Peas and Beans, I usually sow Parsnips in rows 15ins. apart, the seed being put in groups of 3 or 4, 6ins. apart; Lettuce in rows 12ins. apart, the seed being very thinly sprinkled down a shallow trench; also Onions and Brassicas.

Onions like to be sown in firm, dry soil, and you may have to wait until March or April for these conditions. Onion seed is very expensive, so do wait until the soil is favourable or else the germination will be poor. Sow shallowly in drills 12ins. apart, firming the seed bed well after sowing.

The early Brassicas such as Red Cabbage, Summer Cabbage, Sprouts and Cauliflower may also be sown in late February, but more about the making of seed-beds and favourable soil conditions for sowing in the Spring Work Programme.

From thoughts of Spring we again return to the Winter fireside. It is great fun looking through the seed catalogues, but do not be over-persuaded by the lovely pictures to buy packets and packets of flower seeds and those new wonder vegetables. Plan your garden on paper first, taking into account its size and soil. Make notes of, or mark on the plan, your rotation, your manurial programme, and the amount of seed and varieties you will need for the year to come. Then, and only then, order your seeds. For many years I was very satisfied with one or two seed firms, but I am now increasingly getting the seeds I do not save for myself from a Compost Seed firm, for I am convinced that to obtain healthy plants the seed itself should have come from plants grown in healthy soil.

In my garden I have established a 5-year rotation. Roots, Legumes, Potatoes, Cut Flowers and Brassicas. Lettuce and Onion have permanent beds to themselves which are interchanged every 3 years. Other crops are grown along the edges, and the permanent crops such as strawberries, soft fruit, asparagus, etc., in their permanent beds.

When making out your seed orders do not forget to look at the Plant Catalogues. From my experience it is well worth while to buy the best plants to start with because you can propagate from them yourself once you have the stock. Chrysanthemums are not difficult to grow and are one of the loveliest of the Autumn and Winter cut flowers. Last Winter we ordered one rooted cutting of each of 24 named varieties. These arrived in April, and by mid-August Lovelace, pale salmon, Daydream, rose pink, and August Red, a fiery red, were blooming profusely, since when there has been a constant succession of a variety of colours and types, and we shall still be cutting those removed to a cold greenhouse when Christmas comes.

When flowering has finished, the "stools" of the plants should be put in good soil and good light in a frame or greenhouse, and as early as January they will be sending up strong, sturdy shoots. As soon as these are 4ins. high, taking of cuttings may begin. Cut with a sharp knife just below a node and insert each cutting firmly in a sandy medium. Water in well with a dilute solution of Actumus and cover with a frame or piece of glass. Shade for a few days if necessary, and turn frame or glass every morning to prevent the atmosphere becoming too humid and mildew-forming. These cuttings will root in 3 weeks to a month, and may then be pricked out into seed boxes or pots. Be sure to keep the varieties separate and label carefully.

So even in Winter there is plenty to do in a garden, and it is up to each one of us to plan carefully for the year to come. Now to all Actumus gardeners I should like to wish you all a Happy Christmas and Health, Abundance and Beauty from your gardens in 1953.

Advertisement for Actumus Grown seeds and plants.

Chapter 19

Money Spinners and Good Ideas

The holiday season during the 1950's was very short – no more than three months, starting with Easter followed by Whitsun and ending with the main summer period, the high point of the year being the Bank Holiday weekend at the beginning of August. No wonder, in an endeavour to extend this period, my parents reminded prospective customers of the beauties of early summer. 'May we book you in for the following season? Remember June is the best holiday month – Sandy Balls is in its full glory and the days are longest'. Although we were open the whole year round, few visitors came at other times and it would have been quiet for us here during the rest of the year without our resident community, who numbered about 50 or so and included many interesting people.

Sandy Balls – Organic Fruit and Vegetable Stall.

We sold our farm and garden produce in a variety of ways; in the campstore (a converted stable), run by 'Grandpa' Harrod, my mother's father; from my fruit and vegetable stall; and from the farm dairy, open morning and evening for fresh milk, eggs and cream. The surplus produce, including cut flowers, went to Southampton market, milk and eggs to the Milk Marketing and Egg Boards, respectively, and pigs to the local bacon factory. The practice of castrating the male piglets of a litter at six weeks old was known locally as 'cutting'. Henry Chalk was called when needed, and with a razor-sharp penknife, did a quick neat job. The piglets squealed from being handled and it was over in an instant. My sister-in-law reports that the knife was then wiped on rather grubby trousers and put carefully away in a pocket, to be brought out later for a luncheon snack of bread and cheese!

There was always plenty to do and, young as we were, and money scarce, nothing was too much trouble. Cockerel and other poultry were reared for Christmas and all the family, except Father, took part and enjoyed the annual plucking sessions.

Welsh onions were another good line for early salad trade in the wholesale market; dug, cleaned and bunched, it was a tedious and time-consuming task. This crop, excellent for family use, makes a neat edging, is completely hardy and healthy, does not die down during the winter like chives, builds up quickly, from a few to a multitude of 'spring onions' or scallions, and can be used in a variety of ways, especially during the winter months. A few put back each year and top-dressed with compost will give a never-ending supply.

I kept a large, three-tiered cage of rabbits for meat, all naturally fed, producing a total of 60 or more for sale each year from three breeding does. These were killed and paunched (by Martin), hung, then skinned and sold to order – whole at 1/10d lb or choice joints 2/6d lb; they were immensely popular.

The garden paths had to be cut regularly during the summer months, so I devised a scheme to utilise the mixed herbage for the rabbits. I figured this would mean <u>no</u> grass cutting and <u>less</u> rabbit feeding, in theory a clever plan! A simple run was designed with wet-weather shelter to cover the three foot pathways.

The estate craftsman was pleased to make one per doe from our own sawn-out timber. Sturdy and strong, yet relatively light, with a plywood sliding door, the bottom and sides covered with wire netting and two handles, I could hardly wait to try one out. Placed in a position with rabbits inside, it could be moved by me alone – an important consideration although, obviously, it was easier for two people to lift it along, especially when the rabbits became large and heavy. By the time they got to killing weight, four to five pounds, another batch of youngsters were ready to be put in.

Rabbit runs converted for Chickens or Bantams.

It was a very happy arrangement for me as well as the rabbits – but no system is perfect and, after a summer or two, coccidiosis appeared. This is a disease usually of chickens (and other birds) but fatal to rabbits too and we were recommended to rest the pathways for at least three years – so, that was that!

The runs were moved elsewhere and, in subsequent years, were adapted for bantams – 18 per run. This also worked well for a time until, first fox, and then badger, came by night to harass them. A fox can be deterred but not a determined badger; nest-box lids were raised, wire netting surround bitten through and the poor creature dragged out. The final straw came when a badger (in the 1970's) lifted up a run bodily, <u>and</u> was caught in the act, but by that time all the beautiful Maran Chickens, except one, were dead. One cannot win!

It is interesting to note that, in the early years in Sandy Balls, badgers were <u>never</u> seen, although their setts proved they lived happily within; they were certainly never the nuisance they later became. As the fox has become suburbanised, in some strange way the badger, too, has been drawn into the human web. (I wonder if this is a local phenomenon or more widespread?).

About this time I bought my first machine, a second-hand Howard Bantam Rotovator with grass cutter attachment. I was primarily a hand worker, so this was a big step forward for me as I was a little frightened of the 'monsters'. Hitherto, all plots had been rotovated by an old Clifford, when needed, by one of the menfolk. Now, with finances under my own control and wanting to be as independent as possible, I did them myself, even cutting the grass; not a perfect job but quite adequate for a large kitchen garden. Indeed, on such light soil, the 'Bantam' proved to be a tiny machine I could happily manage and its use gave me added confidence.

Chapter 20

Holiday Interlude

October in the Dordogne - France 1952

In 1922, Ernest Westlake, as a special concession to Philip Oyler, lessee of Sandy Balls Gate Farm, (Martin's first farm in 1949) allowed him to erect a dwelling for his Mother-in-Law, a Swede. She wished to end her days in surroundings reminiscent of her native land.

After her death in 1928 it came onto the market and was purchased by Forest School and became known as Woodcot. Later it was to be our home in Sandy Balls.

After the 2nd World War we were interested to hear that Philip Oyler, now living in France, had written a book about his life there entitled *'The Generous Earth'.

After reading the book – lent to me by Father – and remembering Oyler's association with Sandy Balls in the early days, I was keen to see 'this land of all good things' for myself. So in the Autumn of 1952 my friend and I, with rucksacks on our backs set off for a walking holiday there. Hitch-hiking, although cheap, was not an ideal way of travelling, and it was not until five days later that we reached Soulliac, a small town on the edge of the Valley, and the following afternoon before we saw the Valley itself.

Standing on the slopes of a young oak plantation we saw the river shimmering through the silver trunks of the yellowing poplars that grew along its banks. Below us lay the flat valley bottom like a huge market garden. Beyond the hills rose steeply, a network of pasture and vineyards; and higher still the wooded hilltops of deciduous trees, mellow and still in the warm Autumn sunshine.

Our first impression of this Valley was of great peace and serenity, the stillness being broken only by the low murmur of the river and the occasional barking of dogs. The Dordogne, with its many sidewaters and tree-clad islands, is indeed a river of great natural beauty. It flows wide and clear, incredibly swiftly over the shallow pebbled bottom, to Bordeaux and the sea beyond. There are few stone bridges, but several not unpleasing suspension bridges had been thrown across in the early war years, and it was over one of these we crossed, to climb to the village of Carennac on the other side. There we found the Hotel La Croix and Madame, a little old lady with 'a heart of gold'. France was very expensive and the exchange unfavourable, but here we found warmth and friendliness, comfortable beds, wonderful French food, plenty of wine and all at a reasonable cost. Here is the

* 'The Generous Earth' by Philip Oyler published 1950 by Hodder & Stoughton.

supper we enjoyed on our first evening; the others there were similar in quality and quantity, although in other hotels we were not always so fortunate.

Soup

Chicken dressed with sliced onion and egg mayonnaise

Fish in oil and red vinegar

Mushrooms

Variety of cheeses

Apples, pears and walnuts

Bread and a large bottle of red wine

This at our request was a 'repas pour 300 francs' (apparently the lowest charge in France just then). The exchange being about 1000 francs for £1, this meal cost about 6s., which, by its excellence and size, even by English prices was extremely reasonable.

For breakfast and lunch we bought from the little village shops, and picnicked by the roadside, thereby sampling the valley's produce.

The day after we arrived in Carennac was Sunday, a day of blue skies and hot sun. We walked by footpaths past farms and villages, through chestnut and oak-woods, crushing acorns and chestnuts beneath our feet, over alpine meadows still starred with flowers, up to the little village of Queysac perched on top of a hill. For this was their Fete des Vendanges. Starting with a church service of thanksgiving in the morning, as the day wore on it developed into a lighthearted, joyous affair of talking and wine drinking, of dancing and fireworks. From miles around the youth of the countryside came to give thanks for the harvest and to enjoy each other's company and the local Vin paille, which was indeed delicious. To our great disappointment we found no traditional dresses, dancing, or music, and stalls not selling the local produce but common triptraps as we have in England.

The farmhouses, the churches, châteaux and villages were a constant joy to us. The houses were old – very old. The tiles were uneven, and a purplish black in colour – the walls of thick mellowed stone, with small brightly coloured shuttered windows. A flight of steps led to the front door, for the ground floor was largely used for storage and for the many animals that wandered in and out.

The farms or cultivated plots were worked in strips. On the rich herbage of grass, clover or lucerne, old women or girls, knitting steadily, tend cows and goats. Artichokes up to 10 feet high were in full flower, their golden heads shining in the sunlight. Enormous Pumpkins, red, yellow, orange and green, stood high above the slightly frosted foliage, while Asparagus was a lovely rich gold. The many rows of vines were colouring and apple, pear, quince and medlar trees hung with ripe fruit. Turnips and broadbeans grew luxuriantly – while drying Tobacco hung in the lofts and barns, On one holding we saw lines of young fruit trees, but we saw no raspberries, strawberries, black and red currants or gooseberries, and only saw one Apiary of six hives on our tour.

The cows had very small udders and no farm appeared to have more than five or six. We saw no calves, very few pigs but plenty of chicken, geese, ducks, turkeys and muscovy ducks, and pigeons which lived in the white towers or pigeonniers built as an integral part of many houses. One morning we saw a full-grown bull ploughing alongside two bullocks and a cow. We saw milk cans hanging in the lanes waiting to be collected and taken to the Fromagerie, for milk is largely made into cheese and not drunk in its liquid form as it is here in England.

At Carennac the valley was about a mile wide – upstream towards St Cere it broadens considerably, while farther down it narrows so that sheer cliffs, reminiscent of Cheddar Gorge, fall steeply to the river below. For this is limestone country, with its abundance of wild flowers and rocky outgrowths and the alluvial soil rich in the valley. By the river and up over the hills we explored the countryside between Bretenoux and Salat, a distance of about 30 miles. On our walks we saw peasants leisurely gathering ripe maize, picking up, washing and drying walnuts, carting manure in miniature carts, ploughing with bullocks or oxen, tending their animals, making hay, baking huge round loaves in their enormous bread ovens, distilling eau-de-vie by the roadside, sawing wood and shoeing horses and oxen in the many local sawmills and forges. Many varieties of toadstools were being gathered from woods, women were washing clothes in the river, and new houses and barns were being built in the same style (except for larger windows) with the same materials as of old – natural rock, oak timbers and red tiles. Everywhere we saw the rich maturity and golden colouring of Autumn side by side with the lush green growth of Spring.

Vines climbed round the walls of many houses, while in the patches that might be called gardens, amid a variety of crops, dahlias flowered in brilliant profusion. Along all the roads and lanes, by every house, and dotted throughout the whole valley, the walnut tree reigned supreme.

Many things surprised us, how the weeds flourished alongside the crops, how the churches were used as church, school, and hall combined, the pot-plants that grew on the steps or on the verandas of many houses, the herds of sheep in the hills with their long thin legs, pointed faces and poor wool, the peasants who never hurried, who in the rain walked or cycled with large black umbrellas, the infrequency of buses and trains, the silence and darkness of a shuttered village after dark, the primitive sanitation and lack of drinking water in a countryside where even the remotest village had electricity.

As a gardener my impression of the valley, seen only as an onlooker, and for a few days only in the Autumn, was this. Their culture is purely of the sheltered unhedged plot in deep rich alluvial soil, or on the hillside where the soil is deep enough. They have no glass to contend with, no management of greenhouses or frames as we have in England. The holdings belong to the peasants themselves and are small and easy to work. There is plenty of labour and varied work for all, from the old grandmother to the youngest child. They manure heavily for most of the animals are stall-fed. The heat of the summer sun is sufficient to oxidise any inert humus and the underlying strata of limestone to neutralise any excess acids there may be in the soil. Coal is seldom used and being a purely agricultural area there are no poisonous fumes from town or factory. Growing a little of everything there is the right natural balance between trees and plants. The climate is favourable and disease rarely known.

It is no wonder then that these people, seemingly untouched by wars or the cares of this modern world, live full, useful, creative and happy lives in this lovely valley where the sun shines.

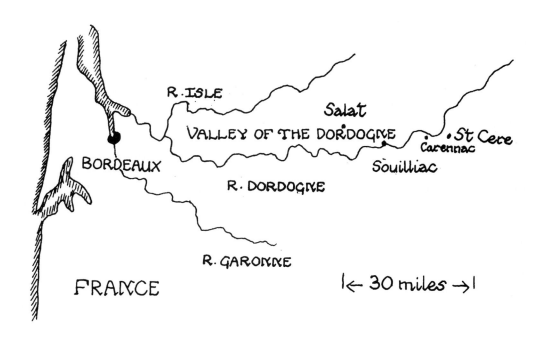

Chapter 21

Snowdrops for Cloches

1954 found me perched on a hillside above 'Sunnyside' (a newly acquired estate property) pulling snowdrops, and frosty evenings saw Mother and me backed by the warmth of a wood fire, a table full of cool flowers in front, meticulously counting and listening to the wireless the while. Correct presentation was necessary for Covent Garden, that mecca of the flower trade – 25 flowers in a bunch with five ivy leaves behind and secured with two elastic bands. On and on we went, bunching and placing the finished article upright in bowls of water for a long overnight drink in our cold barn of a bathroom. Next day, carefully packed in flat boxes, labelled and invoiced, they were speedily taken on the back of a bright, new scooter to catch the 4.25 – two miles away. This train, slowly puffing its way up the Avon Valley, later assumed a more challenging aspect for it was the one we <u>had</u> to catch for certain morning delivery of our fresh-picked produce to the Whole Food Shop in Baker Street.

The Snowdrop money, as much as £40 in a good year, was a most welcome source of income in early Spring (cold fingers forgotten) and, indeed, financed my first venture into something different – the purchase of 100 cloches. These were the Chase growers' barn type which arrived in crates of glass and wires; the puzzle was, how to put them together? Finally, with good advice and help from all sides, the job was mastered and I surveyed a sea of tiny glass houses and, with a sinking feeling, thought 'How could I have been so foolish!'

I eventually bought another 200 and found them wonderful for early crops and those needing extra warmth during the summer months, e.g melons, cucumbers, tomatoes, etc. You might say, after my initial feeling of misgiving, I took to cloche management like a duck to water. I bought the book by J.L.H. Chase on 'Commercial Cloche Gardening' and studied it assiduously – visited his gardens at The Grange, Chertsey where crops and layout were superb and was convinced – if I needed convincing – of the excellence of the triple combination of cloches, compost and trickle irrigation for the production of quality vegetables. Now, 40 years later, I still have 66 cloches left and value them immensely for the benefit they bring. If a wooden side had not collapsed during storage and, in a moment of generosity I had not lent <u>more</u> than a few to 'budding gardeners' within the family, who, when enthusiasm died, neglected them, I would have had many more.

Glass cloches have many advantages over the modern day plastic ones or even, I think, the small greenhouse, especially when you are young and able. They are portable, stable, long lasting, able to be ventilated, easily irrigated, there is little chance of pest or disease build-up, for they can be used to cover three different crops a year and, during the short period when not in use, occupy a very small space. Obviously, being glass, they need careful handling but, if aligned in rows with shaped glass ends, are able to withstand the strongest gales. Quite a consideration, when greenhouses themselves are lifted bodily by the wind and thoughtlessly smashed to the ground!

Organic gardening – where the plant's living environment is continually studied, needs great attention to detail and this is true in cloche management, too. Broken glass should be mended immediately and this involves use of aluminium cloche menders or replacement of smashed panes. Overlapping paper sacks or other ground cover material can be used for stacking, as bare soil, with its inevitable weed growth, causes green algae to form. Fewer now need a yearly wash, although even this can be quite a tolerable job on a fine Spring day and a delight to see the bright glass sparkling once more in the sunlight.

From this time on, I adopted the strip-bed system in my garden. One plot at first, a double row of cloches in a 4ft bed with a 2ft pathway with beds for rotation on either side – then, gradually eliminating all side paths, I cultivated the whole of the garden in this way. The centre path remained but was now installed with standpipes at regular intervals along its length, thus making it possible to use the trickle irrigation in every bed. The original piping was made of black rubber which soon perished - thankfully so, for I emerged from my garden coal black, like a sweep, every time I handled it, much to the astonishment of the holiday visitors. An improved type, bought from Camerons in 1966, is still in perfect working order and something I would not be without.

Little children love to tease and when, many years later, I saw my elder son, Eden, as a toddler, crawling carefully through a row of cloches, I knew the time had come to store them for a few years. So this is what I did, with disastrous results for the stacked glass, but, more importantly, the child was safe and I had peace of mind.

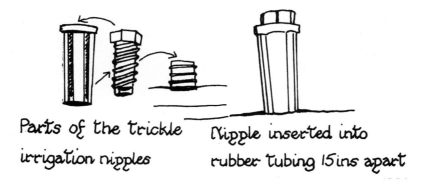

Parts of the trickle irrigation nipples   Nipple inserted into rubber tubing 15ins apart

Juliette de Bairacli-Levy
Herbalist, author, traveller and pioneer of holistic veterinary care.

Chapter 22
Juliette de Bairacli-Levy
Herbalist and Author

It was in the 1950's that I first came into contact with a colourful character called Juliette de Bairacli-Levy. She was staying in a tiny caravan near to my Aunt Margaret on Godshill Ridge – the Ridge property, 40 acres of heath and purlieu land was the first purchase of land in Godshill by Grandfather, Ernest Westlake. My Aunt and her family continued to live there after his death, the wooden dwelling little changed since those early days. Juliette was of mixed nationality; she was proud that her Grandfather had been a Turkish Gipsy King and her Jewish blood was evident. She had a young son called Rafik whom she was in the process of weaning and as with many primitive peoples she was masticating all his food before she fed it to him. This piece of information, imparted to me by Cousin Christopher, I found intriguing – the more so when I heard that she was a herbalist, an author and knew Augustus John, the famous artist who lived locally. She was introduced to me, for, being vegetarian and eating most of her food raw, she was keen to buy my organic produce. A friendship grew up between us, respect on my part for her knowledge of herbal lore and by her, for me, as an experienced and enthusiastic gardener.

The Ridge – Godshill.

Father at this time was medical adviser to Augustus John, giving him the benefit of the new medicine that he and other doctors were pioneering and developing; they had another mutual interest – the Gypsies of the New Forest. Augustus John was President of the Gipsy Lore Society and was concerned about the Gypsies of the Forest who in 1926 had been forbidden mobile camping, and had been rounded up and put into compounds with no services and from which they could not move – the result had been deterioration and degeneration and more especially universal round worm infection.

Many were concerned at their plight and Father, as Chairman of the Ringwood and Fordingbridge Rural District Council, with the help of other bodies drew up a scheme which was submitted to Augustus John to send to the Gipsy Lore Society. Juliette was also a champion of the Gipsy whom she contacted in whatever country she happened to be living. Her intention was to live in the Forest and to research a book about the Gypsies. Faber and Faber had already (1952) published her 'Herbal Handbook for Farm and Stable' and were keen to take more.

Expecting another child and not wishing for it to be born out of wedlock, she decided to marry the father, (of both children) before the baby was born. The prospective groom, working as a journalist in North Africa, was asked to come to England to marry her. It was a bitter Spring and I do not know what this handsome young Spaniard expected (so very much younger than herself) but he arrived in plimsolls and

Rose Cottage – Abbotswell.

136

light weight clothing and promptly caught cold. Never before or since have I been to such a bizarre wedding. Juliette obviously 'with child' turned not a hair as Rafik ran round and round the Registry Office table and the groom spoke little English. It was very strange but entirely in keeping with Juliette's character – she knew what was right for her to do at any one time. Later I heard that a Gipsy wedding had been celebrated with her gipsy friends – Augustus John presiding.

…The weather worsened and snow fell and after a few weeks, the husband, pining for warmer climes, left for his journalistic job in North Africa – I never saw him again. Juliette now became concerned that her baby would be born in England, where hanging was still the ultimate penalty in law. (Rafik had been born in Tunisia). So she left for Spain where she caught Typhoid from infected water and nearly died. When she returned to Godshill she had lost all her hair and the baby, a girl Luz*, was covered with impetigo. Staying in a tiny wooden dwelling adjacent to Sandy Balls the family recovered their health – my produce was certainly very welcome at this time.

My next memory is of being asked by Juliette to look after her children for a few days while she represented herself in a law case in London. She maintained that some of her herbal recipes were being manufactured by another and she was seeking to redress the wrong. I moved down to Rose Red Cottage at Abbotswell where they were now living. Abbotswell is mentioned as far back as 1217 in the 1st Perambulation of the New Forest, so is of very ancient origin. Juliette drew her water from this well. The tiny cottage – cob built, was little more than one room. Originally there had been a loft above and the tiny window was still visible below the eaves, however, the staircase was unsafe and blocked with debris. Two beds occupied most of the floor space – a high and a low one

Spanish donkey boy.

*From Andaluz (light), pronounced Luth.

THE ILLUSTRATED HERBAL HANDBOOK FOR EVERYONE

❄

Juliette de Baïracli Levy

illustrated by Heather Wood

which could be pushed under the other during the day. I remember little other furniture but can still recall the eye-catching woven baskets of different textures and patterns hanging from the walls. The inglenook fireplace had been boarded up at sometime and now was replaced by a stove.

There was no electricity, no running water, in fact it was very primitive indeed.

A long list of instructions was left for me which included care of the Afghan hound, the children's constant companion – the gentle Tullipan. First thing each morning I had to wash the children on the porch with Abbotswell water; ice-cold at that time of the year! Then followed a raw fruit breakfast sitting on the bed. Both children had perfect teeth, white and even; I think that I was a little envious of such perfection. The weather was cold – very cold, the stove difficult and on one of our walks over the Hyde Common pushing the pram, flurries of snow made me fear we would be snowed up. But all was well and Juliette returned safely form London to the joy of both children and the dog. Her only comment about the case was that the English Legal System

was prejudiced against women representing themselves. She never mentioned the matter to me again.

Living by her pen, Juliette spent long hours typing late into the night when her children were in bed – but finally with the manuscript finished she prepared to leave the New Forest: her task was completed and she had to move on. Rafik was now five, Luz three years old. 'Wanderers in the New Forest' with a preface by Augustus John was published in 1958, with many beautiful photographs of the Forest and the children.

Luz and Rafik and the gentle Tullipan.

138

The following Christmas I received a card from Spain; a photograph of Rafik. The scenery and vegetation were in complete contrast to that the family had left behind in England. Over the years I received news of Juliette but I only saw her once again......

Our goat, Emma, had kidded and was not cleansing satisfactorily. Eden and I were studying the book 'Herbal Handbook for Farm and Stable' on the kitchen table, when who should walk in but Juliette herself. She was over in England to sign copies of her recent book at the New Forest Show. We were surprised and she was delighted to see us referring to one of her books in this way. She looked at the animal, gave us sound advice and all was well. Another contact was second-hand, as it were. A young friend, Heather Wood, trained at Kew as a botanical artist, who with her family had stayed in the camping huts in Sandy Balls on holiday for many years, told me she was joining a Kibbutz in Israel. I suggested she should contact Juliette who was living there at that time. The result of their association are the beautifully drawn illustrations in the Herbal Handbook brought out later as a paperback.

Heather also did work for the Israeli Government, illustrating their endangered plant species as eye-catching posters.

...And what of the plight of the New Forest Gipsy? The communes were closed down and those that wished were offered sub-standard accommodation by the Council and integrated slowly (with much opposition and prejudice) into the community. Increasing health regulations, site-licensing measures and changes in the management of the New Forest meant that the other ideas mentioned in the original scheme were not felt to be justified in any way. The New Forest Gipsy would never again be free to wander as he had once done in the past.

...And what of the two children I had felt so honoured to be entrusted with, in those far-off days – News in the Spring of 1998 from the Azores: Juliette, now 84 years old, with 18 books to her credit and three more still to come. She writes of her children – 'Rafik and Luz both married. Rafik chose career of a deep sea diver for many years, and is yet on that sort of work, on the oil rigs. He has married twice, a child with each marriage. He lives in Aberdeen, a base for work on the rigs. Luz married an architect, lives in Switzerland, has a little daughter who calls herself 'A friend of the trees'.

It is good to think that those uniquely brought up children should find happiness and fulfilment in today's world and that Juliette remains undaunted by life – her vision still clear, her mission undimmed.

Chapter 23
Braziers Park

At the Centenary Camp held in Sandy Balls to mark the Founder's birth, I was introduced to Dr Glynn Faithful, an early member of the Order of Woodcraft Chivalry at the age of 12 years in 1924 and a student helper at Grith Fyrd during the winter of 1932/33. He was now a close friend of Dr Norman Glaister who had acted as Keeper of the Fire (Spiritual Leader and Counsellor) to Father's Chieftain (Leader) in the early formative days of the organisation and a Director with Father on the Forest School Committee. Serving throughout the Second World War and rising to the rank of Major, Glynn Faithful was now a lecturer in Italian at Liverpool University and between whiles (weekends and holidays), Director of Studies with Norman Glaister, founder of an Adult Educational Centre in Oxfordshire – its full title being Braziers School of Integrative Social Research! Glynn was separated from his Austrian Countess wife and had one daughter called Marion who lived with her mother in Reading. She was later to become the well-known Marianne Faithful, friend of Mick Jagger and the Rolling Stones. She was eight years old at the time.

Marion Faithful (later Marianne Faithful) Age 8 years in the Water Meadows at Sandy Balls.

With Marion by Ernest Westlake's Memorial.

Glynn was as enthusiastic about Braziers as I was about Sandy Balls, and his glowing reports of the courses, community life and surrounding countryside persuaded me to attend one of the weekend courses later on in the Autumn; although pleasant walks in the lovely Chiltern countryside were marred at this time by the sight of so many suffering rabbits overcome by myxomatosis. This disease had not yet appeared in the New Forest.

Exploring the grounds, the morning after my arrival – for breakfast was not until 8.30am – I found a Victorian greenhouse, complete with boiler room and potting shed. The shaped glass panes in the roof suggested that care, quality and durability had been considered when building it. Inside, at a turn of a handle, the windows opened effortlessly. Alas, it was empty of crops.

Beyond, protected by three high walls, lay the garden sloping gently towards the South. Although neglected and overgrown with weeds, it still retained a gracious dignity with its wide, central path flanked by an avenue of espalier apple trees. The walls too were covered with fruit trees of many kinds – peaches, pears, apricots, plums and nectarines, their Victorian labels still hanging from the wires. Some trees were dead, others dying, all in need of attention. Looking through the early morning mist I saw a golden haze, which proved to be an old quince tree laden with large golden fruit, the ground already littered with many windfalls. It was sad to think that this once productive garden had become such a wilderness that nobody loved it or valued its potential.

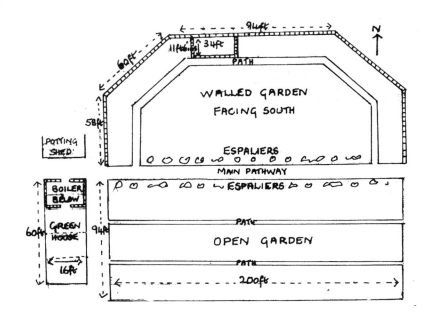

Plan of Braziers Kitchen Garden walled on three sides.

Discussing the matter with Glynn later, I said that I would be pleased to help plan the work if somebody volunteered to be the gardener. I had always wanted to work in a walled garden, and this was too good a chance to miss. Later, back home, Glynn wrote to say that Fred Clarke, a young man in his early twenties, a member of the house-team – 'a thoroughly dependable young man' had volunteered to care for the garden under my direction. He turned out to be an apt and willing pupil, eager to learn and keen to manage the garden organically. Compost heaps were built, undergrowth cleared and burnt and by Spring the four main beds were dug and ready for sowing. It was an incredible transformation. The greenhouse too was given a thorough Spring-clean and prepared for early crops. The good work continued and much fresh organically-grown produce was used in the kitchen from then on. Later, the farmland under Glynn's management with sheep, cows and poultry gave meat, milk, butter, cheese and eggs and became a valuable asset to the whole community venture. What could be better than to provide fresh, wholesome food for one's guests?

Braziers Park – School of Integrative Social Research.

Braziers Park was a large country house set in rural Oxfordshire with 40 acres of surrounding land. Originally a 17th Century Farm House it had been extended over the years in the Strawberry Hill Gothic Style and was now a grade 2 listed building. Many of the beautifully proportioned rooms were oak-panelled and log-fires burnt in the grates. I was charmed by the country-house atmosphere (only once experienced before at Oaklands – the Westlake family home, when a

The Oak-Panelled Hall at Braziers.

distant cousin of Father's had a family get-together and we were invited); the changing for dinner in the evening and the stimulating conversation with intelligent, cultured people over leisurely meals in the oak-panelled dining room.

After supper, Glynn took me on a tour of inspection. We saw the adjacent pantry where volunteers washed up in large teak sinks, the roomy kitchen with scrubbed beech work-table and four-ovened Aga; the cool marble-sided larders with gauze-covered windows; the store room with sacks of brown and white sugar and shelves full of sundries; and the tiled scullery where saucepans were washed and vegetables stored in large wooden bins......and I imagined life as it had been in the past when families were large and servants plentiful. Then up the broad sweep of staircase to the light airy bedrooms, six beds apiece in the larger rooms; then by a twisting narrow stair to the attic rooms, once the bare-boarded servants' quarters. Descending to the Hall, we found everybody gathering there for after dinner coffee.

The Hall was the heart of the house with its open wood fire and this was Norman's special responsibility; he exercised considerable skill by keeping it in day and night during cold weather. Now crackling merrily it brought a warmth of welcome to this cool autumnal evening.

Braziers was run by a Committee of Management: Dr Norman Glaister and his second wife Dorothy, Dr Glynn Faithful and Miss Bonnie Russell, a friend of Norman's; later Honor Fawsitt joined the group. They were all highly intelligent individuals, many with Woodcraft connections. The day-to-day work was done by a small 'house team' who consisted of students, many of them foreign, who came for a 3-6 month period to learn the language, and other young people searching for peace of mind or what to do next with their lives. They were paid a nominal sum of £3 per week, had one day off, but never at weekends. There was a rich and varied programme of weekend courses, to which tutors gave their services free: the centre had been running for six years.

Bonnie led the Art courses and did much of the office work. She was a talented artist and teacher, preferring to live in her own cottage close by and work long hours at the house. Later I was to see her studio where the art courses were held. This was another of the well-built assets within the grounds and ideal for its purpose. Close by the studio was an apple and pear store, reminder of the days when many gardeners would have been employed and in-season dessert fruit supplied daily to the kitchen. There were many outbuildings, four cottages, a terraced area, a water garden with fountain and statues, and a raised Victorian garden with yew hedge surround and summer house, completed the picture. It was a considerable challenge for that small nucleus of dedicated people in those early years.

Over the next three years I spent many weekends and longer periods too at Braziers, including three Christmases. At first helping in the garden and greenhouse, then branching out in other ways where I could see help was needed. Having little self-confidence myself, I had the ability to put others at ease and this gift, combined with a capacity to see what was needed at any particular point in time, made me a valuable addition to the household. Weekends were often very demanding and an extra pair of hands was doubly welcome.

The house, especially at Christmas, was full to capacity (55) and with limited helpers and everything needing to run smoothly, much forward planning was necessary and early preparation of the festive fare. I felt honoured to be asked to help…and there were carols and music and presents from the tree for all, and country dancing and party games, charades and plays, walks and plenty of good food and social fellowship and I was part of it and felt part of it too, for it was Christmas at Braziers and it was unique …

On my first visit, a little nervous and apprehensive, for I did not know what to expect – I was met at the cross-roads with other paying weekend guests and transported by a member of staff up the long lane to the house and welcomed at the front door. From now on I was to come by scooter, a lovely 1$^{1}/_{2}$ hour

The Author and Glynn Faithful waiting to meet guests at the bottom of Braziers Lane.

cross country journey from home arriving at breakfast time, and increasingly welcomed by the whole community as a friend of Glynn's.

Nor did my work at home suffer, for the Winter was always quiet and the garden being my own concern, I was free to choose what to do with my time. Mother was pleased that I was meeting interesting people and making new friends but there was a slight feeling, on my part, that in some way I had joined 'the enemy camp' – for all my childhood I was conscious of the fact that Norman Glaister was in some way involved in Father's decision to resign from the Order in 1934.

So, my visits continued and my enjoyment of the place. Sometimes I was free to join one of the art or craft groups – lino cutting, silk screen printing or painting in the grounds or studio with Bonnie. One Life Drawing weekend, when the model failed to turn up, I was asked to pose for the group – quite an experience! The more intellectual and sociological subjects I did not feel able to cope with, nor did I ever really feel at ease with the ideas on which Braziers had been founded. It seemed to me to be talk, talk, talk, even to the extent of taking scant notice of lunch or dinner gongs and then the whole group trooping in late for the carefully prepared meal.

Jenny, the cook, appreciated my help in the kitchen. We made puddings and pies, mincemeat and cakes, both to her recipes and to mine; and often in the afternoons when the staff were off duty, I had the freedom of the kitchen to make preserves – chutney, jellies, jams; in my note book I record 'Quince Jam for Braziers – Oct 31st – Nov 4th. 2 x 7lb jars, 8 x 4lb jars, 5 x 3lbs jars, 1 x 2lb jar + extras: Total = 68lbs. 40lb of Quince cheese, 9lbs of jelly = 117lbs'. After Christmas the Seville oranges arrived and a whole year's supply of marmalade was made as well. It was good fun and many guests volunteered to help cut the peel and prepare the fruit and vegetables.

…Then back home again and Mother and I did the same with equal success. It was no wonder then, that when I started to supply the Whole Food Shop in Baker Street, London, with produce, I should suggest home-made jam as one of the things I could offer them. When Jenny suddenly left for family reasons I was able to take charge of the two German helpers and the catering until a replacement was found.

It is truly amazing what a little appreciation does for one's confidence, for when I was asked whether I would lead a course on Garden Design I readily agreed and took it seriously enough to contact one of my tutors at the University and discuss the format with her. Alas, the course was never to take place, for on the way over, one Friday afternoon, a car waiting at a side turning drove straight into me and my red scooter and I found myself minus several teeth, with a badly split lip and in a state of shock. From that time on I began to question the wisdom of 'splitting myself in two' and, although I continued for another year, I knew a decision had to be made … Braziers or Sandy Balls, Sandy Balls or Braziers, I could not do both.

About the same time in the Summer of 1958 my favourite brother, Keith – a brilliant Doctor – died. He was only 33 years old. The whole family, especially Mother and myself, were shattered and I was needed at home. At this time Father, now 66 years old, badly shaken by the death of his eldest son, was conscious that he needed to make sure that the family were not penalised by massive death duties on Sandy Balls, if he should die. His cousin Leslie Rutter, whom he was brought up with as a child, was his Solicitor and he left it in Leslie's capable hands to work out a satisfactory scheme. A Family Company was suggested, which, if Father lived 7 years, simplified the Tax situation. 100 £1 shares were split between the members of the family.
We were all a little naïve about legal matters and left it to the experts, little

realising then that a Company, even a Family Company, is a business and is profit-orientated and that the ethos of Sandy Balls and the vision of Ernest Westlake and Father (that meant so much to me) would become increasingly threatened by commercialism and materialism in the years to come.

However, the following year, 1960, brought many new challenges for me – a new status, Director of Sandy Balls, a new garden and my meeting with a young Scot in the Royal Air Force based at Old Sarum, William Cormack, and later my marriage to him: Both Honor and Glynn came to my wedding. The choice was made!

Braziers is now approaching its 50th Anniversary (founded 1950). It is the only adult college that is run by a community and the oldest surviving lay community in Britain. Although none of the original group I knew so well are still alive, the work of Braziers continues and its Research project remains: 'To make conscious in ourselves the shape of the process of which we are a part, so that we may facilitate its development more efficiently and harmoniously'.

Front View of Braziers Park.

Chapter 24

Intensive Gardening

In the Autumn of 1959 I decided to visit Stratford on Avon, staying at a nearby guest house, 'Edstone' close by the village of Wooten Waaen. This was one of the longest journeys I had been on my Vespa Scooter – from Hampshire to Warwickshire, and after the long drought and recent rain, the roads were slippery and care needed. My main memory of the holiday is not of the hazardous journey or the many Shakespearean productions I saw at the Festival Theatre, including Paul Robeson as Othello and Sam Wannamaker as Iago, or the other places I visited in and around Stratford, but the book I bought at the guest house bookshop prior to leaving.

The book caught my eye because it was called *'Intensive Gardening'. It was about an organic system advocated by the author, Rosa Dalziel O'Brien and tried out with great success by her over a 12 year period. So much so, that it was thought worthwhile to write it up in the greatest detail – including a motion study routine indicating the correct movement of hands and body in the various operations needed! The method was particularly applicable to Dutch Light structures for getting crops a few days earlier for market; so essential for profitability in those pre-supermarket days of seasonal produce.

I had experience of this with my cloche crops, especially in the wholesale market. I grew five varieties of Sweetpea, 'Startler', a flame, 'Captain Blood', a crimson, 'Swan Lake', a white, 'Elizabeth Taylor', a lilac and, 'Mrs Bolton', a pink. They were sown on October 4th each year, as a double row under the cloches with a row of lettuce between ('Attractie' being an excellent variety). The lettuce matured first and the sweetpeas grew on, and were either sticked or later I used a 3 inch mesh for them to climb up. They were sent to Southampton Market in self-coloured bunches – 12 to a bunch, the bottom flower just out. At first I received 2/6d a bunch; a large sum, then, as if to emphasise 'Summer is here', a heat wave arrived and returns showed 'No Sale'. The prices never recovered. After this time large bunches were picked for the holiday visitors and in those days, being fragrant, they were immensely popular. The secret of success with sweetpeas is to pick every day; this keeps them producing long stems and young growth, otherwise they will quickly set seed and go over.

The Intensive system could obviously be adapted to any garden of any size – protected or in the open. Having turned my garden successfully into areas of strip beds for cloche cultivation, I could see the benefit of extending it to outdoor crops as well.

Intensive Gardening – R. Dalziel O'Brien, Faber and Faber 1956

The Author picking Rhubarb in the Market Garden.

Soon after my return from holiday the inaugural meeting of the newly-formed family company 'Sandy Balls Estate Ltd' was held with Father, Mother, Martin, Valerie and myself as Directors. One of its first decisions was the proposal to extend the area available for touring caravans and my garden was felt to be the ideal site.

After the initial shock of learning that I was to lose my garden – my pride and joy for the past 10 years, I was somewhat pacified by the assurance that when it was transferred to the new field, the 1½ acre one, in front of my bungalow 'Rosemarie', every help would be given to me to set it up. This included moving the garden shed, cloches and other equipment, installing standpipes for irrigation (so necessary on such a light sandy soil), planting up a new soft fruit bed, rhubarb and asparagus and ploughing and harrowing the whole area. There would be a year's run down on the other garden to facilitate the change.

Gradually I became enthusiastic about the new garden and could see the benefits of being so close to my bungalow and to the family home 'Woodcot'. However, I was now an employee of the Company and was paid a weekly wage of £8.00 – this was not so easy to accept. In some strange way I felt that I had lost my independence and freedom and to justify my wage I needed to work harder and harder. One of the results was that my Autumn trips and weekends away from home ended abruptly from that time on.

Q.R. was the basis of fertility used by Rosa Dalziel O'Brien in her Intensive Gardening system, later called 'Veganic Gardening'. It differed from Organic because it contained no animal manure; instead, humus from vegetable matter only was used in the compost heap, activated by a mixture of herbs added in a solution. The Q.R or Quick Return Activator was pioneered by Maye E.Bruce. She was an early member of the Anthroposophical Agricultural Foundation (later – the Bio-Dynamic Agricultural Association), inspired by the work of Austrian-born Scientist/Philosopher, Rudolf Steiner (1861-1925) – founder of Anthroposophy.

She was inspired to perfect a composting method, feeling that Dr Steiner's was not widely available (for members only) and not simple enough to follow for general use. A further stimulus came from an inspirational thought on awakening one morning, and the words ringing in her head: 'The Divinity within the Flower is sufficient of Itself'.

The herbs she chose: Wild Chamomile, Common Valerian, Dandelion, Yarrow, Stinging Nettle, together with Oak Bark, were exactly the same as he had recommended for his compost preparations in 1924, but included no animal element which he felt to be essential. On analysis these herbs, were found, by her, to contain all the elements – in a living form – necessary for plant growth.

So, after many trials and experimentation stretching over a ten-year period (1933-1943) Miss Bruce evolved her perfect formula which included a drop of honey in a dilution of 1 in 10,000. The honey was mixed with sugar and milk and added to the other ingredients. Initially she produced and marketed the product herself, but later she associated with Mr Chase of Cloche fame who took on the enterprise, selling a much finer powder containing a small quantity of sea weed as well. 60 years later this product is still available, mainly for the home gardener and produced and marketed by Chase Organics.

I knew vaguely about the Q.R method, for Father had Miss Bruce's* books in his library and others too about Composting, and I had every intention of trying out the Intensive system in my own garden. How was it then that I never bought one packet of Q.R? The reason was quite simple – I had a plenteous supply of my own compost activator from happy healthy bantams and rabbits and pig and cow manure from Martin's organic farm and I was happier to continue with this than buy in an alien product – Q.R. not produced on the holding. If I had understood then the importance of these herbs and of Steiner's work I might have taken a little more notice, but I continued in the same way producing a fine mature compost which I hoed into the surface of the beds with the little scrapper hoe, as recommended.

From Vegetable Waste to Fertile Soil 1940, Common Sense Compost-Making. M.E.Bruce Faber & Faber 1946.

It was not until 15 years later that I joined an Anthroposophical reading group and 25 years later that I felt impelled to join the Bio-Dynamic Agricultural Association. Awareness, it appears, is a maturing process and the time has to be right.

However, compost bins to the measurements and design advocated by R.Dalziel O'Brien – firstly using straw bales for the walls and then a more permanent slatted wood structure, were erected and I was particularly taken with the concept of rotting down the coarse, woody material in a 'rough' bin first and using it much later as the soil layer in the compost heaps.

Gradually, (with help) I laid out the new strip beds – 32 at first in four rows of eight, the length of the field. The beds were 4ft wide, 22ft long with 2ft pathways between. The bedsize that I had originally used for the cloche crops in the old garden was now extended to outdoor vegetables, soft fruit and rhubarb as well.

The pathways were lined with straw to facilitate working conditions but so much corn germinated that it was removed and composted and replaced by bracken. This in turn proved to be rather prickly to kneel on using the little scrapper hoe (the symbol of the system) so I soon reverted to my usual upright precision hoeing, buying a narrower hoe blade for the close-sown beds.

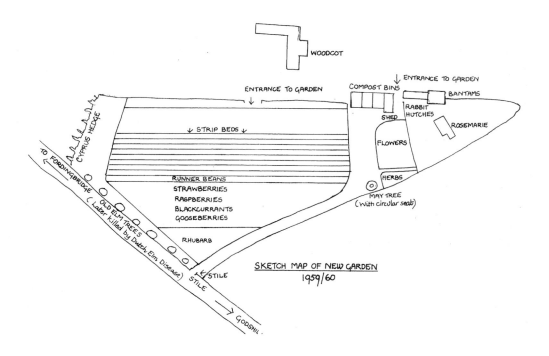

SKETCH MAP OF NEW GARDEN
1959/60

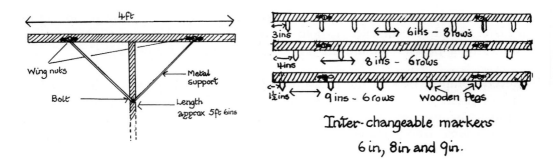

Inter-changeable markers
6 in, 8 in and 9 in.

I practised 'no digging' from this time on and avoided treading on the soil unnecessarily. Fortunately my light, sandy soil was workable in most weathers and did not pack or puddle after rain as would a clay or loam. In many ways I adapted the system to my own particular circumstances and made it my own.

In the 'Intensive Gardening' book a seed-sowing marker was illustrated. I was so taken with this labour-saving device that I consulted the woodwork teacher at evening class who helped me construct a 4ft handle, with metal supports, and inter-changeable heads for sowing 6, 8 and 9 inch rows. Ten rows, 4½ inches apart could be made if the 9 inch marker was drawn twice over the bed; so useful for sowing cloche carrots. I still use the markers in my kitchen garden today.

Soil preparation was easy – the mature friable compost, resembling a rich dark earth, was spread and hoed into the top 3 – 4 inches; the amount used depending on availability and crop grown. With such an intensive system, rotation within the beds was of paramount importance, especially as two or even three crops could occupy the same bed within the year. Green manure crops were sown after a final crop clearance and the resulting growth used for composting or animal feeding. Tares, a leguminous plant, was recommended, giving one and sometimes two cuts in a good Autumn.

At first many perennial weeds appeared in the new beds; these were carefully loosened with a fork and removed bodily. After a few years a remarkable change was obvious, the coarser weeds disappeared, the annuals lessened and were easy to control. Under the 'no digging' regime, dormant weed seeds remained dormant in the subsoil below.

Greatest attention was paid to watering. This I accomplished to my own satisfaction with the use of my trickle irrigation, using water from four standpipes newly installed down the length of the garden.

Looking back I can see I took many ideas from the 'Intensive' system and adapted them to my own holding. The result was that my garden had never been so productive, so healthy or so easy to manage. I was well able to supply a number of crops to the Whole Food Shop in Baker Street, and was told that my lettuce were the best that they had ever had. This continued for three years until the Fordingbridge Railway closed down in 1963. By this time the Holiday Centre was becoming increasingly popular, the family community was expanding rapidly and any surplus went to Southampton Wholesale Market.

In the end I had few regrets for the old garden; the only casualty was the prolific asparagus bed which could not be moved and was never replanted. Later, my children ran daily through the garden over the stile to school in Godshill, a few 100 yards away, and on their return would find me happily tending my crops in the garden, now cut to manageable size.

When we left Rosemarie and the garden in 1972 (later to become an Adventure Playground) and moved to Sandemans, originally the school house of Forest School, I rejoiced that the property was ours and I would not be subject again to the expansion plans of a Holiday Centre and have to move on.

Strawberries and soft fruit in the New Garden.

Chapter 25

The Organic Farm - Exciting Developments

The sudden death in 1959 of Jimmy Witt meant that the farm in Godshill on which Martin had trained came up for sale by public auction in the Spring of 1960. The lot included both Street and Arniss, farms about 100 acres in all, owned by him and farmed as a single unit. (Arniss Farm had been purchased in the early 1950's since Martin's apprenticeship). Street farmhouse in Godshill Street, an unattractive box-like dwelling on the opposite side of the road to the farm yard, had been occupied by the farmer Jimmy Witt with his wife and daughter; the more isolated Arniss farmhouse, by two farm workers and their families. Father and Martin were interested to attend the auction in Salisbury but had no other thought.

When the sale began Arthur Dalgety put in an opening bid of £16,000; there were no other bids. Then Robert Jeffrey, the Auctioneer, said he had had instructions from Dalgety to immediately offer Street Farm for re-sale, less three fields which he wished to retain. Both Martin and Father were astonished by this turn of events and thought there might now be a chance to make an offer for this smaller unit. Father quickly contacted his solicitors, Rutter and Rutter of Wincanton, who asked firstly, did he know what he would be buying and secondly had he seen the title deeds? On returning to the Sale Rooms he satisfied himself on both points but was told that an interested party, closeted in another room, had already put in a bid. Father, with great presence of mind, asked what the reserve price was and, on being told that it was £8,000, said he would offer this for it. At this point the Auctioneers were not quite sure what to do; so telephoned a senior independent Solicitor who said that the first person who offered the reserve would be accepted. The other party had offered £200 less, so Sandy Balls became the new owners of Street Farm. This was the first purchase by the family company formed the previous Autumn – Sandy Balls Estate Ltd – with Mother and Father, Martin and Valerie and myself as its first Directors (I resigned in 1966).

A further payment was required for the standing crops, (Winter sown wheat and hay in barn) and an immediate deposit of 10%. Without previous notice of intent, Lloyds Bank of Fordingbridge were not particularly happy with a demand for £800, but all was amicably settled. It was nevertheless a considerable outlay for the new company, so it was reluctantly agreed to sell off the Farm House with adjoining orchard and pasture. £4,000 was received from the sale, thus halving the burden of debt, and Martin took possession of the land he knew so well.

The farm buildings included a milking parlour with standings for 23 cows, a concreted collection yard, stabling, calf sheds, a rat-proof grain store and a large modern hay barn. The farmyard was well laid out and serviceable so, from then on, the milking and dairy work were transferred there, although for a year or so the dairy in Sandy Balls continued to open for the sale of farm bottled milk, morning and evening to the holiday visitors.

Sandy Balls Gate - Traditional New Forest Cottage.

SANDY BALLS HOUSE

Mother and Father's new home on Prospect Point.

In 1961 we were still registered as Producer Retailer – a licence being necessary to sell home produced unpasteurised milk. Originally milk was sold from a churn measured out into customers' jugs, but legislation put a stop to this. Then followed farm-bottled milk with all the work involved in washing and sterilising the bottles and persuading people to return them, rinsed if possible.

However, at this time the country was not only 'awash' with milk but there was a growing awareness that Channel Island milk with its high butterfat content was not as health-giving as tradition made out. In 1956 the premium for this type of milk was withdrawn by the government and the heart went out of our breeding programme. The government now began to favour beef production and in line with this thinking and with Forest grazing in mind, two in-calf Welsh Black heifers were purchased in 1958; an ideal dual-purpose breed for rough conditions. Gradually demand for our farm-bottled milk declined, the holiday makers were happier to buy pasteurised which they were familiar with and ours was sent off by churn to the Milk Marketing Board. In 1963 Mother moved to her new house in Sandy Balls and the dairy was used for other purposes. The Camp store with cold room now sold pasteurised milk.

Later Planning Permission was given for a farm house in Sandy Balls, and in 1963 a Colt cedar house in kit form was purchased and erected by Martin and the estate workers for his family. Up to this time they had been living in Sandy Balls Gate Cottage at the estate entrance – a traditional New Forest cottage with large open fireplace and bread-oven, two up and two down with annexe attached: it was cramped accommodation for a family of eight!

Up to the mid 1950s our Jersey herd was gradually being increased by selective breeding. Milk Recording had been in operation since the first purchase of two pedigree heifers, Rosebud and Pleasure in 1950, and a small herd was soon being milked. On such a small acreage, 16 acres, quality of breeding stock was recognised as the goal. Rosebud unfortunately died of bloat, although everything was done to save her; Pleasure exceeded all expectations by receiving a Certificate of Merit in 1954 from the Breed Society and her heifer calves promised well.

From the beginning Mother had taken the greatest interest in the farm and particularly in the Jersey herd, studying the records and becoming very knowledgeable about breeding lines. She took over the dairy work while it remained in Sandy Balls and had great pleasure in serving the customers. Even in those days hygiene regulations were very stringent and no one was more careful than Mother. However, one morning when the milk cooling system broke down and some water accidentally leaked into the churn, by 'Sod's law' an Inspector called. It was a very traumatic experience for her!

The Colt Cedar House – Sandy Balls Farm House.

Our new neighbour, Arthur Dalgety, had ranching interests in Australia and was applying this policy to the New Forest. By buying up strategically placed holdings, he could take advantage of their Common Rights to graze a large number of animals on the open forest all year round. With right of PASTURE, or for pigs, right of PANNAGE, any number of animals could be grazed. Branding was obligatory and a payment of 10/- a head required. Harris, with similar interests in Australia, had the same idea.

Arniss farm was Dalgety's third purchase and by retaining three fields belonging to Street Farm he not only had Forest access but also access onto the main Southampton road (B3078) as well. It was an ingenious scheme. The first criterion was a thrifty, hardy breed. Arthur Dalgety chose Galloways, while his brother, Christopher, chose Welsh Blacks and Saddleback pigs. For successful management and to get the best out of the extensive acreage, an understanding of the Forest was needed and close attention to animal husbandry. This was very soon found to be lacking.

Various ailments were bound to appear under such rough grazing conditions and a close watch needed to be kept on the herd. New Forest Eye could cause blindness in a week if left untreated. Red Water, which is a tick-borne disease, is equally serious, adder bites could be fatal and by 1970 there was public outcry against him for neglect and a large proportion of his herd were lost to worm and fluke. Liver fluke, often endemic in the water meadows of the Avon Valley, appeared in the Forest and untreated animals died of emaciation and starvation. In fact fluke became a serious threat to Forest grazing.

At Street Farm, hand milking gave way to machine, and as the herd increased to 20 milking cows and followers, a part-time worker was employed. Jeff Noble was a countryman of the old school, loyal and dedicated to the master 'Mr Martin'; while his wife, who helped me in the garden, was more formal still and called me Mrs Cormack, over our fifteen year association.

During this time, 1960 onwards, we too were putting our expanding herd out on the Forest, driving them up the main road in the morning and back in the afternoon for milking. We had no access other than the Forest gate and the inhabitants of Godshill, no longer country-born villagers, complained bitterly about the herd congregating there in a 'menacing fashion' and fouling the footpath.

However, in 1970, Dalgety decided to sell up, and the adjacent landowners, Mr Bob Fosh of Godshill Green and ourselves, Sandy Balls Estate Ltd, were approached with a view to purchase. Mr Fosh, who had already bought the three fields with road access from Dalgety, was not interested: so we became the new owners of Arniss Farm with Forest access and our cattle nuisance immediately ceased.

£16,000 was now asked for the 40 acre farm, the same as both farms had been sold for 10 years earlier. However, it was valued by the local Estate Agents for £10,000 and the bank was only prepared to loan £8,000 of this, which had to be repaid within three years.

It was understood that the Bank Manager had given an unsecured loan of £30,000 to another person in Godshill, so it seemed strange that they were only prepared to offer Sandy Balls half the amount required. At this point the family were asked to contribute as much as they could, interest-free, and the loan was paid back within six months! The Bank Manager said to my Father that it need not have been paid back so quickly and Father replied 'You did not want to lend, and I do not want to borrow' – and that was that.

The first major work on the new farm was the draining of the low-lying land by the brook – the fields from earliest times filled with rushes and liable to flood. Then the farm buildings were taken in hand, the lovely old barn utilised for the cattle in winter and, when my youngest brother, Richard, a civil engineer, requested a stable base for his growing family, Father offered him the farmhouse. When modernised it became a spacious dwelling suitable for a large family, for Richard had three step-children and three tiny children of his own. The present house was built in 1881; the large open fireplace and bread oven were retained, although for safety the well was filled in. The Manor of Arneys (Arniss) is recorded in the 'Perambulations of the New Forest' of 1218, 1670, 1682, 1801, and 1939 - so 'Arniss' is of very old foundation and enjoys many Forest rights.

Arniss Farm and Welsh Black Cows 1975.

Chapter 26

The Farm - Difficulties and Disappointments

Martin experienced all the Forest problems - also continuing deaths on the roads, where animals in fact had right of way. This was partially addressed in later years by traffic-calming measures and a 40 mile per hour speed limit. A cow was lost from an adder bite, several were treated by the Vet for Forest Eye (fortunately in good time), worming was a routine matter and the cattle inspected every day if possible. While we had a milking herd this was no problem but after the death of Mr Noble, when it was decided to go out of milk and gradually build up a suckler beef herd, supervision was more difficult. However, after a while the herd established its own territory and herd instinct. With access on to the Forest from Arniss they were fed with hay and silage during the winter months, put out from the trailer on the farm fields in the day time and the animals let out on the Forest at night. All Summer they grazed on the Forest day and night.

One of the longest established and best managed herds on the Forest was owned by Col. Le Marchant of Fritham with a herd of Sussex cattle. The regime was:- the cows calved in June or July and were brought back off the Forest to get back into calf in October – so there was no acorn poisoning problem. During August and September the calves were calf-minded by nanny cows who changed from day to day, enabling different mothers to forage away from their young calves – this was something that developed from the herd instinct. They were weaned at eight months old and thereafter kept on the farm until served by the bull and they were in-calf heifers. Then the cycle began again. With the death of the owner in 1987 the farm was sold up and the cattle dispersed. This was the herd on which Martin based his management.

The following incident in the late 1960s is a good example of the care and attention given to their animals by Martin and Valerie and indeed the whole family. Valerie had been ill and I, to help, offered to give the children supper every day while she was recovering. On this particular day my garden peas were ready, so I picked, shucked and cooked sufficient for the nine of us, eight children and myself; with thin bread and butter and grated cheese on top we were waiting for the kettle to boil (to begin) - then into the dining-room came Martin and Valerie: 'Up and Out', they said and with one accord the children got up, trooped out and we, my two young sons and myself, were left to eat supper alone! Obviously animals came first and everyone was needed to go hunting cows.

The idea now was to breed high-quality, hardy, Welsh Black cattle for sale and resell them in their native country.

At this time the Forest was T.B. - but not Brucellosis - free and while we were waiting for the 'all clear', so that animals could be sold outside the area, the herd built up so that even with the Forest grazing, the farm was heavily overstocked. In the Spring of 1976 the Forest was declared Brucellosis-free and at last selected animals could be sold, but then came the disastrous drought; from Easter until August Bank Holiday no rain fell. The farm fields dried up and the suckler herd, out on the open Forest, disappeared for six weeks, moving on in search of food and water. Sitings were reported but not substantiated, although the whole family, Martin and Valerie and their six children, went out searching. It was a worrying time. At last they were found in poor condition and in the following year there were deaths from heart disease. Post mortems showed an abnormal crystallisation of the heart which the Vet thought might have been caused, not only by the previous year's inadequate diet, but to eating prematurely shrivelled-up bracken which was palatable to them but poisonous.

At the first opportunity two lorry loads of Welsh Blacks – all pedigree – set off for Abergavenny in Wales, Martin and Valerie accompanying them. Unfortunately at auction they failed to reach the reserve price and both loads returned. This was a bitter disappointment and a nail in the coffin of the organic farm.

Another blow was to follow: Megan, purchased in 1958, one of the original Welsh Blacks, a cow with great character and a good milker, produced a heifer calf which Martin and Valerie could see was the best animal they had ever bred. Perfect to type she showed the greatest promise as an in-calf heifer. When the herd was tested for Brucellosis, she was the only one to react to the S19 vaccine so was immediately isolated. She reacted to a second and then to a third test and in a Brucellosis-free area reactors were not tolerated. Reaction can sometimes occur from vaccination alone, no disease being present and even the Ministry Vet thought that this might well be the case, but there could be no reprieve: the law was the law and this lovely animal was slaughtered. The heart went out of the farm.

From this time on the viability of the farm was questioned and the Company decided that <u>if</u> planning for change of usage could be obtained a Riding Stable would be the answer. It was hoped that this would also benefit the Holiday Centre. The Planning Officer advised that it would be wise to apply immediately; another farmer in Godshill with the same idea had put in an application. Both permissions were given but the other was never implemented.

Arniss Farm was chosen for the venue and in 1977 the Riding Stables were opened and a manager installed.

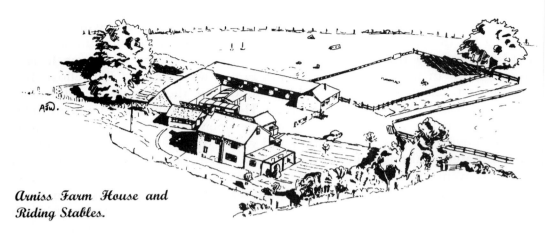

Arniss Farm House and Riding Stables.

Riding on the New Forest.

Saddling up the horses.

The cattle were gradually sold off and by 1983 only four calves were born. In 1984 a fire at Street Farm gutted the modern hay barn – full of the season's hay – and when compensation was paid, a replacement barn was erected at Arniss. By 1986, from a total of 200 cows and followers ten years earlier, none were left except a brindled cross-bred bought in as a house cow.

Two members of the family, my sister Carol and Richard's wife Patricia, were interested in spinning and a selection of rare breed sheep were bought – Shetland, Manx and Jacob. Most of the fields were sheep-wired but interest for sheep waned and they were discontinued. Obviously the organo-phosphorous sheep dips had to be used and Martin developed a serious illness which Valerie put down to their use and he was off work for more than a year. Neither of his sons wished to farm and it was a sad and difficult time for him, but once a farmer always a farmer and in 1989, now well again, both he and Valerie, liking the breed, bought a Welsh Black cow, Miracle and her calf Quest to graze on their own watermeadow land at Holwell Marsh (five acres) and in the one acre field by their home – Sandy Balls Farm House at the entrance to the Estate. Here a small unit with barn and other buildings developed, but obviously hay and fodder had to be bought in on such a small acreage.

Most of the field work at Street and Arniss Farms was now done by a contractor, Clifford Diben – manuring, ploughing, seeding, spraying, hedge-cutting, making hay and silage for the Riding Stables, and all this work had to fit in with the local summer show. The Fordingbridge Show, established in 1921 (originally a Horse show), was finding it difficult to find a satisfactory site in the area, so Sandy Balls offered the Show Committee the use of a few Street Farm fields alongside the B3078 at Godshill Cross. They were used for the first time in 1977 and with a break in 1988, when Sandy Balls grew ten acres of wheat for thatching, continued there on an expanding scale until 20 years later, in 1997, the Show ground covered over 50 acres, mainly over Street Farm, extending into Arniss and neighbouring fields.

In fact, the Show, held each year on the third Saturday in July, dominated any farming practice, for all these fields had to be free of crops for a fortnight for preparation and dismantling, and the hedges neatly cut long before the berries and seed enjoyed by wildlife were ripe. Afterwards, due to compaction, dandelions and docks appeared, their tap roots doing their best to restore the soil structure, but spraying, especially for the docks, was often found to be necessary. The heritage of the organic farm and family involvement in Sandy Balls seemed to be a thing of the past.

Chapter 27
The Family Community

The photo above shows the Westlake Family in Sandy Balls in 1966, Mother and Father with three of their five children, myself Jean, Martin and Carol with our families; Keith the eldest, a Doctor, had died in 1958, Richard the youngest, (11 years my junior) was unmarried and working away from home. My sister, Carol and her husband, Peter joined us in 1961. He was in charge of Estate maintenance

Sandy Balls Gate Cottage - enlarged and modernised.

and the woodland, and became very skilled and knowledgeable. Carol, as her children became older, took over the management of the Camp Store, moving into Sandy Balls Gate Cottage vacated by Martin's family in 1965 – the cottage being extended and modernised for them. Martin was the farmer, I was the gardener. The family was synonymous with Sandy Balls and everyone worked for the greater good of the whole. Helpers were taken on as they were needed.

Food, warmth and shelter were provided; a small wage to each family, depending on the number of children, and a weekly grocery allowance from the shop. My two young sons and myself were the smallest unit – I lived in a little wooden bungalow, 'Rosemarie' – we received £8.00 per week, £2.00 worth of groceries, milk, eggs, meat and potatoes from the farm, wood from the woodland and fruit and vegetables from my garden. We had everything we needed and a purpose and vision to our lives, inspired by Grandfather, Ernest Westlake, and Father's far-seeing ideas and philosophy. The organic farm and garden were an integral part of the whole.

Although we did not realise it at the time, the formation of the Company, Sandy Balls Estate Ltd. (primarily for tax purposes), was to change the feeling of good-will and community, created by the hard work and dedication of the early years, in a subtle way. Gradually, the loving relationships between the families became less tangible and in 1975, with mother's death, without her warmth of personality and unifying influence, began to break down.

Emphasis was now focused on the modernisation and development of the Holiday Centre under Richard's expertise and drive as Managing Director, receiving many awards for excellence over the years – and the final accolade 'Best in England' award from the English Tourist Board.

The older Grandchildren, keen to help, were told that if, when they left school, they qualified and gained experience, there could be an opportunity for them in Sandy Balls. Later this policy was overlooked and they began to feel discouraged. Few were welcomed in, although there could have been a number of openings.

After father's death in 1985 at 92 years old, a dividend was paid for the first time on shares held in the Company – all owned by family members. This was felt by the Directors and their advisors to be recompense enough for being part-owners of the Estate, other benefits having long since been discontinued.

A way of life here in Sandy Balls had disappeared perhaps never to return.

Chapter 28

Greenwood, Wardenship and the Order of Woodcraft Chivalry

In the early 1960's, the OWC decided to look for a permanent camping headquarters and this was the subject of much discussion and search. So, when the recently formed company (Sandy Balls Estate Ltd), at Father's suggestion, offered them a 10 year lease of the Riverside Greenwood Camp - originally Grith Fyrd (later, simply known as Greenwood), it was carefully considered by the Council of Leaders and at the Folkmoot of 1963, the decision was taken to accept. Many members felt that not only would they be returning to their original home but they would be able to facilitate the educational work of other bodies as well.

The accommodation was very basic. It consisted of three bunk houses, a common room, a dining-room, a kitchen, an elsan block and other storage sheds.

The bunk houses had two tiers of wide wooden bunks within. These had been constructed in the early days of Grith Fyrd from freshly-cut tree trunks and over the years the wood had become iron-hard. However, the floor boards were rotting and the first, job, after the lease was signed, was for a retired member to spend several months there and with the help of others at weekends to jack up the timber framework and replace the floor timber with concrete.

As can be seen from the photographs, the windows were originally glazed – later shutters replaced the glass. Much other repair work was needed and it was not until 1965 that it was ready for the first School Journey party, and the Order felt that they had begun to fulfil their double purpose of providing a permanent home for themselves and helping the educational work of others.

The large common room had a spacious open fireplace, Calor gas lighting and the windows had plastic screens for daytime use. Over the years a collection of sofas and easy chairs appeared and with a roaring woodfire, it was a warm and friendly place to relax in.

The dining-room was left open and unshuttered. The attractive windows had come from a house being demolished in Bermondsey. They had so taken Father's fancy that he paid a nominal sum for them and they were brought down to Sandy Balls by my Uncle, Ken Harrod, the carrier, and later used at Greenwood. At the far end of the dining-room was a hatch which opened into a spacious kitchen with Calor gas lighting and cooking facilities, a deep sink with a cold water tap, space for

The Dining Room.

The Common Room.

Ernest Harrod - Steward of Sandy Balls.

The Bunk House.

dixies, saucepans, crockery and cutlery and a spacious workside. It was all very primitive but had great appeal to a wide range of groups over the following years. Close by was an outdoor fireplace which could be used for open-air cooking and a plentiful supply of hot water for washing-up. Fallen wood was abundant in the surrounding woodland and the children delighted in collecting it for the kitchen and common room fires. Water came down by pipe from the Holiday Centre above, and care was needed to turn off stopcocks during the winter period.

The site was 6 acres in extent; this included the Federation Camp Site, named after the Southampton Federation of Boys' Clubs. They kept their equipment in a large store hut and camped in marquees during the summer, under the able and friendly leadership of Mr Boucher: as a child I remember him well. Many of those young men so happily enjoying themselves in the late 1930's were called up when war was declared – some never to return.

The hutted site was occupied at this time by an American sect called the Mazdaznans, who, on hearting that Britain was at war with Germany, quickly packed up and left for America on the first available sailing – their visit still had some time to go! For the duration, the site was let to the Southampton Federation of Girls' and Mixed Clubs. The Boys' Club, now wishing to return, found it was disallowed as being too close to a camp of girls! So it was, that the Federation Site was left vacant until included in the Greenwood lease of 1963.

Now, as I was a member of the OWC, *and* living in Sandy Balls, what could be more natural than for them to ask me to hold the keys and show groups in when they arrived. This I was pleased to do. Later I was officially recognised as Warden of Greenwood, and part of the Greenwood Committee which included the letting Secretary, the Steward who was responsible for the upkeep of the site, and my brother Martin representing the Estate.

I took my job seriously, not only showing new groups in, but visiting them at other times and making sure everything was left well at the end of their stay. The burnable rubbish was dealt with at the Camp, but later, as plastic increased, it was brought up to the Estate rubbish bins. At the beginning of a stay, I asked for food refuse to be kept separately and brought up to me for my bantams. It worked very well.

Many groups returned year after year. They included Youth Clubs, School Groups, Cubs, Scouts, Boys' Brigade, Brownies and Guides - Groups from Hospitals, including the blind and partially sighted, the mentally handicapped and deaf, Folk Dance group, and Operatic Society and a Scottish Pipe Band, whose haunting music echoed up the valley and delighted the Holiday makers above and all benefited immeasurably from their stay.

One incident I remember vividly. It was a Friday evening in May, the trees were green and lush in their spring loveliness; a heavy mist had obviously made driving difficult and it was dusk before the school party I was expecting arrived in two mini-buses. Accompanying them to Greenwood, I was surrounded by chattering 7 year-olds but not one word could I understand, for these were Asian children talking in their native tongue. At the 'Top of the Hill' we began to descend into the mist-filled valley. As we carefully wound our way into the green depths a silence stole over the excited children. A silence so profound that it remained unbroken until we arrived at camp and the head-lights piercing the mist picked out the buildings ahead. The mini-bus stopped and the spell was broken. It was a moving experience for me as it obviously was for them. Later I asked the Headmistress if she had any white children with her – "One or two," she said.

An article appeared in the Inner London Education Authority magazine, 'Contact' of 7 June 1974 under the title 'Babes in the Wood'. It may well have included this group I describe above.

I quote -

"This weekend,a party of Camberwell seven-year-olds will set off for a few days in the wilds of the New Forest. The children, from Brunswick Park Infants School, will for four days sample a life in the country which for many of them is a totally new experience. Accompanied by a party of adults – teachers, school helpers, friends and students – a total of 80 children will spend four days each in a camp consisting of four wood cabins.

The children – all of them about to go up into th junior school – will go in parties of 30 at a time. Once they arrive, each group of three children will be looked after by an adult. Many teachers would be daunted by the prospect of taking such young children away from home, but Headmistress, Miss Wendla Kernig, dismissed the problems. She said: "Naturally a good deal of organisation goes into it, but the children themselves give us no problems. We operate team teaching here so the teachers and helpers know the children they are with very well."

"Four days and three nights away is about right for children of this age. We took about 30 last year and not one of them was homesick. There is so much for them to do, they don't have time to miss home. However, we always have a car here, so if a child wants to come home, he can do so straight away." The benefits for the children she believes are incalculable. "Some of these children have never been in the country before in their lives. They find so much out for themselves, becoming aware of different plants and animals and so on," she said.

In small groups the children climb trees, explore, build dams and bridges and play games and collect wood for the evening bonfire. "But it is the change of environment which means so much to them; they can run and run and sometimes we will find one of them just standing in the middle of a field taking it all in."

Parents are enthusiastic about the scheme too. "Very few of them don't want their children to go, and most are very keen," says Miss Kernig. "Really, we have found it so easy to organise and so rewarding for the children that we think other infant schools could try something like it".

The Woodcraft themselves used Greenwood at least five times a year, and, when not let to an outside group, both sites were available for members' use. A list of lettings was included in 'Pine Cone'. The year began with the Easter Work Camp, supervised by the Greenwood Steward. This was a mixture of work and social fellowship and always well attended. The Spring Bank Holiday followed with both sites being used, for, now that the emphasis in the Order was on family groups or kindreds rather than leader-led children's groups, as in the early days, families preferred to camp together on the Federation Site, although they usually joined in the communal catering and other activities based at Greenwood.

The August Bank Holiday was traditionally the high point of the Woodcraft year – embracing the AGM or Folkmoot. This began with an opening ceremony in the Folkmoot Circle, a natural ampitheâtre chosen by Grandfather – a special place halfway down the hillside between the top plateau and the river, surrounded by majestic pines; bounded by 'Giant's Grave', one of the woodland's distinctive rounded hills.

Here, over Folkmoot the Opening and Closing ceremonies took place, presided over by the Chieftain and the Keeper of the Fire, with other Chiefs in attendance all clad in ceremonial cloaks. During the weekend business sessions took place followed by a grand feast, and camp fires, both Merry Moot and Inspirational led by the Gleeman – while on Ernest Westlake's Memorial on Woodling Point the Sunrise Service remembered the Founder and others who had passed on to the Great Adventure; ending with the 'joyful eating of apples', Grandfather's favourite fruit. Father and I always attended the Sunrise Service when Folkmoot was held in Sandy Balls.

Hallow-e'en became established as a fun weekend for all the family. Pumpkins and marrows were carved, candles inserted and when darkness fell a long procession of lanterns issued forth from the common room and wound up the hill and round the caravans and chalets, to the surprise of the holiday visitors and the delight of younger members who pretended to be hobgoblins and witches and other foul fiends. Father and Mother and later Father on his own in Sandy Balls House looked forward to this yearly visitation.

Many of the young, adventurous members also chose the New Year period for a winter camp. The common room fire was snug to sleep by on a cold winter's night!

On our frequent visits to supervise Greenwood, my sons and I often took in the broad expanse of Sandy Balls. This lovely woodland that we came to know and love so well was closely observed. We noted its flora and fauna and I became so enthusiastic about its beauty and wildlife that I offered to write a series of Nature Notes for 'Pine Cone', illustrated with simple line drawings. Later these were published in booklet form entitled 'Sandy Balls for all Seasons'.

They were good years, natural and unspoilt, a time of innocence of which we were part, a time of nostalgia in which we participated. Neither Radio nor Television stole our time and over the years my sons and I made many friends!

Chapter 29

Those Halcyon Days of Childhood

The next years were good ones for the Order, membership increased and they now had a permanent home. Over the next 10-year period our association with them was not only in Greenwood but at the annual Family Camp as well. The camps were held for a fortnight in August and generally embraced the Folkmoot festivities on the last weekend.

I declined an invitation to join one in 1967, for my younger son, Ashley, was not yet 3 years old, I had not camped since I was a child, I could not drive and had no tent.

However, I spend the next year in preparation; I bought a pneumatic 'Igloo' tent with built-in groundsheet and zip-up opening. A little tent was borrowed for Eden, who would be 6 years old, simple enough for him to erect, and later both boys saved up to buy their own. I made 3 sleeping bags out of eiderduck down from old quilts bought at jumble sales, complete with feather-proof casings and washable covers. The question of transport was also resolved for, as we were to include other family members, Peter, my sister's husband, was pleased to take us to camp and collect us at the end.

The 1967 camp had been held in the grounds of Bearwood College, near Wokingham in Berkshire. The camp was such a success that the site was re-booked and extracts from 'Country Life Magazine' about the house and grounds were printed in 'Pine Cone' to attract other participants and made interesting reading.

Bishops Berewood had once been part of the Hunting Forest of the Bishops of Salisbury; in 1574 it was taken by the crown until the early nineteenth century when it was sold to John Walters II, Chief Proprietor of the Times. A country house was built but later demolished by his son, John Walters III, and the great palace-like structure of today was begun in 1863. In 1870, the 20-year-old heir apparent to the Times, also John, was drowned in a skating accident on the frozen lake at Bearwood; his Father never really recovered from the loss of his son and heir and even before the house was finished (1874) the Times had started to go into decline. In 1917 a considerable portion of the Estate was sold and by 1919 two leading Ship owners bought the house and 500 acres of land and presented them as a new home for the Merchant Seaman's Orphanage. Now a public school, it includes Merchant Navy children and has taken the name Bearwood College.

This, then, was the site of the family camp. Our first glimpse was impressive as we approached down a wide avenue of Wellingtonias - the Giant Redwood trees of North America. There were woods and meadows, two large lakes with five islands, diving boards, swimming, boating and fishing, even the school learners' pool filled a-fresh for our use. The woodland was full of unusual trees, plants and wild life abounded: it was a wonderful place to camp and we had it all to ourselves.

Ashley was perhaps a little young for his first camp, he found the earth latrines, deeply dug trenches, intimidating, as well he might, and being so adventurous and used to the freedom of Sandy Balls, I needed to keep a careful eye on him when he wandered near the lake.

However, our little group was welcomed by all, and indeed we received approbation from the Chieftain in the following issue of 'Pine Cone'...

> "Another source of encouragement was that this year we once more had members of the Golden Eagle kindred camping with us. We were delighted to welcome Jean Cormack, together with her two small sons, Eden and Ashley, and niece Fern: joined later by three nephews, Leigh, Clive and Vincent. With all six children and any troubles that camp life threw up, Jeannie coped, to our growing admiration, with utmost cheerfulness and poise, like a true grandchild of the Founder." High praise indeed.

My abiding memory of this camp was of the Sunrise Service by the lakeside, recorded for others to share in 'Pine Cone'.

Sunrise Service

The sky was already lightening and the dew wet and cold as we silently left our sleeping companions and made our way to the landing stage. The change from soft squelchy mud to grass and then to gritty gravel made our tread sound curiously loud.

As we stood facing the lake we were conscious of many things. The slight rippling of the expanse of water stretching away before us; the coo-ing of pigeons contrasting in strange harmony with the more strident voices of the crow, jay and more melodious songsters; coots, just distinguishable by their white beaks, splashed from the shadow of rush and waterweed and a single tiny spot of white moved swan-like across the furthest side of the lake.

We looked towards the rim of distant trees and the narrow band of cloud above gradually became suffused with a rosy glow, the reflections in the water echoed with rippling variation the sunrise we had come to see. Any moment we expected the sun to push back her covers and startle us by her brilliancy.

Bearwood College (photo taken by Ashley)

Woodcraft Camps

Woodcraft Fancy Dress using natural materials.

Bearwood – the tracker Hike.

Bearwood – the lake and Memorial Island from the landing stage.

Charmouth – space invaders.

*Devil's Bridge – Ashley outside the Igloo
tent with two little friends.*

Arran – rock, sand, sea and sky.

Butterfly hunting on the cliffs.

Then four ducks with long straight necks, tiny black shapes, glided from the Memorial island. Suddenly a loud honking disturbed our contemplative absorption and a strange discordant "Arise Song" shattered the tranquillity of the sunrise before us. Very soon we saw the longer shapes of geese entering the water by the larger island - woken by the ducks; the sunrise; who can say! Majestically in formation they glided across the lake, thirteen in all, the four largest bringing up the rear. Then with a flapping of wings and water they turned, rose into the air, turned again below the sun-awakened trees and curved back and away.

A soft greyness was now all around us, the water sombre and uninviting. The Sunrise was over. Ragged storm clouds were beginning to gather and a dozen or more sand martins wheeled and wheeled again, high on the wing, catching innumerable unseen insects in their beaks.

Our thoughts were drawn back to the Father of the Order, to the Adventure of Life and to those who had already passed on to the Greater Life. As we munched our apples we found that our fingers and faces were chill and cold. A breeze began to take form, whispering through the trees and sighing along the willow leaves to the dark water below.

A couple of us stayed behind for a morning dip. We found the water warm to our bodies as we dived, swam, reached the log and then returned. An exhilarating warmth and chilliness accompanied us back to camp where we were met by the sound of clan activity, the all-embracing smell of wood smoke and a welcome cup of tea.

We returned four times to Bearwood 1968, '69, '72 and '74, each camp unique, each different but all traditionally 'Woodcraft'. The children were divided into age-groups, as at Forest School, Elves 5 - 8 year olds, Woodlings 8 - 12, Trackers 12 - 15, Pathfinders 15 - 18, each group with their own activities and volunteer leaders. Catering was communal, in clans over open wood fires and I can well remember the day I helped prepare supper of liver and bacon and fried onions with vegetables and a sweet to follow in pouring rain – the heavy drops splashing into the hot fat and dripping off our waterproofs; but the 'full monty' was delivered to the hungry campers waiting in the shelter tent to much applause. This was a 'one wet week', 'one hot sunny week' camp and when the change miraculously occurred my nieces put everything out to dry and even the sleeping bags steamed in the hot sunshine.

This was not an easy camp; I had taken 8 children with me – so keen were they to come, that the adult/child ratio was unbalanced. Later a ruling was brought in, 'Only four children per adult'; a sensible precaution.

Other Order camps took us further afield: once to Devil's Bridge in Welsh-speaking North Wales, where we had the exciting experience of going by train with rucksacks on our backs. Luckily my 'Igloo' tent, too heavy for me to carry, had gone in advance with the camp equipment stored at Greenwood. After several changes the afternoon saw us chug-chugging up the Welsh Valleys and arriving late; the children by now tired and fractious were shown where to pitch their tents … then out of the half light came smiling faces, helping hands and a welcome cup of tea. It was not long before Ashley, 3 years old, was sound asleep in my tent and the others soon afterwards in theirs. The camp had started well.

Wood was very short for fires, so much time was spent daily combing the steep hillsides and hauling it to the top. Ashley, too, was keen to join in this dangerous activity. The scenery was breathtaking and a pair of rare red kites soared effortlessly over the campsite day by day.

Often we stayed on after the official camp broke up and enjoyed cooking for ourselves and exploring the immediate environment. Fossils abounded at Charmouth and the cliff tops in the warm sunshine were alive with an abundance of wild flowers and butterflies.

In Pembrokeshire we camped in a little green valley called Brandy Brook, where the stunted hawthorns had become ivy trees, the Royal Fern flourished majestically in the bogland and glow-worms (once so abundant in Sandy Balls) lit our way along the narrow green lanes at night.

At Bucks Mill, on Barnstable Bay in Devon, the shingle beach was at the bottom of a long steep descent and the sea unsuitable for swimming, so there were many excursions to spacious sandy beaches. Here we made sand castles and played beach games and, back at camp, I made the mistake of playing volleyball, (for the first time in my life) and tore a ligament in my knee. Camp life was a little difficult for me then.

OWC
SUMMER CAMP ON ARRAN
6th August to 20th August 1977

LENAMHOR FARM KILMORY

177

A patient of Father, Francis Sutton, a Quaker artist living at Bucks Mill, invited me in to see his chapel conversion – the result, a charming studio and home. Later, this 'grateful patient', wishing to thank Father for 'saving his life' with the new Psionic Medicine, came to Sandy Balls to make preliminary studies for a portrait of Father, capturing his likeness and 'far- seeing' look to an extraordinary degree. I have both pictures in my home today.

Our last camp together was to the Isle of Arran in Scotland. Needing a light-weight tent I decided to make one from a First World War parachute segment belonging to Ernest Westlake – using a pattern from an old 'Pine Cone'. When finished, the wigwam type tent was a little high but the super fine material was still perfect after more than 50 years and I hoped for the best.

The following extracts from a letter written to Father, now on his own in Sandy Balls House, (Mother died at the end of 1975) gives a good idea of the Arran camp.

Arran
Saturday 13 Aug. '77

Dear Dad and all at home

---- The journey from Glasgow to Ardrossan took an hour and the ferry was there, and the journey across took another hour. It was pretty rough and cold with seagulls wheeling and turning above us. The bus was there to meet the ferry and another 40mins on the South Arran bus to the Kennanhor Farm turning. We were all pretty tired and took the further half mile walk down to the campsite with only half our luggage, walking back to the farm to get it later.

The wind was very strong, and first of all we thought it would be impossible to get the tents up especially mine, but we managed in the end. ----

It certainly is a lovely site – on the machae or upper beach, and most of the tents are against the sea wall as this offers a little protection from the wind. The kitchen is in a curve in the cliffs, which jut out in layered orange - yellow rock all along the coast into the sea and are much beloved by geological students who coming drilling cores for their Theses and PhDs The beach is very sandy with many big orange lichen covered boulders and beautiful rock pools exposed at high tide filled with innumerable seacreatures. The beach slopes very gently, but is noticeably zoned, (We had a talk and survey of the beach one morning) the greener seaweeds at the top, the red and brown ones farther down and the different varieties of periwinkles, welks, barnacles, limpets, brittle stars, sponges, sea urchins etc. etc. each in their own place.

The Irish or carragheen moss can be found also the variety made into laver bread (much beloved by the Welsh). We learnt that limpets are browsers and after feeding, always move back to their own exact spot on the rocks. On one walk we saw a field with many stacks of tripodded hay, tied and weighted down with ropes and bricks.

Lennamhor Farm has one or two holiday cottages and the farmer's wife lets her own house at this time of year, moving into the scullery, (presume there must be sleeping quarters as well for her two sons 23 and 13 and herself), her husband died in an accident some years ago. This is primarily a dairy farm, milking 36 Ayrshires and running several 100 sheep, but obviously making a good income from holiday letting during the summer.

The peaty, soft water comes down to us by a long polythene pipe brought many years ago by Forest School Camps Ltd and left here for future camps – all £100 worth, so we are indeed fortunate as the farm is a long pull up of about ½ mile. We had £16 worth of wood delivered and the son who now manages the farm, under his mother's close supervision, brought it down in two trailer loads. It is dry and burns well. The latrines are earth, not elsans, for the ground is sandy, rock free in places so easy to dig and very satisfactory. We are constantly reminded about hygiene as the camp above has a tummy bug and we do not want to get it.

There is plenty of   tap water and with the hot sun every day – so far, the overground hose gives on-tap <u>hot</u> water for a long period; not so good if you want cold, but lovely for washing and washing up.

There are 5 clans, which means that most days you have one meal to prepare, followed by a free day. However it is quite a responsible job if you are clan leader, and if you are on for the evening meal, you may start at 2 o'clock and not be finished until 7.30 or even later. The milk comes down from the farm and the last job is to empty out the milk that is left, ready to collect the evening milking. We have 36 pints a day and the large plastic containers have to be properly cleaned before going to collect it.

The food is very good, an infinite variety, plenty of salad usually for lunch and a cooked supper and breakfast, finishing the day with cocoa and biscuits.

We have had many activities – The Beach Survey; walk to the Black Cove, Camp Cooking in little groups. We were provided with enormous lamb chops, new potatoes, onions, spaghetti and mushrooms, followed by scones and orange and a cup of tea. The four boys and I were very efficient, sitting down to a beautifully cooked, tender and tasty dinner (the Scotch meat is really superb) at 1.20pm — by far the first. We went to Lamlash Agricultural Fair (the nearest town of any size about 10 miles away). It was just the day for a Show, hot and sunny, the show ground beautifully situated between the mountains and the sea. There were classes for cattle, horses, riding, jumping and gymkhana events. The W.I (Scottish equivalent) tent had some good cooking and a high standard in craft, embroidery and art. We came back with the Pringles and had a picnic by Arran Forest (Forestry Commission Land) and saw one of the waterfalls of note in the district.

Most evenings there have been camp fires, a beach one with the Woodcraft Folk camping above, Merry Moot to-night when all are asked to contribute an item. The Sunrise service is 5.30 tomorrow - Sunday morning, and the Inspirational camp fire in the evening. Yesterday we had a coach trip all round the island. We saw high mountains in the North, walked up one of the lovely glens, ending up at Lamlash for a 6-o'clock Fish and Chip supper - large helpings'. There are miles of beach with nothing to see but rock, sand sea and sky, a few sheep and the mountains rising above. Brodick is the largest town where the ferry comes in. There are about 4000 residents on Arran, swelled in the summer by tourists, but still relatively unspoilt.

<u>Sunday morning</u>. George Alexander led a very thoughtful Sunrise Service - but only wind, cloud and rain, no sun. The weather looks to have broken. The sun has shone unbrokenly throughout the week and was almost too hot on the coach trip. The changing sea and sky have been very lovely, at first we could see Ireland quite clearly, but recently Ailsa Craig was covered with a sea-mist and vanished from sight. Usually it dominates our view, a strange limpet-like island, rising sheer on both sides to a height of 1,110 ft.

The Brittania passed us on her way to Ireland, and there was much activity during the day - submarines, frigates patrolling and a mine sweeper preceding. I'm glad the visit passed off well; rather a headache for all concerned.

My tent appears to be fairly waterproof, although this paper is getting damp from a very fine spray and the groundsheet I am leaning on is also damp. I think it is waterproof enough so I won't have to bother the boys — although Ashley has said I could go in with him. We all have the waterproof trousers and jackets I bought at the wholesalers so we won't get too wet; although none of us were able to carry wellingtons. A little rain always makes for a better camp, and the parents who came by car have bought a variety of indoor games, so all should be well.

I have been trying to identify a few of the great variety of sea birds that one can see along the cliff and sea line. The oyster catchers and kittiwakes have a a call that is easily recognisable. The gannet plunges into the sea after its food. Through binoculars I saw a cormorant waiting patiently on a rock, many types of gull, herons fishing, a flock of enormous white - fronted geese swimming, a buzzard hovering and the little rock pippits busy among the rocks.

The wild flowers are very fine, enjoying the marshy conditions where the many little streams come tumbling down deep crevices in the form of waterfalls to the sea below. Betony for instance, which I know as a flower of the Forest grows luxuriantly on the lower cliff, so I could hardly recognise it as the same plant. Margery (my craft teacher at Forest School) has brought a Flora with her, and I have a bird book, others have brought sea-shore ones, so we are well provided with reference books. — This is indeed a lovely place.

Ashley's tent is a great success, the fly sheet that Margery made him has kept everything beautifully dry.

The camp is costing us £37-0.0 each, not bad for the distance away and the quality and duration of the camp.

We shall be arriving in London at 5.30 a.m. on Friday morning. August 19th and will catch the first tram home.

love to all — Jeannie

Ashley absorbed in a game of Chess at Camp

Chapter 30

Folkmoot Ceremonial

In the early 1970's I was nominated as MC and as such was responsible for Order Ceremonial. At this time, many of the newer members felt that the wording was archaic and indeed ceremonial unnecessary, so in preparation for the special Jubilee camp of 1976, (The OWC had been going for 60 years), I wrote a spirited defence for its continuance.

As M.C. I should like to say a few words about Ceremonial. The purpose of Ceremony is to make a group emotionally one; a true congregation and not a collection of individuals, enabling them to experience in an artistic and symbolic setting the great truths and ideals of life which unite them.

There may be some among you who think that the Order Ceremonial is unnecessary and rather old-fashioned at the present time. On the contrary, I feel that it is an essential part of the Movement and at this time, as at all times, anything that helps to crystallise within us a deeper understanding of the mysteries of life is of infinite value. Listen to the beauty of the words, and you will find that they are timeless words, and embody timeless concepts. Enjoy the colour, the music, the warmth, the feeling of belonging and you will begin to understand a little more of the original ideals and aims of the Order to which you belong.

No Woodcraft Camp is to me complete without the two ceremonies, the Arise and Goodnight Songs. They make each day a complete whole, giving it a beginning and an end. The central idea around which the Folkmoot Ceremony revolves is LIFE, that living vital force which is the spirit of existence, and this is represented by that most ancient of symbols, fire. So with the lighting of the Council Fire, Folkmoot is born, is brought into being, and each one of us, in so far as we are part of it, share in its rebirth and fresh out-pouring of life.

We are concerned with two things, with the source of the life which lights our Council fire, and the nature of that life. This Life is passed to us as "a love gift, from our brethren of the North, East, South and West", symbolised by a burning torch carried by a messenger who, in each case, describes the nature of the life he brings. These messengers also represent the four seasons. That from the North or Winter showing life in its resting state; from the East or Spring in its newborn state, from the South or Summer in its full, potent glorious aspect and from the West or Autumn in its mature or completed state. The four thus represent the complete circle of life in all its phases, and it is with this full, complete life - this love gift - that our fire is lit. Once lit, the Keeper of the Fire places on the Fire the remains of that of the previous year 'that our Fires be the same though always new'. Other representatives come forward and the Keeper of the Fire places the embers that they bring on the fire with the words: "from London Guild (or other group) to the Greater Life". During the interval, while the Fire is burning up, the whole assembly hold hands, that all might feel that they are part of the life cycle.

Now follows a phase of calm, of quiet prayer when we stop to think about this gift that has been given us, and pray that we may use it aright and use it fully. We pray that the flame of life may burn intensely, socially and spiritually and, lastly, that we may pursue the way of life to which we are now called as Adventurers. It will be noted that this part stresses one of the principal ideas of the Order, that of integration, the bringing together of all aspects and their practical working out in life.

The Closing ceremony follows the same general pattern – the central idea is still LIFE, symbolised by the Fire. With the Council drawing to its close, we hand on the life by returning the torches, relit, to the four messengers to take to their Brethren, enriched by our contributions. This emphasises the idea of fellowship and brotherhood with all mankind and the bond of common life, in which we

The Opening Ceremony of Folkmoot

live and move and have our being! Then, with the Fire burnt low and embers saved for next year's fire, we pray again for wholeness and fullness of life, with the whole vision in theory and practice, and with the Folkmoot blessing echoing in our ears, we go our several ways.

We can now see that the Order ceremonial, if rightly and sincerely presented, can inspire the group with a common and lasting vision and imprint on their hearts the main truths for which the Order stands in a form which can be enjoyed by all, regardless of age, experience, ability or intellect.

In conclusion, I should like to say this:- Anything that enriches our life, anything that brings us closer to each other and anything that gives us a deeper understanding of the purpose of life, is of the greatest importance and should be encouraged. This is what the Order ceremonial does for me, and has done over the years. It is a living, vital part of my childhood, and I wish it to be part of my children's memories too.

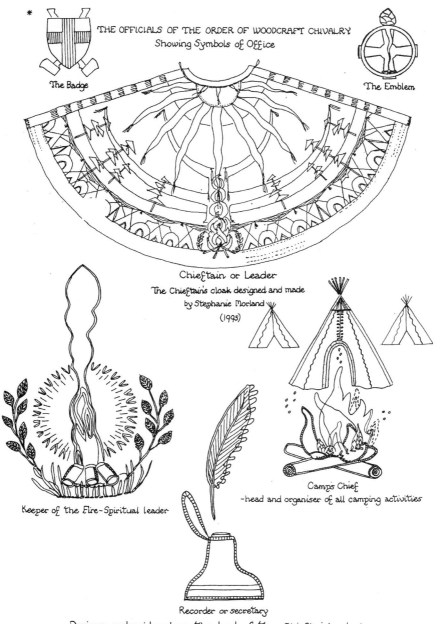

THE OFFICIALS OF THE ORDER OF WOODCRAFT CHIVALRY
Showing Symbols of Office

The Badge

The Emblem

Chieftain or Leader

The Chieftain's cloak designed and made
by Stephanie Morland
(1995)

Keeper of the Fire - Spiritual leader

Camps Chief
- head and organiser of all camping activities

Recorder or secretary

Designs embroidered on the back of the Chieftain's cloaks.

★ Appendix 3

Marshal—Deputy leader,
chief organiser and head of other officials

Keeper of the Purse or treasurer

Herald—propagandist
or advertiser of the movement

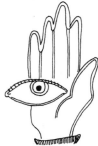

Craftsman—adviser and organiser
of all types of craftwork

Gleeman—leader and organiser
of song, dance and drama

Keeper of the Wardrobe
—responsible for dress
and ceremonial regalia

Keeper of the Honours Tally
—responsible for tests, trials and honours

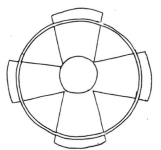

M.C.—Master or Mistress
of Ceremonies

Reader—to keep members in touch
with important literature

Editor—Editor of Pinecone
the Bi-monthly magazine of the Order

Chapter 31

A Time of Grief and Loss

Mother died suddenly but very peacefully on Wednesday, December 10th, 1975; both Father and I were with her. This was a profound and moving experience for me, for I had never been in close contact with death before. Looking back I can see a well-defined period of preparation for this important event, for which I was predestined to play a leading role.

Our Steiner Study classes were discontinued during the Autumn, so every Tuesday morning Father and I took the opportunity to sort through family papers. Thus it was that we were both there when Mother said how ill she felt, and again on the Wednesday when she died. The Doctor did not think her condition to be serious and recommended a week in bed. She had a perfect night and next morning I found her sitting up in bed looking relaxed, surrounded by her books, her papers and her embroidery, happily anticipating a week of rest … But this was not to be, for soon after 11 o'clock she had a major coronary and by 1.10 p.m. she was dead. Passing through the Gate of Death (according to Rudolf Steiner) is an awe-inspiring experience, similar to being born. It too needs loving support, and words of comfort and quiet encouragement, and this I think we were able to give her.

The human being is made of four bodies, separate yet forming a unity. The substantial Physical body we know so well, the Etheric or Life body, the Astral or Soul body and the Ego. While we sleep, the Soul and the Ego freely leave the body to journey into other realms, re-uniting again on waking. When we die, the Life-body leaves as well, the silver thread is broken and can no longer return. Death gradually releases the Etheric into the cosmic ether, taking three to four days. During this time the Etheric body, still being present, causes the past life of the dead person to be spread out before it as a vivid comprehensive panorama! Thus it is important during the period of lying in state for the physical body to be surrounded by loving thoughts and prayers, by family and friends, and grief too is natural and relevant at this time.

During the three days that followed Mother's death, the house was never left. Each evening the family gathered round the bedside for a short service of remembrance led by our friend Kitty Trevelyan. Mother looked so very peaceful lying there in state surrounded by flowers, the room lit by candle-light and sometimes filled with the poignant scent of incense, the blue smoke rolling and curling round the bed. During these days I supported Father and escorted close friends who came to say goodbye. I slept on the sofa in the room below and clearly remember the firelight flickering all night and the clocks striking the hours. I slept fitfully, for our loss was so sudden, our desolation and grief so great. We were existing in an unreal world, a kind of limbo that had no end.

The outside activity was also intense and this was my brother Martin's responsibility. The funeral had to be arranged; friends and relatives contacted; the Order of Service printed. Our Estate workers laboured like Trojans to clear the chosen site; the J.C.B. digger-man, as a special favour, came to dig the grave among the tree roots with his machine. Martin made several journeys to Lyndhurst and finally on the Friday afternoon (with the Funeral arranged for 2.30 p.m. on Saturday) the Public Health Officer visited and gave the "go ahead". There was a great feeling of relief: for where else could Mother be rightly laid to rest, but here in Sandy Balls!

Sitting quietly by Mother on the last evening, I could hear the wind roaring up the valley and sighing through the tree-tops. With the open window it was bitterly cold, but there was a great peace in the room. It was as though her presence was all around, supporting and sustaining me.

At 2 o'clock on Saturday, the Quakers, the family and close friends gathered at Father's house and waited. Time seemed to stand still, and grief hung heavily around us as the simple coffin was carefully manipulated down the stairs and placed on the Parish bier. Covered with a brilliance of flowers it preceded the funeral cortège. We followed slowly behind, past the Office, round the Ghost Oak and the waiting group of grandchildren to the large congregation gathered silently round the graveside. I remember looking up at the delicate network of branches silhouetted sharply against the clear, cold blue sky in the brilliant sunshine, and thinking how lovely Sandy Balls looked on this day of all days - the 13th of December.

The Service was very simple. One friend described it as "a delicate and moving event - your Mother would have approved" - another said it conveyed the concept of "essential simplicity". Kitty Trevelyan supported us throughout and while the coffin was being lowered, she recited with great feeling a passage from the Dream of Gerontius, by John Henry Newman (1801-90).

"Go forth upon thy journey, Christian soul ! ..."

I truly believe that while this was happening here on Earth, so in another realm Mother's soul was being welcomed by those spiritual beings to which she now belongs. Her soul will be kept constantly nourished by our sleeping thoughts, and as a Lady Bountiful on Earth, so in Heaven she will be able to help those poor souls lost in the spiritual realms between death and rebirth.

Mother's Memorial on Good Friday Hill.

...And now a full month later the pieces of our shattered lives have settled back into position - a different pattern emerged for me. A new home - a new life! The days of the weeks have returned. Life goes on, but we are even more aware that time is a limited and precious commodity, and there is still much work to be done.

On Saturday, January 25th, a Memorial Service was held in the Folk House. This was an opportunity for all who wished to pay their last respects to a gay, warm and optimistic personality, and to remember the full, active life of a courageous woman, who was ever a loving wife to Father and a true Mother to us all. Later a Memorial was erected on Good Friday Hill, the inscription written by Father and painted by me, but the 75 year-old piece of Elm was unseasoned and needs a replacement.

My sons and I stayed 8 months with Father in Sandy Balls House, but as he settled into a new routine, working on his autobiography and medical research, the clattering of teenage feet up and down the many stairs disturbed him; so we moved back home and I established a routine that suited both him and us.

Good Friday Hill.

At this time, 1976, Father was nominated and elected Chieftain of the OWC - after an interval of 40 years! To his delight I became MC. Being Chieftain again was a wonderful thing for Father, he felt honoured and appreciated and was able to give advice and guidance. I think this recognition did a great deal to ease his sense of loss and loneliness … and was even more welcome because the Holiday Centre was entering a phase of major development under the Managing Directorship of Richard, my youngest brother, which distressed Father greatly but which he was powerless to prevent.

To
Dr.
Aubrey
Westlake
with admiration

Father continued in office for 5 years, then, in his 1981 Folkmoot Address said, 'I feel the time has come when I should retire and let a younger person take over as your leader'. For the last 4 years of his life he was honoured as Grand Chieftain and the Council of Leaders continued to meet monthly in Sandy Balls House, as before.

I enjoyed looking after Father, and over this 10-year period, learnt a great deal about many fascinating subjects – complementary therapies, including the Bach Flower Remedies, and his particular interest – Psionic Medicine, which he and other qualified medical practitioners were pioneering. I observed at first hand the International regard in which he was held, acting as hostess to visitors from many parts of the world, and Sandy Balls House was a lovely setting in which to welcome them and provide organically-grown produce for their enjoyment.

Christopher Bird from America I remember well, a giant of a man, co-author of 'The Secret Life of Plants' and later 'The Secret Life of the Soil' and other books.

One of Father's books 'The Pattern of Health', published in 1960 by Vincent Stuart, London, was a considerable success and Swiss, Italian and German editions appeared. The American Publishing House Shambhala brought out a 2nd edition in paperback and Element Books a 3rd edition, which included a further chapter by Father, published in 1985 shortly before his death.

I had one further sojourn in Sandy Balls House. In April, 1983, I suffered a back injury with motor nerve damage and, being in considerable pain and on my own all day, Father offered to care for me while I was recovering. (Eden being in his final year at Kent Horticultural College, and Ashley at College in Salisbury). On 1 July, Father celebrated his 90th birthday with a grand family gathering but I was still unwell and unable to attend. However, by Christmas I returned home. Later, fitted with a splint I became reasonably mobile again.

Greenwood continued to be used throughout this time, but as I was unable to act as Warden, vandalism began to be reported by visiting groups. The first real casualty was the Dining Shelter; the uprights were sawn through and it was lowered to the ground and in 1990 the Common Room was burnt down as well. In the October 1991 'Pine Cone' the Chieftain writes: "The news from Greenwood is depressing, and following a discussion with Richard Westlake, we have agreed to terminate our lease at the end of the year. This is due partly to the safety aspect of the continuing works by the Estate, but mainly to the fact that we will be unable to let the site to groups next year without either a Common Room or a Dining Shelter; this would leave us liable for the rent with no income to help to pay for it." The Herald writes in a more hopeful way: "The uncertainty of our future there has hung over us for so long that now departure is definite, I no longer feel any sadness at leaving, but with the possibility of new land, my feelings are all of hope, excitement and very, very positive that the Order has a future. We will be different, have a new home, perhaps not permanent, but we will be." So the Order left Greenwood after almost 30 years, and there was some resentment and much sadness. The remaining buildings were fired under Estate supervision, the Greenwood site levelled and grassed down and the Federation area planted up with trees. At the same time huge machines bulldozed a road partway round Sandy Balls, halfway down the hillside, which left a great scar for many years.

Mrs K. Allen, Hants

The carved pine root guarding the Greenwood site.

Now nature has clothed it once again and it has become a lovely woodland walk. I did not see any of this happening. My sons said to me, "Don't go down Mum, it will only upset you". It was several years before I saw Greenwood again – a green glade framed by yellow, red and gold beech leaves, peaceful and smiling in the Autumnal sunshine; the southern approach guarded by a carved uprooted pine root – surely a permanent reminder of Woodcraft.

In 1995, the Estate, wishing to celebrate its Silver Jubilee as a Holiday Centre, (the first camp of the Smoke Tribe was held in 1920), invited the Order to share the occasion by holding a special Festival Camp on the new Greenwood site – the Folkmoot Circle being used for the Opening and Closing Ceremonies as before.

The Camp was, understandably, not quite as well-attended as in other years, but the ceremonies which included the presentation of many of Ernest Westlake's Great grandchildren to the assembled company were impressive, ending with the bestowal of a ceremonial name – a high Order honour on me with the following words:

"Fellow Adventurers, now is the time when we shall bestow a Ceremonial name upon one amongst us. This is our gift to show our faith in its winner as the finest type of Adventurer. Jean Cormack, daughter of Golden Eagle and Apple Blossom, has remained steadfast to the Woodcraft Way, and shown friendship to all Order members over many years. For her

A great-grand child of the Founder presented to the assembled company.

'GREENSLEEVES' - crowned with a garland.

devotion, great skill and knowledge of all things living, for artistic talent and friendship, we bestow on her the name of Greensleeves - Blue Sky."

Then the Chieftain placed a garland of oak leaves upon my head and the Gleeman, in her beautiful soprano voice, sang several verses of 'Greensleeves'. Although I was prepared and expected to be moved by receiving such an honour, standing there in the sunshine in the presence of the whole assembly, listening to the lovely melody flowing over me, I was completely overwhelmed: it was another poignant moment in my life.

In the words of the affirmation the 'Woodcraft Way' is "To respond to the call of the world of nature, seeking from it simplicity, good sense and fortitude: to pursue bravely and gaily the adventure of life, cherishing whatever it holds of beauty, wonder and romance; and endeavouring to carry the chivalrous spirit into daily life."

Chapter 32

Memories of my Father

Aubrey Thomas Westlake – Golden Eagle

1.7.1893 – 30.10.1985

My very earliest recollection of Father was in Sandy Balls and, strangely enough, close to Greenwood (formerly Grith Fyrd). As a tiny child I was put down from dizzy shoulder height and told to wait; as I waited, a tiny lone figure in a sea of green loveliness, a bearded giant from Grith Fyrd approached me and said: 'Little girl are you lost?', and even then I remember thinking how silly he was to think that I could be lost when my Daddy was coming back for me.

Another memory from those early days: a lovely afternoon, we three children, Keith, Martin and I enjoying the summer heat, sitting in the heather by the Old Boxing Ring, listening to the crack-crack of the pine-cones and watching the ants. My Father passed by and asked us to take 'Bertie', a heavy two-wheeled cart, down to Grith Fyrd. The two boys disappeared, so always a dutiful daughter, even at 8 years old, I decided to take it down myself. At the top of the hill I got inside the shafts and very soon gathered speed. Faster and faster I had to run, as trapped inside I careered madly down the loose gravel road.

Fortunately for me, Father was working on the slopes above cutting timber. Hearing my frantic cries he rushed down the hillside and in the nick of time saved me from certain injury at the next bend. My badly-cut feet were bathed, the boys reprimanded and all was well, but the feeling that my Father had saved my life remained with me and a special relationship developed from that time on.

Thus when Mother died it seemed only right and fitting that I should be the one to look after him. Although dedicated to the Woodcraft ideal of 'learning by doing' he never mastered domestic skills; instead his time continued to be occupied with medical work, writing and research and he relied upon me for good meals, understanding support and companionship.

He was a very kind man, always showing forbearance and patience and generously giving his time, help and advice to all who asked for it. His patients respected and admired him, for he had the ability to stand back and view dispassionately life's everyday problems. Dedicated to the family, he could not relate to them with the same human warmth as Mother had; he had no small talk, and as Sandy Balls rapidly developed as a thriving Holiday Centre, he became increasingly isolated from them, and indeed fought a lone battle against such rapid development. Many Order members who knew and loved Sandy Balls in those early days will sympathise with his spirited defence of such natural beauty.

He had many interests, but the O.W.C meant the practical expression of his Father's ideas and they were of paramount importance to him. The fact that it had been a living vital force for almost 70 years gave him continued hope for the future. In his last years, honoured as Grand Chieftain, he died happy in the knowledge that with the guidance of our present Chieftain all would be well in the years to come.

The Funeral

Let me first say how very touched I was by the sympathetic and generous support of the Chieftain and the Keeper of the Fire as they helped me keep vigil in Sandy Balls House during Golden Eagle's three days 'lying in state'. The newly-polished house, empty since he became ill in February, welcomed him home. Surrounded by flowers, he lay there in the beautifully-made oak coffin, his hands serenely folded across his breast, clothed in pure white.

It was a strange sensation for me the first night to be there alone, and over the next three days to see and feel the gradual withdrawal of his spirit, leaving the lifeless

insert pic page 167 of original. 'Lying in State' in Sandy Balls House.

195

The Parish Bier on the way to Good Friday Hill.

The Committal.

The Portrait of Aubrey Westlake by the Quaker Artist Francis Sutton.

physical body an empty shell behind. Not a time for grieving but more of rejoicing that after 10 months of decline he had passed on to the Great Adventure into Spiritual Realms. Ten years previously, when Mother died so suddenly, we were in a state of numbed shock and grief, but this time I marvelled that everything had been planned so well, even to the death on a Wednesday, the funeral on a Saturday, just as it had been for her.

The Saturday dawned just such a brilliant day, the cold not perhaps so intense; the simple Quaker Burial Service on Good Friday Hill just as Father would have wished. In the presence of a large congregation I read William Blake's moving poem 'The door of death is paved with gold'. The hymns, led by the Fordingbridge Choir Master, reverberated out over the valley and the grief of the grandchildren touched our hearts as it had then.

Those at the graveside will agree that it was a deeply moving experience, and as the coffin was gently lowered into the deep cool earth, the cold wind stirred, and a blackbird sang OEPEI MATEPI MAIDA (Thou broughtest the child back to his mother). There he now lies, overlooking his beloved Sandy Balls, united with Apple Blossom my Mother, enfolded by the loving thoughts of all who knew and valued him.

A fortnight later a Memorial Service was held in the Folkhouse; every chair was taken, the room full to overflowing. In the centre a single candle lit up his portrait, painted in 1977 by the Quaker Artist, Francis Sutton, and many were the tributes to the life and work of a remarkable man. The service ended with the 'Dance of the Blessed Spirits' by Gluck from his Opera 'Orpheo ed Euridice'. The serene, radiant music transported us into Elysian fields, paradise of the ancient Greeks; where eternal sunlight shone on green glades and cool streams and the happy spirits danced in everlasting bliss.

I would like to end with this tribute from a friend:
'He was a man who saw his duty according to the will of God and no man could have performed it with more energy and greater understanding. A man of compassion, especially for the less fortunate. A man of peace. A man who will be missed more deeply than simple words can ever express. A man who came among us, and left us when his work was done. A man whose memory will live long after the earth has taken back the life it once gave. A man, a Father and a friend'.

Chapter 33

An Introduction to Bio-Dynamics

…And so the years passed, gardening organically at home on the family estate, now an increasingly popular holiday centre. I married, had two sons and was divorced. For many years I supplied the Wholefood Shop in Baker Street, Central London, with produce until the Fordingbridge railway was closed down and it was no longer possible. I also sold fruit and vegetables to the holiday visitors from a garden stall until the organic produce was swallowed up in a larger shop.

The Thatched Shop at the entrance to Sandy Balls.

Since Mother's death in 1975 I had been looking after Father and was at this time only cultivating a kitchen garden for our own use. I devoted myself, firstly to my family and then to bringing out three booklets for Sandy Balls, entitled 'Sandy Balls for all Seasons' 1977, 'Gipsy Caravan – A 100 Years' Story' 1982, and 'A Handbook for Sandy Balls' 1983.

In 1983, my elder son, Eden, qualified from Hadlow, the Kent College of Agriculture with an OND in Commercial Horticulture; the course included two years practical experience, firstly at Hillier Nurseries, Winchester, with nursery stock, the second year on a commercial fruit and vegetable holding in Kent – both run on conventional lines. After qualifying he decided to return home to grow organic fruit and vegetables for sale, although at College the idea that there could be an organic option was 'persona non grata'.

Three books about Sandy Balls by the Author.

Father had been a founder member of the Soil Association with Lady Eve Balfour and had come into contact with the work of many other organic pioneers. He had studied Rudolf Steiner's Anthroposophy in depth and my home had been the venue for a Steiner study group in 1976, but neither Father nor I had felt any inclination to join the Association, although it was the earliest organic movement and the agricultural expression of Anthroposophy. This was now to change…

A compelling thought in the Spring of 1985 decided me to join the Bio-Dynamic Agricultural Association and I had a very welcoming letter from David Adams, Acting Secretary at that time.

Attending my first Bio-Dynamic Conference at Hawkwood College, near Stroud in Gloucestershire, in July 1985, entitled 'On the Road to Bio-Dynamics', I was greatly impressed and inspired by the speakers; among them were David Clement, Chairman of the Association and a Bio-Dynamic farmer, Alan Brockman, also a Bio-Dynamic farmer, and Dr Lotte Sahlmann of the Sheiling School at Ringwood (Medical Advisor for the Camphill Rudolf Steiner Schools in Southern Britain). I returned home with two messages: 'One alone cannot do anything; you must have a group around you', and secondly, 'There must be a purpose beyond the actual work itself'. So I decided that rather than let Eden do his own thing, I would actively support him in a combined venture.

At this time we were cultivating a large kitchen garden by our bungalow, Sandemans, given to me by Mother in 1972, originally the school room of Forest School; and Eden had the use of 1$\frac{1}{2}$ acres of land from the Family Company, Sandy Balls Estate Ltd. He was 100% behind my interest in Bio-Dynamics and indeed had a natural understanding of Steiner's concepts.

We decided firstly to apply for the Soil Association Symbol and then to work steadily towards Demeter, the quality symbol of the Bio-Dynamic Agricultural Association, our goal. The practical application of the Bio-Dynamic principles took us a couple of years to understand and achieve and it was only at the 1987 Conference that we finally became aware of the role of the Silica spray 50l, which we had not previously used.

Our first step along the Bio-Dynamic path was to send for a set of the Compost Preparations, prepared by a dedicated member and marketed by the Association. I understood that they lay at the heart of Bio-Dynamic practice.

On arrival the package contained a number of small plastic tubs containing brown substances of varying textures, labelled 502 Yarrow, 503 Chamomile, 504 Nettle, 505 Oakbark, 506 Dandelion and 507 Valerian, a dark brown liquid with a strange smell.

These six made up the Compost Preparations and the set was completed with two spray materials – a larger amount of a crumbly black substance, 500 Horn Manure, and a fine white powder in two tiny capsules, 501 Horn Silica.

A newly made compost heap was ready and we followed the enclosed instructions carefully. The easiest way was to form each substance – and only a teaspoon of each was necessary – into a ball with a little damp soil and roll it down the deep holes made by a crow-bar in the sides of the compost heap. In this way they were in intimate contact with the heap itself; then then the holes were filled with soil and packed down well. The Valerian, (just sufficient to colour the water), was mixed vigorously for 10 minutes in a gallon of warmed rainwater, and sprayed or watered evenly over the heap. The whole was then covered with soil, grass mowings or other material to keep off excessive rainfall.

Preparation	Herb	Bears relationship to:	Result
502	Yarrow Flowers	Sulphur (S) Potassium (K)	Enables plants to attract trace elements in extremely dilute quantities for their best nutrition. Matured in the bladder of a red deer
503	Chamomile Flowers	Calcium (Ca) Sulphur (S)	Stabilizes Nitrogen within the compost. Increases soil life which stimulates plant growth. Matured in bovine intestines
504	Stinging Nettle	Sulphur (S) Potassium (K) Calcium (Ca) Iron (Fe)	'Enlivens' the soil, which provides plants with the necessary elements for plant nutrition. Matured in the soil
505	Oak Bark	Calcium (Ca)	Provides healing forces to combat plant diseases. Matured in the skull of a domestic animal
506	Dandelion Flowers	Silicon (Si) or Silicic acid Potassium (K)	Stimulates the relationship between Si and K so that the Si can attract cosmic forces to the soil. Matured in bovine mesentery
507	Valerian	Phosphorus (P)	Stimulates the compost so that the phosphorus component will be properly used by the soil. Juice of flowers stored in jars

Rudolf Steiner suggested these particular herbs (plus oak bark) as those in the plant kingdom holding the particular element(s) in the best possible form and/ or ratio for use by the soil

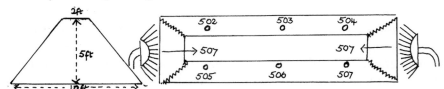

BIO-DYNAMIC COMPOST
PREPARATIONS

All this was straightforward and we mastered it without difficulty. The two sprays were a different matter and we did not use them for some time, for the time of application was important, also the conditions prevailing on the chosen day. The Horn Manure was to be applied in Spring, avoiding frost and rain, when the soil began to warm up: it promoted root activity, stimulated the micro-organisms within the soil, regulated its lime and nitrogen content and helped in the provision of trace elements! However, the one hour's initial stirring creating vortices within the spray liquid was of the greatest importance to its efficacy. So we were a little daunted and sought advice and a demonstration of how to proceed.

Eden later became adept at stirring and using both sprays. The Horn Silica was beneficial as a foliar spray of the summer time, enhancing the light, warmth and ripening processes within the crop, but was only to be used if preparation 500 had previously been applied earlier in the season. There was much to learn! - but Eden was young and we were both keen and enthusiastic.

At this time we had no knowledge of how the preparations were made, but in the following Autumn we were invited to the Preparation making day at the nearest *Steiner Camphill Community, Sturts Farm at West Moors in Dorset, and this invitation was renewed yearly. Each Spring we helped the Community lift them from their Winter resting places within the soil and were given a share of each for use on our own holding. In this way we gained a knowledge both of their simplicity and their complexity.

Michael Schmundt, inspired leader of the Community, expanded and refreshed our knowledge of Bio-Dynamics and Steiner's work at these 6-monthly gatherings and we gained immeasurably from this contact. The young handicapped members of the Community may not have understood intellectually but they were enthused with a deeper understanding and listened to their leader with reverence, awe and respect.

As the preparations worked most effectively with cattle manure we decided that to run a small Bio-Dynamic Holding successfully, we would need to keep a cow. This was rather naïve, for we were still negotiating with the family company to rent or buy a piece of land for Eden's organic project and indeed 1/2 acre had already been planted up with fruit and vegetables. Even for a small breed, e.g. Dexter, we would need another 2 acres to be self sustaining. But when we saw an advertisement in the local paper for a 15 month-old Pedigree Dexter Heifer, we were undaunted by our lack of pasturage, and decided to go ahead.

The black, short-legged animal was still suckling her Mother; sleek and plump she

The Bio-Dynamic Agricultural Method is an integral part of the Camphill movement both at home and abroad.

looked the picture of health. (How were we to know then, that the long-legged, rundown mother, who was also for sale, would have been the better purchase?) So we decided to buy Netherwell Sara and with her tied securely to the back of our Honda Pickup, we made our way home - swaying a little as we went. But no mishap occurred, although I suspect it was illegal to transport an animal in this way. Arriving home we tied her to a fence, gave her hay and water and went home to lunch. Imagine our consternation when on our return found that she had disappeared and was discovered several fields away being pursued by horses belonging to Arniss Riding Stables.

We joined the Dexter Cattle Society and also the Hampshire Cattle Breeders, based at Lyndhurst, chose a suitable bull, ordered semen from the Society and when Sara 'came on bulling' had her inseminated using A.1. All went well and great was our joy when our first calf was born – a little heifer, Ytene Charlotte – our own breeding, the mother of our future herd.

In 1987 we were able to buy 3½ acres of old watermeadow land outside Fordingbridge – one mile away. Our aim was to build up a single-suckler herd of Pedigree Dexter cattle, having a sound constitution by being fed entirely on home-produced fodder from land worked Bio-Dynamically. This we were now able to do. The system was proved to our satisfaction by easy calving, few health problems, and minimal vet's bills; in complete contrast to orthodox farming methods which were to come to headline prominence with Salmonella, B.S.E. and other self-inflicted ills.

Chapter 34

All Muck And Magic

In the late Spring of 1988, the fieldsman, Jimmy Anderson, who visited us yearly to inspect, phoned to ask whether we would be prepared to take part in a TV programme, in the series 'All Muck and Magic' as an example of a small Bio-Dynamic garden and holding; Oaklands, a Camphill Centre, was to be asked to represent a larger unit. Although we were so new to the Association we agreed to do our best, but were dismayed to hear that Oaklands did not feel that they could take part. However we liked the researcher, Jane Wales, from HTV, Bristol, who came to discuss the programme with us and at her request sent detailed plans of our holding.

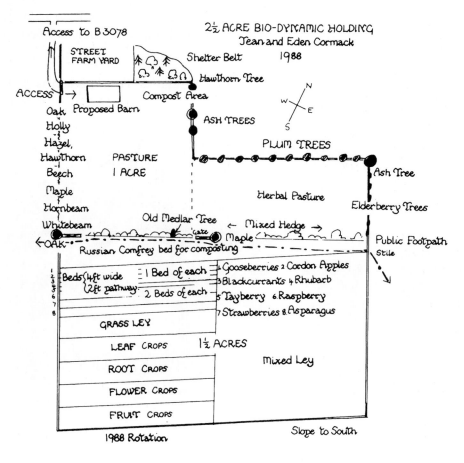

2 1/2 Acre Bio-Dynamic Holding.

The land which we now owned (August 1988) was 6¼ acres in all, – made up of 1½ acres of pasture and 1 acre of land growing market garden crops overlooking the New Forest, from which 6 acres of bracken were cut annually for litter and mulching material; 3½ acres of old water-meadow land 1½ miles away in the Avon Valley, and the ¼ acre kitchen garden. Most of our produce at this time was sold from the door, because we were situated on the busy B3078, and at the entrance to Sandy Balls.

Determined that our garden should be perfect for the programme on Thursday 7th July we worked tirelessly and on the day I felt justifiably proud of our lovely garden and Eden's field. The morning was showery but in the afternoon the sun shone hotly from a blue sky, and Eden made a striking picture in a black and red striped shirt, spraying the 50l Silica Spray from a blue and yellow knapsack sprayer onto green potato plants with a background of towering cumulus clouds, and our Dexter cows contentedly looking on. Jimmy Anderson gave a wonderful interview to Alan Gear from the Henry Doubleday Research Association and they seemed satisfied with my hesitant contribution.

The Researcher, in thanking us, wrote on 17th August. 'Transmission is due in the Spring'.

Gatekeepers Restaurant at the entrance to Sandy Balls - Opened 1988.

Ytene Gardens - The Bio-Dynamic Nursery.

1988 was an exciting year for us – I was offered the floral contract to supply and arrange flowers at the newly-opened Holiday Centre Restaurant – Gatekeepers – and Eden was asked to supply quality produce; my younger son, Ashley, qualified with a good BSc Honours Degree in Horticulture from Reading University; our home-bred Dexter, Charlotte gained 1st in her class and Reserve Champion at the Fordingbridge Show: and in August we heard we had achieved the Demeter Symbol of quality for our produce!

We are creating a holding with a difference. Open to the public from 10am – 6pm every day from May 31st – October 31st, it is a riot of cottage garden flowers, herbs, kitchen garden, greenhouse, goat, bantams chickens and beehives, where visitors are welcome to look round. There are herbs, shrubs and hardy herbaceous plants for sale and a small stall selling a wide range of freshly-picked Demeter quality produce and flowers at reasonable prices. Cut herbs are free and indeed the chef from the Restaurant is encouraged to pick fresh herbs daily.

The work is demanding but infinitely rewarding. There is a vision and purpose beyond financial considerations and I feel that we are sustained and supported by a greater Power.

Two quality symbols are held, the Soil Association symbol and Demeter from the Bio-Dynamic Agricultural Association.

Food bearing the Demeter symbol has been grown by Bio-Dynamic agricultural methods and has met specific standards within these methods. The aim of Bio-Dynamic agriculture is to restore and maintain the vitality and living fertility of our soils, and in so doing produce foods of the highest nutritional value.

We have many plans for the future, and look forward to passing on in a practical way our knowledge and enthusiasm for Bio-Dynamics and the work of Rudolf Steiner to the increasing number of people who visit us.

Sara, our original purchase, was not destined to have a second calf, perhaps due to her late weaning and having the tendency even then, to lay down fat, she continued to get fatter and fatter, her womb became floppy and she could not conceive. The vet recommended sending her on as a barrener.

Chapter 35
Practical Bio-Dynamic Gardening

YTENE GARDENS
(At the entrance to Sandy Balls)

At the end of 1993 I was asked by the *BDAA whether I would be prepared to write a series of practical gardening articles for their twice-yearly journal 'Star and Furrow'. I said I would be pleased to. In my first article for the Summer number (1994) I explain the origins of our unusual name – Ytene Gardens. When we first started to keep pedigree Dexter cattle in 1986 we needed to choose a prefix for our herd. I suggested Elysian (a state or place of perfect bliss!) but this had already been used by another breeder. The Saxon name of the New Forest was Ytene (pronounced to rhyme with Brittany), meaning 'furzy waste', so, as our land overlooked the Forest, we decided Ytene would be an appropriate prefix instead. Subsequently we renamed our bungalow Ytene Gardens. I commented to Ashley when he expressed a wish to change the name, that few would know how to pronounce it and indeed this has proved to be true.

I wondered how best to approach the proposed articles – for gardening is such a vast subject, as too is Bio-Dynamic Farming. I thought the best way would be to write about our work and show how, in practice, it was linked to Bio-Dynamics and

* *Bio-Dynamic Agricultural Association*

indeed each article illustrated a particular point of interest. I started with an article introducing the readers to my background and the holding which would form the backdrop to them. Subsequently I was to write about hedges, chamomile lawns, kitchen gardening, herbaceous borders and herb gardening – all subjects I knew a great deal about and ones I felt would be instructive and of interest to others.

The Nursery and Show Garden

Our garden includes a half-acre of light sand over gravel, sheltered and early and close to our home. We specialised in producing hardy herbaceous perennials and herbs for sale and have a number of show borders – this means that customers from Sandy Balls can see the plants growing in a garden setting. The large cold greenhouse, (36 x 24 ft) empty of nursery plants during the Summer months, enables us to grow a selection of crops – e.g, tomatoes, cucumbers, melons etc; both for sale and home consumption. A fine monkey puzzle tree takes pride of place in the garden.

The Kitchen Garden

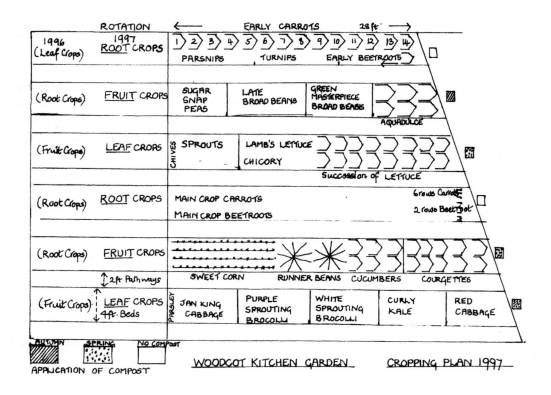

A few minutes away we have another quarter of an acre surrounding my son, Eden's little property 'Woodcot'. Here the soil is equally light but exposed to cold, easterly winds especially in Spring time. Managed intensively as a kitchen garden with a strip bed system and a number of chase barn glass cloches, it provides the household with a succession of vegetables throughout the year.

The Agricultural Land

The rest of the holding consists of one and a half acres of pasture and one acre of land for growing stock plants and Demeter quality field crops, including a 4-course rotation, maincrop potatoes, onions, strawberries and a ley. Although bleak and exposed during the Winter months and the soil a stony loam, the Forest landscape delights us daily with its changing moods of colour and light.

In complete contrast one mile away we have five and a half acres in Holwell Marsh, which is old water meadow land close to the Hampshire Avon. This is divided into three equal-sized paddocks with access from each to a sturdily built animal shelter. Liable to flood in Winter, its rich alluvial soil overlying London clay gives Summer grass even in drought years and sufficient hay for our small suckler herd of Dexter cattle.

The paddocks are managed on a rotational basis so that the cows always graze clean land making chemical wormers unnecessary.

During the Winter months, the two cows Ytene Charlotte and Ytene Clover and their followers are housed in a large airy barn, the deep litter being composted in the Spring with B.D preparations. The resulting compost when mature is the basis of our fertility. As mentioned before, 6 acres of bracken are cut annually in Autumn for mulching and litter.

We have one house-goat and some chickens; thus we have a tiny 8 acres holding in an ideal environment, with a variety of soil types, crops, and animals. Also the ability to put into practice all the farm and garden work necessary to establish and maintain a Bio-dynamic unit.

Both my sons are horticulturally trained, although only Ashley had previous B.D experience, for he worked for 6 months at Tablehurst Farm, Emerson College (The Anthroposophical College) Forest Row.

In 1993 we joined the BDAA Apprentice Training Scheme and sponsored an apprentice. Rebecca, aged 20 years, was with us for 15 months. She had previously been at a Camphill Community in Ireland. On leaving us she went to another community in Norfolk where she had the confidence to put into practice a great deal of what she had learnt with us. She is now working for a degree in Horticulture at Wye College.

Visit of Victoria to Ytene Gardens. April 4th – May 4th 1993
Purpose of visit —

Originally my purpose for being here was to deepen my knowledge and understanding of Bio-Dynamic Agriculture through practical working experience; but it seems rather that in coming here I was to grow and develop in ways never before experienced or expected. It has been the most incredible six weeks of my life yet. I only hope that I am allowed to take this peace of both heart and mind, into my life in the metropolis. I love you both and shall miss you deeply. Thankyou.

Yours in peace and love, Victoria

Letter from Victoria.

We also had an MSc postgraduate student from Salford University who was preparing a dissertation on BD Agriculture. Our task was to show her in six weeks as many BD procedures as we could, so that the practice illuminated her study. We read Rudolf Steiner's book 'Occult Science' daily following *Dr Manfred Klett's suggestion that it should be the Bible of BD. She had access to our comprehensive library which included many books by Steiner and allied authors.

Director of the Agricultural Department of the Natural Science section at the Goetheanum in Dornach, Switzerland.

1993
Friday May 28th – Bank Holiday Monday 31st & June for 1 week.
Visit to Ytene Gardens of Mercedes Merimaa
           gänese farm
           Soomra village
           PÄRNUMAA
           ESTONIA
           tl. 372-44-63658

    I have been in England 9 month, taking Brody-nannic Agriculture course at Emerson College. My individual project is Healing Herb Garden.

    I wanted to know as much as possible about Herbs and art of healing, because I came here to Ytene Gardens.

    During these days I enjoyed to live in family community. I meet openess and love carring, on with everyday life and I feeled myself happy to be here, to lear lot of things working together with Jean, or Eden or discussing with you, or reading together 'Knowledge of Higer Wolds'.

    I gained lot of ideas an strenght how and what to do at home in my farm. I hope to meet you soon. It was too little time for me, to learn all what I have meet here. Thank you!

               Lot of Love
                     Mercedes

Letter from Mercedes.

Then, as part of her study at Emerson College, an Estonian came who wished to work with healing herb gardens. We were able to provide her with much valuable information to take back to her own country, especially on the Bach Flower

Remedies for which we had Newsletters going back to March 1950! Other interesting people came who learnt from us and we from them.

The letters on previous pages, received from Victoria and Mercedes, more than compensated us for all our hard work – and indicated the contribution we could make in the future; unique to Ytene Gardens. For this we would need help, especially in regard to accommodation, and we looked to the family company to allow us to use the old Tracker hut next door – empty for many years.

But help was not forthcoming and with the advent of BSE, the collapse of the pedigree cattle market and other problems, not the least being that I was fast approaching my 70th Birthday, much that we had worked so hard to achieve had to be discontinued. This included my Steiner Study Group meeting weekly in my home since 1976, the relocation of the Southern B.D Group and finally, at the end of 1996, the nursery closed for the Winter, perhaps not to re-open.

Two of our Pedigree Dexter Cattle.

Chapter 36

Hedges in Relation to a Bio-Dynamic Holding

A voluntary helper at the Ringwood Waldorf School asked me if my son and I would give a few pupils each week a little experience of landwork. We said we would. The question was what to do with twelve-year-olds, in January, which would not only be meaningful to them but enjoyable as well.

Around our two and a half-acre holding in Godshill, in line with Bio-Dynamic practice, we had planned to establish a mixed hedge of indigenous bushes and trees – holly, beech, hawthorn, hornbeam, hazel, maple and whitebeam. So, hedge planting was the first job we decided to share with the children.

Except for 100 holly (which were our own), 50 of each species had been ordered from a local tree nursery; they were bare root plants, 45-60 cm size, classed as whips in the nursery trade. In fact when we collected them, only the hawthorns were small; some of the others were at least 3-4 years old, and for this we were grateful.

Bare root holly is difficult to transplant, so it is not surprising that most nurseries only offer pot-grown plants which make them expensive for hedging purposes. Over the past two years we have experimented and find that they can be successfully transplanted, even in drought years, if the young plants are defoliated before planting. The removal of *every* leaf, leaving the leaf stalk and dormant bud intact, is time-consuming but we felt it was a task eminently suitable for nimble, young fingers; indeed it gave us just the right opportunity to discuss with our helpers the benefits of mixed hedging on a Bio-Dynamic holding and what we were trying to achieve.

Historically, hedges fall into two broad categories. Firstly, the ancient ones; those that are relics of old woodland, present since before Domesday; even perhaps having a direct link with the woodland cover of Britain before clearance by man. And secondly the more recent enclosure hedges planted in the 18th and 19th centuries, when the common fields were enclosed and the peasant farmer was deprived of his common rights.

These enclosure hedges were planted with a single species, often hawthorn or elm, (although there were many regional variations), their boundaries were straight and formed part of the regular pattern of fields. It is this type of hedge, concentrated in the arable east, that has suffered most from hedge removal since the Second World War. The loss to the nation was about one-fifth of the total acreage.

Luckily many of the mixed ancient hedges are still intact, for many of these formed part of farm or parish boundaries and as such had a good chance of survival. Indeed most hedges, although mangled by hedge-cutters, are safer now than for some long time, for the whole nation has become environmentally conscious.

Old hedges can be approximately dated by a rule of thumb method by counting the number of species present in a 30 yard run; every shrub represents 100 years. Even the enclosure hedges have had time to be invaded by some of the good colonists – such as blackthorn, ash, elder or rose. With this knowledge I went to look at the hedge close to my boundary and found the following – ash, hazel, spindleberry, hawthorn, wildrose, blackthorn and maple. Knowing a little about the history of Godshill, I was not surprised that this showed the hedge to be about 700 years old!

These mixed hedges make ideal nesting-sites for birds, are especially suitable for tiny mammals who revel in a warm, wind-sheltered habitat and for the many sun-loving insects. Throughout the season they provide a succession of flowers from blackthorn in Spring to late-flowering ivy in Autumn; while on the banks and hedgerow bottoms flourishes a wide range of hardy plants. The humble nettle is particularly rich in insect species and is the food plant for the caterpillars of red admiral, peacock and small tortoiseshell butterflies.

Hedges are not only valuable for the containment of stock and habitats for wildlife but they have an influence on the field's microclimate and soil erosion as well. Grown as wind breaks, the increased crop production from the rise in temperature more than compensates for the loss of yield by the hedgeside.

Trimming a hedge only every 2-3 years *and* in winter is recommended, to avoid harm to nesting birds, as is practising the traditional art of hedge-laying for a thick, stock-proof hedge. Another method needing minimum attention is by 'coppicing' or cutting to ground level every 8-10 years. This retains wild life interest, a vigorous base for future hedge-laying and timber for woodburning stoves.

According to Rudolf Steiner, for the healthy growth of crops, the close proximity of forest, woodland, orchard, hedges, wetlands and meadows all play their part in providing an ideal environment. He speaks at some length about their intimate relationship with the other kingdoms of nature; for example, mammals have a kinship with bushes and shrubs, mushrooms with meadows, birds with coniferous forests.

It is when the environment becomes unbalanced that widespread invasion of pests and diseases occurs.

By planting a framework of mixed hedges around our fields we are extending this concept to our smallholding and it is good that this vital balance can be achieved by all of us in our gardens, with their infinite variety of species and accompanying insect and animal life. As Rudolf Steiner says: "You cannot truly engage in a pursuit so intimately connected with nature as farming is (or gardening) unless you have insight into these mutual relationships of nature's husbandry".

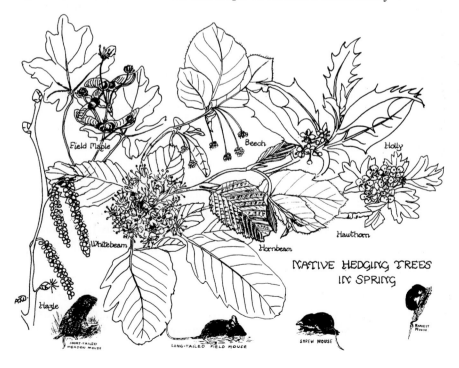

Field Maple · Beech · Holly · Whitebeam · Hornbeam · Hawthorn · Hazel · Ash

NATIVE HEDGING TREES IN SPRING

SHORT-TAILED MEADOW MOUSE · LONG-TAILED FIELD MOUSE · SHREW MOUSE · HARVEST MOUSE

Chapter 37

Herb Lawns and Chamomile

Many of my readers may well have a small area in their gardens that they wish to make into a new lawn – so why not plant one that is 'easy care' this time? Herb lawns have may advantages over grass: they are easy to establish, fragrant to walk on, need cutting only once or twice a year, and, if you choose the right plant, will remain green through Winter frost and Summer drought. If the garden is small and it is your only lawn, all you need is a pair of shears or perhaps borrow your neighbour's 'Flymo', so it is environmentally friendly as well.

Chamomile springs first to mind, it likes a sandy loam, while our native thyme, *Thymus serpyllum*, flourishes on chalk or an alkaline soil, and for the heavier moister situation, the dwarf mint or pennyroyal, *Mentha pulegium*, is ideal. When in flower the wild thyme will be covered with honey bees searching for nectar and this may be a hazard if you have tiny children in your care.

Chamomile.

If you are in no hurry, because sensibly you wish to make sure the area for planting is weed-free, the cheapest way is to buy a few plants in Spring. Last year we had chamomile for sale and, at our suggestion, one customer divided a single pot into 51 tiny plantlets which she individually potted up into a sterilised compost and later planted out into her prepared bed, 6 x 6 ins apart; or a nursery bed can be used, and when Autumn comes will provide sufficient plants for a fairly large area.

We have two lawns in our garden, both of chamomile. One of common chamomile, *Anthemis nobilis*, with its daisy-like flowers and aromatic, feathery foliage, and the other, the non-flowering form '*Treneague*', which makes a denser sward. The double-flowered '*Flora Plena*' can also be used.

I have a note in my flora that I found the common chamomile in a New Forest village in 1967. Passing through last Summer I was interested to see it still flourishing by the roadside – trampled and manured by the Forest ponies, not looking very lawn-like, but persistent and healthy nevertheless.

In the past, chamomile was much prized and a feature of many old gardens where the flowers provided a tisane or soothing tea for the household.

One July, a mother with two young children asked me if they could pick the chamomile flowers each week, when they collected their weekly vegetable order. She said they bought a lot of Weleda tea and it would be nice for the family to 'pick their own'. I was delighted, so they diligently snipped off every head. The following week, very apologetically, she said they didn't want any more; the tea was bitter and the children didn't like it. She brought me a packet of Weleda so that I could taste the difference myself.

I was disappointed, but as a result learnt several interesting facts: both chamomiles are to be found in the *Homeopathic Pharmacopoeia* and are used frequently in diseases of children where peevishness, restlessness and colic give the needful indications. *Anthemis nobilis*, the common or Roman chamomile, is a hardy perennial and contains a bitter component. *Matricaria recutica*, the German chamomile, with its delicate yellow and white heads of flowers and turned-down petals, is a fast-growing annual. This is the one used by Weleda. It contains the same nerve-soothing, sleep-inducing properties but no bitterness. In fact it is very pleasant and I shall grow some myself this year.

Incidentally, it is the German chamomile which is one of the five herbs chosen by Rudolf Steiner in 1924 which are used in the Bio-Dynamic compost preparations – the others being nettle, valerian, yarrow and dandelion (together with oak bark).

The Q.R (Quick Return) Compost Activator, originated by May E. Bruce in 1935, contains the same herb but this time a drop of honey is added to the formula. Miss Bruce was an early member of the Bio-Dynamic Agricultural Association – but found Dr Steiner's system too complicated and decided to branch out on her own. When it was suggested to her that it seemed strange that she should choose the identical herbs, she explained that the solutions used in her method were entirely different from those made by the societies connected with Dr R. Steiner's name. Indeed, as there had never been any secret about the wild flowers used, she felt free to use them in her experiments!

There are many differences between the two systems but both have factors in common, firstly the herb and secondly the employment of the homeopathic principle of 'the power of the infinitely little'. Miss Bruce found that a dose of 1 in 10,000 was the ideal potency; the higher the potency, the less (if any) physical matter remains and the archetypal pattern of the substance is released. This is a fascinating concept and we are dealing here with an unfamiliar dimension.

Steiner, in his series of lectures given in 1924 entitled *Agriculture,* comments thus on the use of chamomile. "By adding to the compost heap the chamomile preparation you will thus get a manure with a more stable nitrogen content and with the added virtue of kindling the life in the earth so that the earth itself will have a stimulating effect on the plant growth. You will create more healthy plants – *really* more healthy – if you manure in this way, than if you do not".

He pointed out how the health of soil, plants, animals and man depends upon bringing nature into connection again with the cosmic creative shaping forces and by so doing revitalising the natural forces which are on the wane.

So from cosmic thoughts we return to earth and herb lawns. What could be nicer than to kneel in Summer sunshine amid a sea of heavenly fragrance of chamomile. thyme or mint and pluck out the little clumps of grass or clover that mar its perfection?

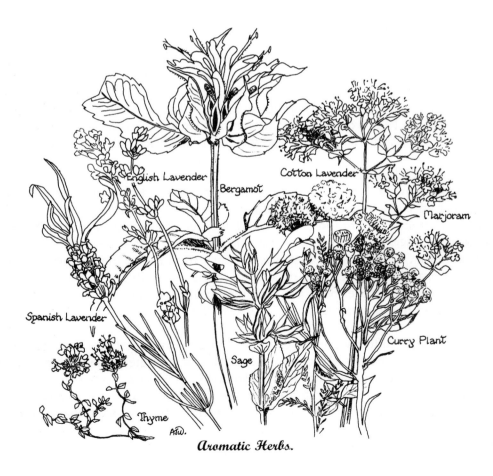

Aromatic Herbs.

A 'Pave and Plant' Herb Garden

Chapter 38
A Bio-Dynamic Herb Garden

Browsing in the Steiner Bookshop at the Sheiling Camphill Community near Ringwood in Hampshire, my younger son, Ashley, came across a photograph in the new edition of John Soper's book *Bio-Dynamic Gardening* entitled 'A Bio-Dynamic Herb Garden'. He instantly recognised it as *our* herb garden and *our* goat Emma in the background. He was thrilled for *he* was the one who had originally bought the goatling in 1983 and who had laid out the garden in a 'chequer board' design several years later.

Indeed, this 'Pave and Plant' herb garden continues to be a source of interest – even inspiration – to the many visitors who come to look round Ytene Gardens during the Summer, and as it contains many evergreens and as seed heads are left on during the Winter, it remains attractive all year round, with its different forms, colours and textures. Rising 15 years, Emma continues in milk and is our compost converter de luxe!

The garden surrounding our bungalow was irregular in shape and when planning the pathways and borders a triangle of land, in full sun and facing South, remained. After consulting the herb books, Ashley decided it was an ideal place for a large herb garden. He levelled the area and cleaned the soil, unfortunately with the enthusiasm of youth not quite thoroughly enough, for couch grass appeared which established itself in cracks and is now difficult to eradicate. A local nursery was being closed down and several loads of good quality paving slabs were purchased; the 2' x 2's being used for the herb garden, and the larger 3' x 2's for the 4ft pathway on either side.

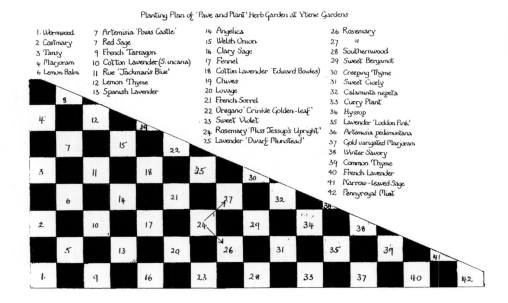

Planting Plan of 'Pave and Plant' Herb Garden at Ytene Gardens

1. Wormwood	7 Artemisia 'Powis Castle'	14 Angelica
2 Costmary	7 Red Sage	15 Welsh Onion
3 Tansy	9 French Tarragon	16 Clary Sage
4 Marjoram	10 Cotton Lavender (S. incana)	17 Fennel
6 Lemon Balm	11 Rue 'Jackman's Blue'	18 Cotton Lavender 'Edward Bowles)
	12 Lemon Thyme	19 Chives
	13 Spanish Lavender	20 Lovage
		21 French Sorrel
		22 Oregano 'Crinkle Golden-leaf'
		23 Sweet Violet
		24 Rosemary 'Miss Jessup's Upright'
		25 Lavender 'Dwarf Munstead'

26 Rosemary
27 "
28 Southernwood
29 Sweet Bergamot
30 Creeping Thyme
31 Sweet Cicely
32 Calamintla nepeta
33 Curry Plant
34 Hyssop
35 Lavender 'Loddon Pink'
36 Artemisia pedemontana
37 Gold variegated Marjoram
38 Winter Savory
39 Common Thyme
40 French Lavender
41 Narrow-leaved Sage
42 Pennyroyal Mint

This design is ideal for any garden, however small, large or irregular in shape. If the soil is light and free of stones as ours was, the paving stones can be placed directly on the levelled area – corner to corner by any handyman. Otherwise a bedding of sand is necessary. For this kind of paving a spirit level is not necessary, but is best used for pathways – irregular surfaces can be hazardous! The areas not large enough to take a whole slab can be fitted with part ones or the area shuttered round with a rough wood surround and filled to a depth of 2ins (5cm) with a concrete mix. Do not forget to point the cracks between the pathway slabs with cement. The tiny areas are ideal for planting up with small herbs such as creeping thymes, mints – Corsican and penny royal – and dwarf artemisias.

Cotsmary.

Your herb garden is now paved and could be planted with herbs; however, it is wisest to plan first and to grow your own plants. If you primarily want them for kitchen use, the main ones that spring to mind are parsley, thyme, marjoram, sage and mint; if more space is available, add winter savoury, fennel, tarragon and chives. The plan of my border, with 42 different herbs, is included for interest. Over the years there have been changes – the rosemary grew too large, despite trimming, and now occupies more than its allocated space and several plants were moved to new positions for a variety of reasons. For instance, costmary with its grey leaves and lovely scent was one year covered with a rosy aphis which crushed as red as blood. The attack was very severe and nothing I did – rubbing off, spraying with a nettle solution, mulching or watering – did any good and the time lag before the ladybirds could appear was too long to prevent all the leaves dying off. All was not happy the following year so in the Autumn I took the plants up and moved them to a newly prepared bed where they have flourished ever since. This may have been coincidence but plants are often very specific in their requirements and a careful note should be kept if plants do not thrive. Golden marjoram scorches badly in hot sun, so should be shaded by taller plants. The crinkled-leaved golden marjoram rarely suffers, so can be grown instead if space is limited.

You will notice that neither mint (other than dwarf ones) nor annuals are included in my plan.

Mints need space: they are gross feeders and will overrun other plants, indeed I had a flourishing 10-year-old asparagus bed completely taken over by Eau de Cologne mint! Mints are best grown in pots or tubs and are happiest in a partial sun / part shade position. Perhaps a tub of your favourite mint by your back door is the answer?

In Ytene Gardens we have 11 varieties, from the tiny evergreen Corsican mint which creeps along the ground, is strongly fragrant when walked upon and flowers at $^1/_2$ inch (1.5cm) high, to the taller varieties – spearmint, applemint or peppermint etc. Spear or lambmint is best known, for in the days when fresh herbs were sent daily to a wholesale market, – e.g Covent Garden for London, it remained the freshest when cut. Our mints appear to be a source of absorbing interest to the many families who visit the garden – the whole family, grandparents, parents and children queue up trying each mint for fragrance and flavour as they pass along the line of tubs.

A Chef at the Ritz, who regularly visited Sandy Balls (the adjacent holiday centre), was keen to know *how to grow* herbs for the first time when he would have an hotel of his own! We had many animated talks and he told me that the Ritz favoured 'Bowles Mint', a very superior flavoured white-flowered apple mint. He enthused over the number of succulent appetisers it enhanced and the superb mint sauce it made. Later he obtained a plant and gave it to me.

Preparation of the tubs must be thorough. Fill the bottom with drainage material and a rich Bio-Dynamic compost mixture. Plant firmly, three of one variety per tub. Spray in Spring with Horn manure 500 and during the Summer with Horn Silica 501. Water well in dry weather and pinch out continually if you want young succulent shoots *or* allow to flower and enjoy the fragrance and abundance of insect-life that rise in a cloud as you pass by on a Summer afternoon.

Many of the popular Summer herbs are annuals and are best grown in pots, in the greenhouse or kitchen garden. Some are not frost-hardy and need early sowing. There are many varieties of basil – even one with purple crinkled leaves. Sweet basil is my particular favourite; it makes neat bushes and can be grown in the greenhouse alongside the tomato crop whose flavour it supplements and enhances.

Sweet Bay

Seed is sown early in heat or even on a kitchen window sill and potted on as required. If planted out later in the garden, wait until all danger of frosts has passed and protect carefully from slugs and snails who cannot resist it. Summer savoury is another half-hardy annual grown in this way. Chervil and dill are hardy annuals, which should be sown at intervals as they quickly mature and run to seed. Parsley is a biennial and will make a useful edging in the kitchen garden, while seed sown in the greenhouse or covered with cloches makes Winter use possible when the outdoor crop has died down. The plain-leaved French parsley has the best flavour and I grow it in preference to the prettier curly-leaved variety. Chives can be grown in a vegetable garden for continuous cutting, but are also very decorative with their balls of bright purple flowers, and blue borage, much loved by bees, is a must and once you have it in your garden it will self-seed with the greatest ease. During the Summer whole families of greenfinches can often be seen eating half ripened borage seed – a lovely sight!

The first year with our newly-paved bed was spent growing the plants we did not have. Seeds were brought from an organic firm, many cuttings were taken from other gardens and there were divisions and gifts from friends. It's amazing how generous people are when they know you are interested in herbs. By the second Spring we had a large collection of plants ready to put into their permanent quarters. During the year of waiting the border was sown with a selection of annual flowers – and very pretty it looked too. If you cannot wait, there are plenty of nurseries to choose from – but in a Bio-Dynamic garden you really need properly grown plants for disease resistance, health and vigour – *and it is really great fun growing your own!* Even on a patio or courtyard you can experiment with annuals in pots and not be tempted to buy the forced ones in the supermarket.

Now the time has come to give each tiny bed its final preparation. With your planting plan in front of you, consider the needs of each herb. Bergamot, for example, is a moisture-lover – the wild ones come from the Everglades of Florida – and needs a deep, rich, moisture-retentive soil to do well. Lavender and rosemary like a light, well-drained alkaline one. Look up your herb books to see the best condition for each and prepare accordingly. Do not over-plant: as a general rule the smaller ones will have five per bed, medium size three, while the larger specimens, angelica, fennel, sorrel or lovage, only need one.

Being open to visitors keeps us on our toes, for the herb garden must look interesting from Easter to Michaelmas and I think it is true to say that our border is as lovely now as it was 10 years ago. The secret is this – propagation material is needed for the nursery, so young plants are always available for re-planting. Some seed heads are removed to encourage fresh growth, e.g chives, or to stop them seeding in the cracks and being a nuisance, e.g fennel. Lavenders and cotton lavenders are cut back after flowering and the border generally tidied up and given a Spring overhaul.

Herbs conjure up for me the scents and sounds evocative of high Summer – the lazy murmur of innumerable bees working the lavender blossom, the heady fragrance of many herbs breathing out, as it were, in the Summer sunshine. The golden afternoons seem to be alive with insects, honey bees, bumble bees, hoverflies, butterflies and day-flying moths all searching for pollen and nectar in the magical environment of a biodynamic garden.

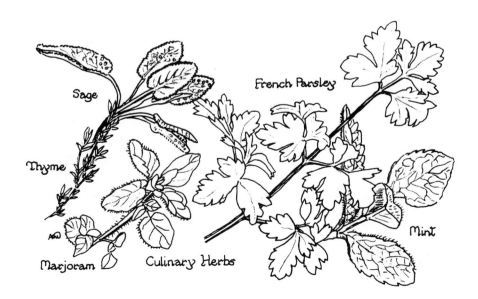

Chapter 39

Practical Gardening

Herbaceous Borders

Here in Ytene Gardens we specialise in growing hardy perennials and herbs and have many herbaceous borders to delight visitors and customers alike – both from the surrounding area and the adjacent holiday centre, Sandy Balls. We open every afternoon from Easter to October 31st and in this article I will say a little about how we establish, maintain and endeavour to make our borders attractive during this time.

In my mind's eye, I can see my Autumn garden rich with the purples and golds of Michaelmas daisy, helenium and golden rod, but how many of my readers have enjoyed such loveliness? How many plants were never mulched, thus allowing the hot sun to bake the soil, or insufficiently staked to withstand those few heavy rains and blustery winds? How many borders have been beautiful from the first opening of the snowdrop and crocus to the last colourful leaves of the peony and cheerful Kaffir lily … I wonder?

The definition of an herbaceous border is an area of ground which is planted with perennial plants to give a brilliant display either for a limited period or for the flowering season. In practice, flowering and coloured shrubs, annuals and bulbous plants are used as well; also half-hardy and tender subjects are often transplanted just before flowering to fill a blank space.

In most gardens ground is limited and you need to make do with the space available. But if you have the opportunity to plan one in a new garden, or decide to change your existing border, Autumn is the time for really getting down to it.

A southern aspect is ideal as flowers will face the sun and front of the bed. The width in proportion to the length needs to be correct: the right proportion gives the impression of length however small the garden; thus a 25ft long border should be 6ft wide, a 50ft, 9ft wide and so on. The best background is a dark hedge, preferably a slow-growing evergreen such as holly or yew, or perhaps not quite so

HARDY HERBACEOUS PERENNIALS

good, the faster growing evergreen honeysuckle or even a fence. In front, a grass path or lawn looks well, but many prefer to have a paving edge between the border and the lawn. This is ideal, for not only can the grass be cut right close without damaging the plants, but those near the front can tumble over, so making them look natural and reminiscent of a "cottage garden". An island bed set in a lawn is also a possibility and is popular nowadays for it can be viewed from all sides and needs no hedge backing.

In Ytene Gardens our hedges are beech and holly gathered from the woodland, and the paths are made from shredded bracken. The build-up over the years has made them sympathetic to walk on and they are in harmony with our timber-clad bungalow close by.

Borders need good preparation, for most plants remain undisturbed for three, four or more years. In all but the cleanest, well-worked soil I would recommend digging deeply in Autumn, growing a cleaning crop such as early potatoes or letting the land lie fallow, continuously hoeing and removing perennial weeds. Planting takes place the following Autumn. A potato crop needs a generous dressing of compost, but otherwise dig deeply in Summer and incorporate it then.

From the time of conception to planting there is much to be done. Firstly plan the border on graph paper, each division representing a square yard. Large groups of colour are best, so place a number of the same plants together giving ample space between for their maximum growth. Individual flowering heights are taken into consideration – plan so the contours flow and try and arrange so you can see beyond. Dwarf early plants can go far back but the tall ones only want to come halfway. Never put early subjects too far forward, except for some of the lovely foliage plants, such as grey-green artemisia varieties which remain attractive the Summer long – and dianthus and other silver-green or golden plants which flower as well.

Form must also be considered; the stately spires of delphinium or hollyhock or later flowering cimicifuga should be mixed with a more rounded bushy group, like the misty gypsophila or daisy family. In this way they will look their best and enhance each other.

Throughout the year of waiting, study your catalogues, visit specialist nurseries and 'open' gardens and get to know your plants, so that when you come to your own border the result will be artistically beautiful and of interest throughout the year. Single plants that are purchased during the Autumn and Spring previous to planting and grown on in a nursery bed will be able to be divided and you will have had the chance to note their form, time of flowering and all the characteristics that make each species unique.

Many perennials can be grown from seed; this is an economical way to begin and you too can select the best seedlings, as the nurseries and plant breeders have done before you. I grew *Erigeron* 'Blue Beauty' and *Chrysanthemum maximum* 'Little Silver Princess' in this way and it was surprising to see the variation in colour and form from a single packet. Other methods of propagation include cuttings – base, stem and root. I always tell interested customers the best, quickest and easiest method to increase their purchase, often showing them how cuttings are taken, and they are surprised to learn that many of the easy ones root within a month and without the use of a hormone rooting compound.

If you are in a hurry and want an instant border (*and* have a deep pocket), use a specialist plan and buy from a specialist nursery. One of our most successful borders was taken from the plan of a square bed at Blickling Hall, Norfolk, a National Trust property, from a book on "Borders" by Penelope Hobhouse. The dimensions are the same as illustrated, being 33ft x 33ft. It builds up in the centre to the 7ft *Rudbeckia laciniata* 'Golden Ball' and the enormous leaved *Inula magnifica*. All the plants were our own and only a few varieties needed to be substituted.

Some of our borders are perhaps less successful, for they have grown "like Topsy" and give the impression of luxuriant abandon or even "cottage garden charm" which delights many – especially those who are trying to wean themselves away from formal bedding.

When everything is ready, mark out your bed and plant carefully, corresponding to your plan. For the Blickling Hall plan we marked out the individual areas with sand and used numbers for the different plants – we overcame the "thin look" in the first year by sowing patches of hardy annuals in the spring. We have never regretted giving each plant and grouping of plants plenty of space. The grass known as 'Gardener's Garters' (*Phalaris arundinacea* 'Picta') was an integral part of the design, but it is invasive and we have since taken it out.

In the 1960s I belonged to a Gardening Book Club, and one of my most treasured possessions from that time is a book by Alan Bloom called *Perennials for Trouble-Free Gardening* (published 1960). This is a gem of a reference book which lists and describes the main hardy plants, giving each a rating out of ten. The points listed for a trouble-free perennial are these:

1. A long period of flowering
2. Shapeliness or beauty of form before and at flowering time.
3. A good appearance after flowering.
4. Completely perennial under varying gardening conditions, e.g. frost, flood or drought.
5. The plant should not flower itself to death or be in need of too frequent division.
6. They should stand up by themselves and need no staking.

So when I started collecting hardy plants I chose from the 10 out of 10 ones and only in subsequent years grew those of lesser merit. These may be just as lovely, but perhaps have a shorter flowering period and are more difficult to grow. For instance, the enormous-leaved *Crambe cordifolia*, with its delightful mass of gypsophila-like flowers, has a relatively short flowering period in July and needs a great deal of space to reach its full glory.

There are many that are not particularly showy but are equally valuable for particular areas or positions in the garden – perhaps under dry shade which is the despair of many. *Tellima grandiflora* and *Geranium phaeum* (the Mourning Widow) are two such plants with "Beth Chatto" charm and good ground-cover potential under difficult conditions. Indeed the deeply veined leaves of *Tellima* are particularly attractive in Autumn and Winter when they turn a rusty red. A shade border backed by trees can be very lovely in a subdued way – but brilliant colours need the sun.

The front of a border needs careful planning and those that flower throughout the summer (with a little attention) should be chosen. *Viola cornuta* species, *Scabiosa* 'Little Blue Butterfly' which if trimmed occasionally flowers from March to November, *Osteospermum* from South Africa, the many varieties of Dicentra with their attractive feathery foliage and "bleeding heart" flowers and the long-flowering veronicas that attract bumble and honey bees in busy profusion – all spring to mind.

Now we come to the upkeep of your border. Each year give a generous dressing of well-rotted manure and lightly point it in. Lime-loving plants will benefit from a light dusting of chalk or calcified seaweed if the soil is acid. Bracken is used for mulching; it saves hoeing, weeding and often watering during the Summer months and is applied in early Spring when the soil is moist. Other mulching materials are available but the old-fashioned dust mulch is still worth considering.

Do stake early – brushwood is excellent for it can be pushed well in among the plants and by flowering time the sticks are completely hidden. Plants like Delphiniums need individual bamboos, one to each stem, the stake being a few inches shorter than the height of the plant. Never stake too lightly; they should be able to withstand a strong gale on a wet day.

Some plants, even tall ones, do not need staking at all, for example the handsome 5ft *Ligularia* 'The Rocket', while *Aconitum* 'Bressingham Spire' is perfect in form and strong enough to resist a tornado! These are the ones to choose if height is wanted and time for care of the border is limited.

Some plants die down early and provision should be made for later flowering ones to cover the space. The beautiful Virginia cowslip (*Mertensia virginica*) goes into a state of dormancy from July – March, the bleeding heart (*Dicentra spectabilis*) dies down in August as does the recent introduction from China, *Corydalis flexuosa*, its blue flowers captivating all who see it; while the Oriental poppy looks unsightly after a short splash of brilliance.

Cut off all dead heads regularly and many will give a second flush of flowers. Penstemons are a good example of this, for they flower on and on, breaking into flowering shoots all down the stem. The wild ox-eye daisy responds to generous treatment, growing to 3ft high with an abundance of large daisy flowers. Cut these down to the green rosette of leaves and they will flower time and time again.

In late Autumn tidy up your border: experience will teach you what to cut down and what to leave. Protect the crowns of those that might suffer in a hard winter: in my light well-drained soil dahlias are best left in situ and covered with a thick bracken mulch for the vulnerable period. Mark carefully so that you know where they are. Many birds enjoy seedheads, so leave some for them.

There are so many lovely plants, all worthy of a place, that it is difficult for the novice to know which to choose – but take comfort from the fact that even the famous lady gardener, Gertrude Jekyll, made mistakes and year by year required her staff to move a plant here, a shrub or tree there until she was entirely satisfied with her creation.

So you can see that an herbaceous border, or indeed any garden, is a real challenge, for you are creating an individuality which will give you, your family and friends much joy. From Easter onward it is a living changing pattern of form, colour and texture, alive with a myriad insects living harmoniously together: hoverflies, ladybirds, bumblebees, moths and butterflies and the hum of the ever busy honeybee searching for nectar in the warm fragrance of Summer!

What could be lovelier or more rewarding?

A cordial invitation is extended to all bio-dynamic members visiting the New Forest. Do come and see our garden – you will be very welcome.

Chapter 40

Kitchen Gardening with special reference to Onion Growing

I am always amazed at the variety of produce in the supermarket; from all over the world it comes. Never before has the busy housewife been presented with such a clean and colourful abundance – everything is made so easy that there is little incentive for all but the most discerning and dedicated gardeners to grow their own. This is a sad and worrying reflection on modern life, for all those lovely fruit and vegetables that look so crisp and succulent, lack the life-giving forces so necessary for human nourishment. Most have been grown with fertilisers and pesticides and many irradiated as well to give long shelf-life, thus destroying any vestige of real goodness. The small amount of organically grown produce available is highly priced (in comparison) and not particularly fresh.

As far back as 1925 when Rudolf Steiner was asked why there was so little spiritual awareness and will to right action even among the anthroposophists of the day, he replied that it was a problem of nutrition. That the food plants no longer contained the forces necessary to build a bridge from thinking to will and action – and that was seventy years ago! It is all very well to think about growing good fresh food for your family and to use the best, the Bio-Dynamic method, but actually getting down to it is a different matter.

Gardeners of old retained the instinctive wisdom passed on from Father to Son. This is no longer the case and we must now make a conscious effort to understand why we do this or that in our gardens today.

In this connection Maria Thun's *Sowing and Planting Calendar : Working with the Stars* is a mine of information. Rudolf Steiner's *Agriculture* should be read over and over again, and no household seriously interested in sustainable husbandry should be without *Bio-Dynamic Farming Practice* by Sattler and Wistinghausen, published by the BDAA.

Over the years I have found that the strip-bed system is the best method to use in the kitchen garden. It simplifies rotation and working practice. Each bed is 4ft wide with 2 ft pathways in between. We use a four year rotation: leaf, root, fruit and flower. Leaf and root crops are self-explanatory but fruit includes the legumes, tomatoes, pumpkins, etc., while early potatoes take the place of a flower crop. A rotation of this kind is easy to plan and guarantees that no crop occupies the same

1994	LEAF	ROOT	FRUIT	FLOWER
1995	FLOWER	LEAF	ROOT	FRUIT
1996	FRUIT	FLOWER	LEAF	ROOT
1997	ROOT	FRUIT	FLOWER	LEAF

4 - Year Rotation.

bed *within* the four years, and rotating within the beds ensures an even longer interval, thus minimising pest or disease attack or deficiencies due to over-emphasis on one particular plant family, e.g brassicas.

Care of the soil is our first concern and compost-making even in the smallest garden is a priority for it is the basis of fertility. Hopefully you have access to manure but failing this, in a tiny garden the essential animal element can be introduced by using the Horn Manure Spray 500. The other preparations are added when the heap is made and it is the use of these six, chamomile, dandelion, oakbark, stinging nettle, yarrow, and valerian (together with silica spray 501) which Rudolf Steiner considered *so* vital for the production of crops containing the necessary forces for the nourishment of man and for healing our planet earth. Here then is the reason for using the Bio-Dynamic method and the challenge to understand why it is so. *Demeter* is the quality symbol of food produced in this way.

1995	1996	1997
CARROTS	ONIONS	PARSNIP
BEETROOT	CARROTS	ONIONS
PARSNIP	BEETROOT	CARROTS
ONIONS	PARSNIPS	BEETROOT

Rotating Crops in the Root Bed.

1995	1996	1997
SPINACH	LATE BRASSICAS	LEEKS
EARLY BRASSICAS	SPINACH	LATE BRASSICAS
LEEKS	EARLY BRASSICAS	SPINACH
LATE BRASSICAS	LEEKS	EARLY BRASSICAS

Rotating Crops in the Leaf Bed.

As beds become vacant during the late Summer, mature compost is incorporated into the soil. This is best done no later than early November, while the soil is still warm and the micro-organisms can work it over before Winter sets in. How much and how deep will depend on the crop planned and the type of soil. On my light sand I lightly dig or hoe it into the surface – potatoes will receive the heaviest amount; carrots the least or none at all. As the day begins to lengthen and there is an unmistakable feeling of Spring in the air, prepare the composted beds for sowing by spraying with 500 and raking to a fine tilth to await ideal sowing conditions for each particular crop.

Maria Thun's *Sowing and Planting Calendar* is available early in the year and here in Ytene Gardens we refer to it continually. To the question 'What day is it today?', the answer is seldom a date or day of the week but 'A root day or fruit, leaf or flower day'. She has shown from many years of research that by every slight movement of the soil cosmic forces are brought in which foster the formation of food substances and influence different crop-bearing parts of the plant.

So for example, by tending and harvesting the onion crop on root days, the keeping quality will be enhanced and onions for kitchen use will be available throughout the year. Over a four-year period we have proved this to be true. The following points may make this possible for others too.

1. **Buy Early**. Onion sets, and these are the easiest to grow, come into the shops as early as January. They are quite hardy, but should be spread out thinly in a cool place to prevent shoot growth prior to planting.

2. **Choose small sets**. I buy from a shop that sells from the sack and they will willingly allow me to spend time picking out my own. Large ones often contain an embryo bud and run prematurely to seed. *Sturon* is a good variety with a rounded base, *Turbo* is equally good but more expensive, while *Stuttgarter Riesen* with a flattened base, in my experience often splits (and later rots) at ripening time.

3. **Plant early, deeply and closely in a prepared bed.** The bed should be composted generously in the Autumn, raked, firmed and sprayed with 500 in Spring. Plant so that the nose barely shows above the ground; worms, or field voles may make little caches of them and it is quite a labour and unnecessary waste of valuable growing time to replant if it can be avoided. Space the rows 6 inches apart with the sets 4 inches in the rows. This makes 8 rows per 4 foot bed, either in the open or cover with 2 rows of Chase Barn Cloches. In 1994 I put the cloche crop in on February 28th – a 'root day' in the 'northern planting time'; the outdoor ones, in heavier soil, almost a month later.

The Author displaying strings of onions.

4. **Encourage early root formation.** Onions come from hot countries and were known in Egypt at the time of the pharaohs. Do not water however dry they get, but let the roots search far and deep for moisture. This will establish a good root system and build up fine strong plants to bulb up later.

5. **Tend throughout their growth on 'Root Days'.** These occur at approximately a 9-day interval (see calendar). Hoe carefully with a scrapper or onion hoe by just disturbing the soil, thereby introducing the earthy or keeping element into the crop (weeds will not be a problem under this regime). Ventilate the cloches as required and remove to another crop when the onions are cloche-high. As the bulbs begin to swell remove soil from the base and start spraying regularly with the silica spray 501.

6. **Ripen naturally**. The old practice of turning over the tops to hasten ripening is not to be recommended. As they begin to die down, natural sprouting inhibitors are produced in the leaves and translocated to the bulb. Bending the tops over prematurely will prevent this happening. At this stage I find a dusting of wood-ash along the rows is beneficial and helps ripening.

7. **Pay close attention to harvesting**. When the tops begin to brown, undermine the roots with a spade and when they are completely dry (necks as well), pull them up and shake off loose soil. If the weather is dry lay out in rows, when rain threatens remove to greenhouse or airy shed. I concentrate mine on a bed of dry bracken under cloches and when the skins are 'rustling dry', prepare for storage by rubbing off loose skins and nipping off the shrivelled roots.

8. **Store in a suitable place**. The ideal conditions of low temperature and humidity are not easy to achieve under home storage. I make them into 'ropes' or 'strings', 10lbs at a time, grading carefully, large at bottom, small at top and hang up in a draughty place. But anywhere which is reasonably cool with a good air circulation is satisfactory. Check over once a week, using first any that do sprout or deteriorate.

It is interesting to note that from a 20ft (cloche) bed-run in 1994 (approximately 300 sets) I harvested 75lbs of good sound bulbs, and still had a couple left a full year later to show to anyone interested.

Chapter 41

Bracken – New Forest to Organic Garden

Over the years bracken has played an important role in my organic garden. It was used then, and now, in two main ways: <u>Firstly</u>, as a mulch – A good mulch is cost effective, readily available, easy to handle and free from weed seeds, and bracken possesses all these attributes, plus one other, so essential to an organic garden – freedom from pesticides and herbicide residues.

A thick mulch smothers annual weeds and reduces water loss from the soil surface, thus making it especially valuable for soft fruit during the summer ripening period, when drought may occur. Herbaceous plants, trees and shrubs do equally well under a bracken regime and are often able to come through dry years unharmed and unwatered.

<u>Secondly</u>, as bedding for stock: During the winter period our cattle, chickens and goat are housed on deep litter – the resulting compost being the basis for the holding's fertility. The difficulty that micro-organisms and worms find in

The Potato Crop - Grown in Bracken Mulch.

breaking down bracken, rather than softer materials, can largely be overcome by making bigger heaps containing plenty of nitrogenous manure, choosing a sheltered site and adding the Bio-Dynamic Herbal Preparations. The result – a first-class bracken compost.

Historically, bracken was once held in high regard. Francis Bacon in 1627 thought that 'brakes cast upon the ground in the beginning of winter will make it very fruitful'. According to Lightfoot in 1777, 'Fern buried beneath potato roots never fails to produce a good crop'; and in 1878 Linton agreed, recommending it especially for potatoes. This has also been my experience over many years of growing.

One July my brother Martin received a bronze medal and 'Best in Show Award' for his early potato entry. The tubers were so perfect that the officials found it hard to believe that they were organically grown in a light sandy soil. Our secret was that they had received a generous dressing of bracken compost at planting time and the seed tubers were bedded on a thick bracken mulch, both above and below. It is an ideal system, for no earthing up is necessary; large tubers are lifted as required, leaving the smaller ones 'in situ' to continue growing. Cooked with mint and served with salt and butter, these potatoes made a dish fit for a King (or Queen) – so good they do taste!

Living so close to the present Forest boundary in Godshill we have Commoners' Rights and this enables us to apply each year to the Forestry Commission for a Bracken Ticket to cut our established acreage. Nowadays, areas also have to be passed by the Nature Conservancy Council who guard the well-being of the Forest flora and fauna. No indiscriminate cutting is allowed, areas are mapped and when accepted a fee is paid.

In the 1987 New Forest Consultative Document, concern was voiced about the little use now being made of this abundant material for bedding as in earlier days and recommended that the use of bracken for horticulture be actively pursued. Yearly cutting means better grazing for the Commoner's animals which are recognised as being essential for preserving the traditional character of the New Forest.

Cutting usually begins in early October when the bracken spores have been released and dispersed by wind and rain and first frosts begin to colour the fern. Bracken should be cut dry and there are many lovely Autumn days which make it possible to cut, turn, bale and carry on the same day. Sodden bales are heavy to handle and little use for animal bedding.

Ashley on the Forest, loading up a large trailer with Bracken.

In the early days of Martin's organic farm in Sandy Balls we cut in the old traditional way – by scythe, then turning and stacking by hand and with a borrowed tractor, proudly driving a huge trailer-load home. The bracken stack was thatched or covered in some way and later, when compacted, cut as required with a hay knife. It was hard work but a lot of fun.

Nowadays things are easier; we own a tractor, a finger-bar mower, an Acrobat hay-turner and a bailer, all given or bought cheaply at farm sales. However, there are many occupational hazards on the Forest, and a few exciting or frightening moments occur: shear bolts break, tyres explode, chains and baler-twine snap and in 1990 our precious tractor sank into a bog at night-fall and had to be winched out.

Conservationists are now concerned that the peat bogs, which supply the Horticultural Industry with one of their basic raw materials – peat - are under pressure and that a substitute <u>must</u> be found. Bark chippings, coconut fibre and even processed sewage sludge have been suggested, but not bracken, as far as I know.

Each year, the fallen leaves in Sandy Balls Holiday Centre are swept up and, at my son Eden's request, are put in some out of the way place to decompose for our future use. By Christmas 1989 they had been deposited in a shady position beneath a large oak tree at the bottom of the wood. By the end of the Summer 1990 Eden was surprised to find the following picture: $1^1/2$ inches of loose dry leaves but below to the full depth of the six foot heap (sunk to half its original height), he found a black crumbly compost, obviously the result of being worked through and through by a multitude of bradling worms, (these are the worms – not earthworms – which do such good work in our compost heaps).

We surmised that the original dampness of the leaves, the condition of the site and the continued high day and night temperature had all combined to produce this wonderful result in such a relatively short time. Usually, without a little help from a nitrogenous activator and the right Ph for worm activity, leaves take a long time to rot down.

With this example in mind, would it be possible to develop a similar process with bracken and produce a peat substitute? A really environmentally-friendly one that utilises and improves the thousands of acres used for animal grazing. I wonder!

Epilogue

Looking back I can see the influences which have shaped my life.

- My deep-rooted Quaker inheritance
- My Woodcraft tradition
- My love for Sandy Balls
- My introduction over the years to different methods of Organic growing and my enthusiastic working with them, culminating in a growing awareness of the importance of Bio-Dynamic Agriculture, the teaching of Rudolf Steiner and his Christ-centred message of Anthroposophy.
- and like Christian in the 'Pilgrims Progress', with divine assistance, I journey on.
.

...And what of the family?

The formation of the Company in 1959 changed the conception of Sandy Balls primarily as a family way of life, and when Father obtained the initial licence in 1960 for 250 caravans, it developed into a self-sustaining family-run business, with Mother as Company Secretary and Father as Chairman. Indeed there was a happy balance between Father's ideas, Mother's business acumen and the organic farm and garden.

Mother's death in 1975 introduced a new direction. Richard (my youngest brother) and his wife Patricia, now living at Arniss Farm House, took on the position of Managing Director and Company Secretary and the idealistic approach changed with increasing momentum to one of business realism in a competitive world.

To Father's great sadness, the old was swept away, including the original cottage, his ideas and work disregarded and over the next fifteen-year period Sandy Balls developed and prospered, gaining many awards for excellence and welcoming tens of thousands of holiday visitors a year.

Over this period the Family, too, grew in age, expertise and experience but it did not seem possible to fit them into the new business structure and year by year the family involvement decreased; so much so, that although Sandy Balls has a workforce of over 100 workers, only two members of the family are senior managers, including one on the Board of Directors – (where once there were seven).

And what of Sandy Balls itself – the lovely woodland that Grandfather saved from the woodman's axe . . . this special centre for ideas and timeless concepts embodied in the Order of Woodcraft Chivalry? What of it? What of them?

> *'Happy he on the weary sea,*
> *who hath fled the tempest and won the haven.*
> *Happy who so hath risen free,*
> *above his striving. For strangely graven*
> *is the orb of life, that one and another*
> *in Gold and Power may outpass his brother.*
> *And men in their millions float and flow,*
> *And seethe with a million hopes as heaven.*
> *And they win their will or they miss their will,*
> *And their hopes are dead or are pined for still,*
> *But who e're can know,*
> *as the long days go,*
> *That to live is happy has found his heaven!*
> *What else is Wisdom? What of man's endeavour*
> *or God's high grace, so lovely and so great?*
> *To stand from fear set free, to breathe and wait,*
> *To hold a hand uplifted over hate,*
> *And shall not loveliness be loved for ever?*

So wrote the Greek poet, Euripides in 406 B.C. over 2400 years ago! How very relevant this message is today.

A misty morning in Sandy Balls by the River Avon
(By photographic competition winner, Mrs Anne Hooper)

THE WESTLAKE FAMILY TREE (1998)

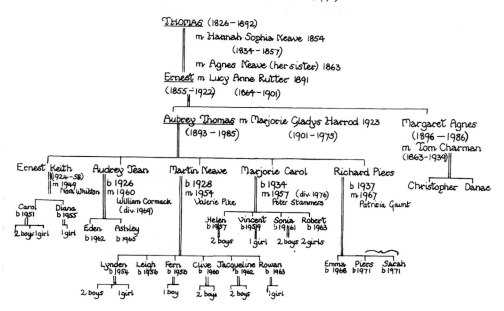

Appendix ②

THE RUTTER FAMILY TREE

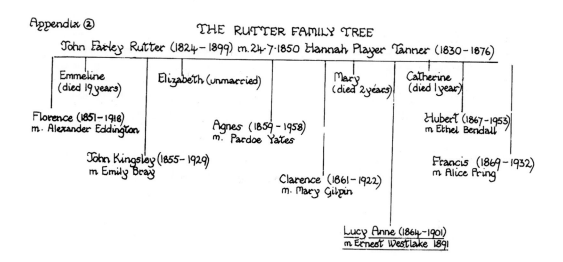

Appendix ③   The Symbolism of the Order of Woodcraft Chivalry

Upon ceremonial occasions the Chieftain wore an orange cloak his Lady a white one. Purple as the colour identified with dignity, rank and power has been adopted for Order officers whose cloaks are embroidered with their symbols of office –

Stephanie Morland writing of the new Chieftain's cloak says :–

"In designing the cloak, we thought it should reflect the woodland background of the Order, and its ceremonies, and include relevant symbols and emblems — sun, blue sky, trees, water, fire & tents.
The fire is framed by garlands, like the Keeper of the Fire's cloak symbol.
The smoke curls round a ray of the sun, suggesting the thyrsus.
The garlands and the Thyrsus express the ancient Greek influence felt by Ernest Westlake (founder of the Order), and his friendship with Ernest Thompson Seton brought American Indian ideas to the Order."

 Keeper of the Fire – A Fire. In its complete form, as seen on the Order's Keeper of the Fire ceremonial cloak, the fire is enclosed within two branches of foliage, the seven leaves on each branch representing the seven age divisions; the five flames of the fire representing the five fold scheme of training carried out in the Order – physical, mental, aesthetic, social and religious)

 Marshal – A Thyrsus
The Thyrsus from Greek Mythology – A staff, usually one tipped with a pinecone borne by Dionysus (Bacchus) and his followers

 Master of Ceremonies – A circle and a cross   Recorder A quill pen and ink-pot   ‖ Keeper of the purse Three gold ingots

 Herald – A caduceus – The winged staff of Hermes
A caduceus from Classical Mythology is a staff entwined with two serpents and bearing a pair of wings at the top carried by Hermes (Mercury) as a messenger of the Gods.

 Gleeman – A harp   Keeper of the Honours Tally Crossed Keys   Keeper of the Wardrobe – a cloak

 'Pinecone' Editor – A scroll   Craftsman – the 'seeing hand' an eye superimposed on an open hand

 Camps Chief Three Tents and a fire   Reader A book and a book mark

The Order Emblem – On ceremonial occasions, the Order emblem is mounted high upon a pole before the assembled people. Directly under it are coloured streamers, one for each of the age divisions, and below is fixed the Order badge. Five symbols are combined in the one emblem.

First the Fire – which from earliest times has been the very centre of man's social and spiritual life.

Second the Thyrsus – a spear or shaft wrapped with ivy or vine bands and tipped with a pine cone, the symbol of the joy of life, here inseparably linked with the Third symbol – the Cross, for the staff of the Thyrsus forms one of the arms of the Cross. Thus is symbolised the synthesis of the two great forces of human life in that exuberance and ecstasy, the urge to lose one-self in the life force, is recognised as equally essential with self-denial, self discipline, service and sacrifice.

Fourth – at the centre of the Thyrsus and Cross – the Sun, giver of life.

Fifth, the Circle or Ring – the symbol of love which embraces the other four symbols

Thus, in the synthesis of these five symbols in one whole, we seek to express our purpose and hold it before us.

The Order Badge consists of a shield resting against crossed woodman's axes. The axes represent Woodcraft and the shield, Chivalry. The shield contains the national emblem of St George.

Order

The Seven Age Divisions

In the Order, each age is symbolised by its own colour as follows :–
Babe (Birth to 5 years) – White is the sign of the pure and innocent. Elves (5 to 8 years) Brown represents the earth, mother of us all. Woodlings (8–12 years) Green is the first colour in nature. It is the colour of woods, leaves and plants and signifies the desire to grow, to do, to accomplish. Trackers (12–15 years) Yellow, the colour of spring flowers is used to represent the Trackers. Pathfinders (15–18 years) – Deep blue is used for the Pathfinders' colour as symbolising a growing awareness of beauty and things spiritual. Waywardens (18–25 years) – Scarlet. Wayfarers (over 25 years) – Deep rose, as symbolising virility, strength and maturity. Witana (sixty years and over) – Grey. The name is derived from the Anglo-Saxon word for Wise One or Counsellor.

The comprehensive school report written by Cuthbert Rutter, Headmaster of Forest School, in his own handwriting.

Forest School Godshill Fordingbridge
Report on Jean Westlake
Autumn 1935.

Arithmetic   Fundamental arithmetic II Long multiplication and reduction of money. Jean enjoys a sound grasp of principles, still regards it as a sin to get a sum wrong and objects to adventuring into new ground. Slow but usually correct in mental arithmetic.

Gen'l Knowledge   She is interested and retains information once acquired. Will enjoy herself more and shine with ease as her general reading gets wider.

Spelling   Good average standard. Should not bother herself so much with comparison with her brother.

Hand Writing   Prints beautifully when she takes care and produces the best work. She needs to develop now a good running hand. Pattern writing is helping to this end.

Story Writing   She has developed a highly imaginative style of Fairy Story with some finish and cohesion. Very readable neat (in both senses) work but somewhat stereotyped

Woodcraft   She has been elected Fire Keeper of the Pack. She is good at most things which the Pack do. She is very competitive and will not be overcome by obstacles.

History   Life in Roman and Medieval England.
          She is doing splendid careful work in her drawings
          and on her Time Chart.

Art   Unusually good. She is very interested and
          easily taught. She has a fine sense of
          composition.

Music   Is taking a better part than at first in
          percussion bands and took some solo parts well.
          She made two pipes with some defects and should
          try again.

Games   She is always energetic and happy at
          games periods. She shines amongst the girls
          at all ball games.
          Her riding has been <u>excellent</u> showing fitness,
          grace, control, pluck and skill.

          Jean's general health has been
excellent. She has gained 2 lbs in weight.
She has seemed more happy and more gay. In her
homecrafts she has been reasonable and friendly and she
has shown initiative. Her own reading has included:
Puck of Pook's Hill, Scarlet Fleming Annual, Girls Own,
and Tales and Legends of Serbia. When she enters
still more into the groups and cares less about
getting on top she will get still more out of living.
She is making a thoroughly satisfactory development.
                                    C. H. Ritter

247

Publications mentioned in the text

The Grith Fyrd Idea by Prof. John Macmurray and others - OWC 1933 46

The Order of Woodcraft Chivalry 1916-1949 as a New Age Alternative to the Boy Scouts by Derek Edgell - Edwin Mellen Press 1992 47

The Living Soil by Lady Eve Balfour - Faber & Faber 1943 51

The Vegetable Garden Displayed - Royal Horticultural Society 1941 59

Saharah Conquest by Richard St. Barbe Baker - Lutterwood Press, 1966 81

Rural Hygiene published by Dr. Vivian Poore, 1903 91

The Generous Earth by Philip Oyler - Hodder and Stoughton 1950 109

Commercial Cloche Gardening by J L H Chase - Faber & Faber 1952 113

Herbal Handbook for Farm and Stable by Juliette de Bairacli Levy - Faber & Faber 1952 116

Wanderers in the New Forest by Juliette de Bairacli Levy - Faber & Faber, 1958 118

The Illustrated Herbal Handbook for Everyone by Juliette de Bairacli Levy - Faber & Faber 1974 119

Intensive Gardening by R. Dalziel O'Brien - Faber & Faber 1956 126

Common Sense CompostMaking by Maye E. Bruce - Faber & Faber 1946 128

The Pattern of Health by Dr. Aubrey T. Westlake - Vincent Stuart 1961 163

The Secret Life of Plants by Peter Tompkins & Christopher Bird - Allen Lane 1973 163

Secrets of the Soil by Peter Tompkins & Christopher Bird - Penguin Books 1989 163

An Outline of Occult Science by Rudolf Steiner - Anthroposophical Press 1939 180

Agriculture by Rudolf Steiner - Bio-Dynamic Agricultural Association 1974 189

Perennials for Trouble Free Garderling by Alan Bloom - The Gardening Book Club 1960 197

Borders by Penelope Hobhouse - National Trust in Association with Pavilion Books 1989 197

Bio-Dynamic Gardenirlg by John Soper - Bio-Dynamic Agricultural Association 1983 200

Working with the Stars - A Bio-Dynamic Sowing and Planting Calendar by Maria Thun
published yearly by the Lanthorn Press 200

Bio-Dynamic Farming Practice by Sattler and Wistinghausen - Bio-Dynamic Agricultural
Association 1994 200

Gardening for Life - The Biodynamic Way
A practical introduction to a new art of gardening, sowing, planting, harvesting
Maria Thun

Biodynamic techniques recognise that plant life is intimately bound up with the life of the soil; that the soil itself is alive and vital and that the degree of vitality has a direct bearing on the health of the crops. Through the nurture and care of the soil you will soon be able to grow quality produce which possesses vitality and has the highest flavour.

Sharing its principles, methods and techniques with organic farming, biodynamic agriculture additionally acknowledges that the plant's growth is also affected by planetary influences like the waxing and waning of the moon.

Whether you are an experienced gardener or not, whether or not you have used permaculture or grown organic produce before, this book offers accessible tips on; favourable times for planting, harvesting and growing; ways of combating pests and diseases; building soil fertility - crop changes and rotation; how planets and stars affect plant growth.

'This beautifully illustrated, comprehensive guide is must for all thoughtful gardeners wishing to work in harmony with heaven and earth.'

Jean Westlake, *gardener and author*

Maria Thun has gardened all her working life and is an authority on biodynamics. This is a collection of her tried and tested methods. Her annual sowing and planting calendar is published in 18 languages.
128pp; 212 x 160mm; 1 869 890 32 9; pb; **£14.99**

New Eyes for Plants
A workbook for observing and drawing plants
Margaret Colquhoun and Axel Ewald

Simple observation exercises interwoven with inspiring illustrations to take you on a vivid journey through the seasons with a fresh pair of eyes. Using the holistic approach of Goethe, this book opens a door 'onto a new way of practising Science as an Art'.
208 pp; 270 x 210mm; illustrations; 1 869 890 85 X; pb; **£14.99**

Water, Electricity and Health
Protecting yourself from electrostress at home and work
Alan Hall

A must for anyone working in health, biodynamics and New Science. This book looks at how the use of biodynamics can be applied to counter the harmful effects of electro-magnetic fields. It also shows how to reduce electro-stress and increase energy.
192pp; 210 x 135mm; 1 869 890 94 9; pb; **£12.99**

The Green Snake and the Beautiful Lily
Play Version - Michael Burton
Original Translation of the Fairy Tale - Thomas Carlyle
The Art of Goethean Conversation - Marjorie Spock
Johann Wolfgang von Goethe

A group of people live in a world turned upside down. They realise that the efforts of one alone can do little to create a new society. But by waking up to each other at the right time, they bring about profound spiritual and social renewal.

Goethe originally told this magic tale in a group of travellers during the French Revolution. Today, this magic still sparkles in Thomas Carlyle's original translation.

Michael Burton's play invites you to enjoy the tale afresh through his punchy dialogue. Jay Ramsay writes that this, ' ... inspiring script is a genuine contribution, combining the grace of the original fairy tale with a brilliant use of the modern idiom'

And when the Green Snake is asked by the Gold King, 'What is more quickening than light?' she replies, 'Conversation!' We come alive when meeting each other in real dialogue. Marjorie Spock's *Art of Goethean Conversation* shows how true conversation has transformative power.

This book is published specially for the 1998-99 European Tour of the Mask Studio's production of *The Green Snake*, a new play inspired by Goethe's fairy tale. It also meets readers' requests for the Spock essay and Carlyle translation in an accessible form.

96pp; 216 x 138mm; 1 869 890 07 8; pb; **£7.00**

Naming
Choosing a meaningful name
Caroline Sherwood

Names matter. They are the fingerprints of the Soul through which we express our nature to the world. Choosing a meaningful name is a lifetime gift.

Included in this thorough, authoritative, and fascinating book is everything you need to choose, or change, a name and plan a naming ceremony. Including; what to take into account when choosing a name; the cultural importance of names; meanings to names - a comprehensive dictionary; naming ceremonies to choose from; holding your own ceremony; taking a new name.

Rosie Styles, of The Baby Naming Society, has written the Foreword for this extensive and insightful book, and says;

' ... Caroline Sherwood's *Naming* is a completely new and far more useful approach in which the meanings of names are the prime focus. With a deep respect for language, she offers a fresh way for parents to set about finding the right name for their child. This is a much needed addition to the naming books already available, and will delight anyone facing the enormous task of naming their child, or those with an interest in names.'

'A true name offers a bridge between 'you' and 'me'. We should be glad of such a book which shows a way beyond labelling towards a naming of essence and potential in the children who come to us.'

Paul Matthews, *author Sing Me the Creation*

Caroline Sherwood works as writer and counsellor. She has researched naming extensively - so as to breathe life into the words, sing the meaning back into a name, and enable the bearer to embody it. Caroline is also the author of *Making Friends with Ourselves: Introducing children to meditation* (Kidsmed 1995).

304pp; 246 x 189mm; 1 869 890 56 6; pb; **£14.99**

Orders

Ordering information from:

Hawthorn Press
1 Lansdown Lane, Stroud, Gloucestershire
GL5 1BJ. United Kingdom
Tel: (01453) 757040   Fax: (01453) 751138
E-mail: hawthornpress@hawthornpress.com

If you have difficulties ordering from a bookshop you can order direct from:

Scottish Book Source Distribution
137 Dundee Street, Edinburgh
EH11 1BG
United Kingdom
Tel: (0131) 229 6800   Fax: (0131) 229 9070

All Hawthorn Press Titles are available in North America from:

Anthroposophic Press
3390 Route 9, Hudson,
NY 12534
U.S.A
Tel: (518) 851 2054   Fax (518) 851 2047